Gift of the Estate of
Robert (1938-2013)
and Gay Zieger (1938-2013)
October 2013

STRIKE

The **DAILY NEWS** *War and the Future of American Labor*

Richard Vigilante

Simon & Schuster

New York   London   Toronto
Sydney   Tokyo   Singapore

SIMON & SCHUSTER
Rockefeller Center
1230 Avenue of the Americas
New York, New York 10020

SIMON & SCHUSTER and colophon are registered trademarks of Simon &
Schuster Inc.

Designed by Karolina Harris

Manufactured in the United States of America

1 3 5 7 9 10 8 6 4 2

Library of Congress Cataloging-in-Publication Data
Vigilante, Richard.
Strike : the Daily News war and the future of American labor /
Richard Vigilante.
p.   cm.
Includes bibliographical references (p.) and index.
1. Daily News (New York, N.Y. : 1920)   2. Strikes and lockouts—
Newspapers—New York (N.Y.)   3. Collective bargaining—Newspapers—
New York (N.Y.)   4. Violence—New York (N.Y.)—History—20th
century.   5. Organized crime—New York (N.Y.)   6. Labor—United
States—History—20th century.   7. Mass media—Objectivity.
I. Title.
PN4899.N42D328   1994
331.89'281071471—dc20   94-5524
                                                         CIP

ISBN: 0-671-79631-3

To my parents,
Dr. Emil C. Vigilante and
Anne Hastings Vigilante,
for piquing my curiosity

ACKNOWLEDGMENTS

MANY people helped me complete this book, but none so much as those who are in it. All the major sources knew that the final product would necessarily tell many tales more comfortably forgotten. And yet they put themselves on the record and at risk in the service of the truth as they saw it. Three deserve particular recognition: Ted Kheel not only talked to me for many hours, but also let me wander through his files without limit of precondition. Ed Gold's novelist's eye produced negotiation minutes as revealing, frank, and colorful about the company's behavior as about his adversaries'. Jim Longson never spared himself in his lengthy account of the company's preparations, even when I got to, as he cheerfully called them, "the set of questions I hate."

George Gilder, Rick Brookhiser, Stephen Weeks, Terry Teachout, and the members of the Board either read or listened to parts of the manuscript and offered valuable comments. Those by Gilder, Brookhiser, and Weeks led to substantial rewrites of chapters 1, 2, 4, and 5.

Alan Randolph signed on as a research assistant and ended up co-reporting chapters 4, 5, 16, and 17. Joan Silverman did some terrific last-minute fact checking; as I release these galleys to the printer my only wish is that I had let her do more.

As the book neared completion I lost both my imprint, Poseidon, and my wonderful editor, Elaine Pfefferblit, to the consolidation of the American publishing industry. Lyn Chu, one half of my husband-and-wife agent team of Hartley and Chu, stepped in to edit the manuscript, on her own time and very ably, truly service beyond the call of duty.

To my book's adoptive parents, Dominick Anfuso and Cassie Jones of Simon & Schuster, thanks for everything.

William F. Buckley, Jr.—mentor, friend, and luminous example of the intellectual life well lived—gave much advice, encouragement, and assistance, as he has throughout my career. The Historical Research Foundation provided financial support for my research.

Maggie Gallagher, my colleague at the Center for Social Thought, read the entire manuscript several times, did major edits or rewrites on most chapters, helped structure the book, and most important, always encouraged me to write the book that interested me, rather than some imaginary average reader—however odd the result. I will leave real readers to judge whether this was good advice.

My wife Susan rewrote chapter 11, making it into one of my favorites. But anyone married to a writer will know that is but a small part of the story. This was my first real book. The work was hard enough, though not nearly as hard as the worrying, and of course it has not been (so far!) a lucrative engagement. I would never have gotten through it without Sue. How she got through it with me I will never understand, but she has my everlasting gratitude for getting us both through it in the end.

CONTENTS

CHAPTER 1

Holy War

THIS is a story about a war for control of a newspaper, until recently and for many decades the largest newspaper in the United States. War is an overused metaphor, but in this war there were real battles and even a measure of real, organized violence. And after the larger metaphorical war was over, one that pitted one of America's largest and most successful communications companies against not only its own unions but against the national labor movement, almost everyone agreed that it was the violence alone—the real war—that finally settled the question of who would control the *Daily News*.

This war was fought in New York, a city not unused to violence. Sometimes, of course, even in quite orderly societies men do throw up their hands and say, "Here is a problem we cannot fit into the system, an intractable and momentous social conflict that cannot be settled under the law." We have had a civil war, with 600,000 dead, because the law could not resolve the contradiction of a nation founded simultaneously on liberty and slavery. In the 1930s American workingmen stepped outside the law to build the industrial labor movement, defying the authorities to drive them out of the factories they had seized until their employers would recognize their right to organize. And in the living memory of most of the readers of this book we have seen a black preacher lead millions of his fellow citizens in a movement for justice, using tactics outside the law until the law made itself again a fit place for men to abide.

The battle for the *Daily News* was not on the scale of any of those civil wars. But it was part of an economic, social, and moral revolution that has already changed the lives of millions of working Americans and their families, and will change the lives of tens of millions more.

It is not the purpose of this book to announce this revolution; it is already probably the most announced, heralded, declaimed, decried, celebrated, exaggerated, minimized, and pontificated-about revolution in the history of the world. I speak of course of the information revolution; more specifically the transition from an industrial to a post-industrial economy that comes when we make our machines not only augmenters of muscle but extensions of mind.

Yet though this revolution has almost been talked to death, most of us have not looked too closely at its human cost, or its human benefits. We know—or are beginning to know as the productivity statistics, so bad for so long, begin to turn around—that the union of mind and machine is the great hope for restoring the "competitiveness" of the American economy. But we also know that the "restructuring" of the economy has, at least for the time being, deprived millions of American workers of that wonder of the mid-twentieth century, the blue-collar job that could pay for a house in the suburbs, vacations, and college educations, and for a while promised to eliminate the phrase "working class" from the American vocabulary. It is precisely because we know these things that we have not wanted to look this revolution too closely in the face. We need the revolution to succeed; we cheer on its progress. But as we cheer we are haunted by the possibility that the mystery at the heart of this festival of progress is a human sacrifice.

This war story, like many war stories, is about men and machines and the bonds and the bad blood between them. Men have changed machines a lot in the past twenty years and now machines are returning the favor. At their best the post-industrial revolution and its machines make men better, not—as the industrial revolution did in some ways—more like machines, but more like men.

In some ways of course men always become like their machines. The dumb brutal machines of the early industrial revolution brutalized their caretakers' bodies but asked nothing of their brains. The meticulously designed mechanical complexes of the mature industrial economy demanded the orderly, efficient, precisely controlled, rule-book following, Taylor-trained work forces of American industry in its golden age. Today, now that we have put mind in machines, we can and must put the minds of men to use in the factory so the machines can reach their potential. That can be a very good thing for the men as well as the machines.

At their best the new machines can evoke some of the best that is in men: creativity, diligence, ingenuity, teamwork, self-governance, commitment to an enterprise larger than the self, purposeful order. But the machines are not always used at their best. Sometimes managers worship the machines, imagining that post-industrial paradise comes from the machines alone and that the men who use them have little more to do than stand next to them or stand in their way. Then the goal becomes not marrying the men to the machines but eliminating as many of the men as possible to save room—and money—for the machines. And sometimes the men refuse the challenge of the machines and turn away from the truth that better machines need better men.

The changing relationship between men and machines is not only changing work, it is changing the social, economic, political, and moral condition of the worker.

In the private sector, union membership is down to less than 12 percent of the workforce. Many people, including many labor leaders, are convinced that the new workplace is incompatible with unions, and that the new machines demand a new individualist worker incompatible with the union ethic of solidarity. Even many friends of labor do not see how the labor union as we have known it can find a place in the new factory, because the unionism that we have known was designed around the old factory.

That leaves us with the exhilarating prospect of a work force freed from the constraints of solidarity, liberated to be as efficient, hardworking, and productive as it can be.

And it leaves us with the horrifying prospect of workers stripped of solidarity, naked and alone before their employers, deprived of all the rights of industrial citizenship won over the course of this century.

Because this prospect, like the whole post-industrial revolution, is both exhilarating and horrifying, there are going to be more wars like the *Daily News* war. Anti-union managers armed with their new machines won a lot of the early battles more or less uncontested before the unions, which have been on the ropes for years anyway, could even get into the game. But as labor lawyer and author Thomas Geohagan has pointed out, the union movement has always had its greatest moments, its most important strikes, its biggest victories, its most rapid growth, just when it seemed about to die, probably because solidarity has always depended in part on insecurity, fear, desperation, and anger.

How we settle the coming labor battles will be among the most important questions this country faces, for it will do much to determine how productive our workplaces will be and how happy and prosperous their workers and their families. To a very large extent, how we settle these questions will determine the social and moral character of this society.

For several decades now, American intellectuals and policymakers have been almost obsessed with the rich and the poor. But now finally there are some signs that we are remembering the working class, and this book is part of their story.

It is a story full of mostly good men, most of them trying enormously hard to do right, passionately convinced they were right, and yet at war with each other. Eventually these mostly good men came to hate each other and tried to bring down upon each other brutal fates including the loss of hundreds or thousands of jobs and the destruction of a great newspaper—the last of which may yet come to pass.

Few of the participants, many of them veterans of other labor battles, have known any more brutal, angry, or desperate conflict. And that is because like many of the most brutal wars of our history it was in the end a war of ideas, a war over right and wrong, in fact a religious war, and that too is only partly a metaphor.

CHAPTER 2

No More Givebacks

For Jim Hoge, the first shot in the *Daily News* war was fired in January 1989, more than a year and a half before the strike. He remembers it well because it was fired at him.

Since shortly after his arrival as publisher in 1984, Hoge had met four times a year with the heads of the *News*'s ten unions. When Hoge arrived morale at the *News* was at an all-time low; *News* management had lost faith in its ability to keep the long-languishing paper alive. The unions had lost faith even in management's intention to do any such thing. The quarterly meetings were part of an effort, now going into its fifth year, to get everyone on the same side, working to transform the *News*, still the nation's largest urban daily, into a modern profitable paper.

At the January 1989 meeting, held as usual in the Patterson Room, named after the *News*'s founder, Joseph Medill Patterson, Hoge reviewed, not for the first time, the *News*'s plans, including building a new $300 million state-of-the-art color printing plant. The money would come from the *News*'s corporate owners, the Tribune Company, and would allow the *News* to acquire all the automated technology that made the *Chicago Tribune* and the company's other papers so attractive to advertisers.

Then he got to the hard part. In the next few minutes he intended to open a conversation that might go on for more than a year. Negotiations would not begin in earnest for many months. But now was the time to start convincing the unions that the game was worth the candle; by the time negotiations came around he wanted everybody in this room to share the same vision of where the *Daily News* was going and what it would cost to get there.

The Tribune Company, he began to explain, would never put up the necessary funds without major concessions from the unions. The *News* had lost more than $100 million in the previous decade on revenues of more than $4 billion. The Tribune Company would not cover such losses forever. The *News* needed labor savings on the order of $50 to $70 million per year, givebacks that would dwarf the concessions the unions made just two years before. The *News* paid out nearly half its revenues in wages. Now, Hoge began to explain, it must reduce that ratio to something like the industry standard of 25 percent. There would need to be dramatic changes in work rules and customs to make the men more productive, raise quality, and improve customer service.

He never got to say most of it. He was interrupted by the riot.

Hoge believed that over the past few years he had made a lot of progress with the men who now surrounded him. He believed he had shown them how unions and management could be on the same team. The feeling was not mutual.

George McDonald, the president of the mailers union, which packages papers for shipment, and chairman of the Allied Printing Trades Council, which coordinated strategy for all ten of the paper's unions, had never been impressed with Hoge. He liked to tell people that on the scale of one to ten Hoge was a four as a publisher, allowing with scorn that he might be a good writer or something like that.

It was not just Hoge whom McDonald did not like. Like most of the men at the table he was angry at what he felt had been a decade of betrayal by the *News*'s faraway owners in Chicago. McDonald is a small, genial, self-effacing, almost grandfatherly figure. But he had been a good enough politician to hold on to the chairmanship of the council for more than a decade, though the mailers are not one of the powerhouse unions. McDonald believed in making deals, not going to the mattresses. His political skills had helped the company win major concessions from the unions in 1984 and 1987. In part on the strength of the 1984 union agreement, which made it appear that the *News*'s chronic labor problems might finally be resolved, the Tribune Company had gone public in a hugely successful offering enriching many of the company's officers. McDonald likes to say he helped make Stanton Cook, Tribune Company CEO, a millionaire—and then the guy didn't even mention the *News* unions in the annual report.

The worst betrayal was that the plants, the horrible, decrepit, obsolete, filthy, unbearably noisy old *News* printing plants, were still there. A

1987 written agreement pledged that the *News* would make $60 million in investments in the plants (as a first step toward replacing them) to match the unions' $30 million in concessions. But two years later the *News* had spent only $18 million, and Hoge was still talking.

Like McDonald, Lenny Higgins, then president of the pressmen's union, the most powerful of the production unions, had arrived angry. Higgins had been badgering Hoge for months about the delay in the promised investments. Higgins believed the unions had been tricked and that George McDonald and his advisor Ted Kheel were sometimes too trusting, too easy on the company. The concessions the unions made were not "investments," they were just plain old givebacks. The company had more, the workers had less, and nothing else changed. Higgins was in no mood to hear Hoge describe the new $300 million plant the *News* could have if only the unions would give a little more.

Jerry Cronin, president of the Newspaper and Mail Deliverers Union of New York and Vicinity (NMDU), the drivers union, the *News*'s second-largest and most powerful union, wasn't "on the team" any more than Higgins and McDonald. Cronin had run away from home when he was fourteen, and had been living in a garage when he made friends with a *Daily News* driver who began taking Cronin around on his route. He eventually got Cronin a union card so he could drive himself. At the time he had "never thought there could be a better job," and in his eleven years driving and eight as a union official he "lived, breathed, and loved the *Daily News*." Like several of the other union leaders, he had known roughly what Hoge was going to say today, but he had also heard something much more ominous. The *News* was considering changing its labor counsel and bringing in a famous union-busting law firm. Cronin feared Hoge was about to get himself and the *News* into a much bigger fight than he realized. Hoge, he thought, often didn't grasp the effect of his words or actions on people around him. "None of us could get comfortable with him," Cronin says. So he had taken Hoge aside a few minutes before the meeting and tried to warn him that the union would not stand for any more givebacks, and that if Hoge wasn't careful he would start a war. But the warning ended in a shouting match, with Cronin screaming at Hoge, "You're going to piss the *News* down the drain. . . . You don't know what the fuck you are doing."

Within a few months Cronin would be out of the union, succeeded as president by Mike Alvino. In 1980 Alvino had testified in court that he had been the bag man for one Douglas LaChance, then president of the union. LaChance made his living in part by taking bribes from employers who wanted to fire unwanted employees without union trouble. In those days the price of a man's livelihood was $3,000. More than three years after today's meeting, the NMDU would become the first union in the history of the United States to be indicted for "enterprise corruption," meaning that the organization itself was charged with being a criminal enterprise, much of its leadership engaged in wholesale theft and bootlegging of newspapers, labor extortion, and numerous other small-time rackets that produced tens of millions in illegal income for the cadre of drivers who ran the rackets. It would be hard to interest some NMDU powers in any grand reforming Hoge plan if it threatened the racket.

Barry Lipton, the short, stocky, curly-haired, mustachioed, perpetually rushed president of the Newspaper Guild, the white-collar union that represents among others the reporters, was as skeptical of Hoge as he was of anybody from management, which is very skeptical indeed. He is by far the most combative of the union leaders, as if, as the leader of a bunch of intellectuals, he constantly needs to prove that he is a real union guy too.

Hoge did not have an ally in the room. The other leaders, from the paperhandlers, the printers, the stereotypers, machinists, electricians, and photoengravers, in greater or lesser degree all felt angry or betrayed. None trusted the Tribune Company's intentions. Most had long been in the habit of thinking of themselves as shepherds of workers in a shrinking industry, whose only hope was to hang on to as many jobs as possible for as long as possible. They were in no mood to ask those men to make yet another round of sacrifices because one more in a succession of saviors sent from Chicago had a bright idea.

Higgins, who would serve only one term as president—to expire in a few months—did not have McDonald's political skills or the strength and intelligence of the man who would succeed him, Jack Kennedy. But he had his own strong points. He could not be intimidated and he had a wicked tongue. He could always "get under Hoge's skin real good," says McDonald. What bothered Higgins the most was Hoge always spouting off with his big dreams. And here he was doing it again. This wasn't a meeting, it was a lecture. This was no way to save the *News:* ten union men who knew more about newspapers than Hoge sitting around listening to Hoge talk about his $300 million fantasy. Higgins decided to create a little dialogue.

Hoge was in the middle of a sentence when Higgins started shouting. "No more givebacks!"

The Patterson room is quite large, more like a small auditorium than a conference room. For these meetings Hoge had four long conference tables laid out in a square, with the union leaders sitting around the perimeter. Hoge was standing inside the square and his back was to Higgins.

Irritated at the interruption he turned around.

"No more givebacks," Higgins shouted again, this time banging his fist on the table so hard it jumped.

Hoge stopped cold and just stared at Higgins. That didn't surprise Higgins. Hoge looked cool, but he was not comfortable around the union guys and he was easy to rattle.

So Higgins shouted again, "No more givebacks." Bang. "No more givebacks." Bang. Bang. Bang. Bang on the table.

Then somebody behind Hoge joined in, rhythmically pounding and shouting.

"No more givebacks. No more givebacks. No more givebacks." Bang. Bang. Bang. Bang.

Though many of the union leaders say they did not participate, soon it seemed to Hoge like they were all doing it. "No more givebacks. No more givebacks." Bang. Bang. Bang. In seconds it appeared to Hoge that his almost desperately calm and rational discussion had turned into a union rally.

The union guys remember it three years later as just a bit of fun and they laugh to recall it. "I blasted him," Higgins remembers with a tinge of glee. Lipton says most of it was in Hoge's imagination: "He put himself in the middle of this circle of union leaders in a real dramatic posture, and he had these big expectations but he could never take criticism, so when a few of them raise their voices it's this big dramatic event."

Imagined or not, Hoge, a man whose friends describe him as cool, reserved, a worshipper of self-control, an "ice cube," hated it. He was "stunned and very angry" that his attempt to reason with the unions could be met with what he calls a "flight from reality of stunning proportions." It was the "height of irresponsibility," he says, except that Hoge says "heighth." But for Hoge this was not just one more union outrage. Lenny Higgins's outburst marked a turning point in Hoge's life.

If Hoge's friends call him cool, and careful, he describes himself as "fairly political"; a man who would much rather negotiate, cajole, persuade, even manipulate, than fight. He so hated what happened to him that day that he turned it into a conversion experience. All of a sudden, he says, it became clear to him that the unions would never cooperate, that he could never get them on the team. Asked years later in the cold, clear light of day to explain what turned the *News*'s differences with its unions into an all-out war, Hoge says it was that meeting.

That was the day Jim Hoge became a hawk.

By all accounts Hoge is bright, driven, and, in the right setting, charismatic; a blond WASP with such chiseled good looks he might be a refugee from a Dick Tracy cartoon, or a steely-eyed Kirk Douglas without the cleft chin. In 1979 he was featured along with George Hamilton and John Travolta in an *Esquire* piece called "The Dangers of Being Too Good Looking." He is the kind of guy the term "wunderkind" was coined for. After graduating Yale in 1958 he had gone straight to Chicago for a reporting job at the city's tabloid, the *Sun-Times*. Within a few years he was city editor; he was managing editor at thirty-one, publisher at forty-four; while he was serving in those posts the *Sun-Times* won a clutch of Pulitzers.

In 1983, when the Marshall Field Company, which owned the *Sun-Times*, decided to let the paper go, Hoge tried to buy it. He assembled a group of investors. But Rupert Murdoch jostled Hoge's group aside and added the paper to his American empire. All of a sudden Hoge was unemployed with a bright red ABORT MISSION sign flashing above the fast track of his career.

Within a few months, however, Hoge was sitting in the Chicago Club talking to then Tribune Company CEO Stanton Cook about coming over to the Tribune Company to save the *Daily News*. By March of 1984 he was in New York.

The *News*, in its day, had been the most successful experiment in the history of American journalism. The *News* was the brainchild of Joseph Medill Patterson, one of two heirs to the *Chicago Tribune*. Patterson was a millionaire and child of privilege with a genuine passion for democracy and such a deep dislike for the social class into which he was born that he spent much of his life trying to leave it. He was also an editorial and marketing genius who transformed his genuine affection for the working class he wanted so badly to join into a formula for the nation's first large urban tabloid. The first picture-dominated newspaper in America, the *News* was a leader in reader-friendliness, stressing short stories and readable type. Widely derided as sensationalist and pandering, the *News* certainly did take a keen interest in sex, sin, money, violence, and the smart set. But the real key to the *News*'s success was not how poorly it thought of its readers, but how well.

Though its editorial credo declared "Nothing that is not interesting is news," for Patterson that simply meant that what his fellow citizens were interested in was a good guide to what was important. Patterson never assumed that working people were witless people. He did assume they liked to read. The famous trademark *News* headlines were joyous in their use of the language. The men who wrote SAYS WIFE MADE TIME/ WITH A NEWSWEEK MAN or 3 JUDGES WEIGH/HER FAN DANCE/FIND IT WANTON or (on an announcement that a verdict in the Gloria Vanderbilt custody trial was due the first day of the week) SIC TRANSIT GLORIA MONDAY were not condescending to their audience. They were celebrating with it.

The *News* was sensationalism with style. Here is reporter Sidney Sutherland's masterful account of buxom blonde Ruth Snyder's execution for the murder of her husband, which she accomplished with the help of her corset salesman lover whose passion had been ignited when "She removed her dress and I tried on a garment to see if it was the right size."

She was garbed in a shapeless green dress and a cheap brown smock, her body reeling between the supporting clutches of the matrons. The priest was whispering.

In Ruth's white knuckled hands was clasped a large yellow crucifix. She stared at it with eyes from which human intelligence had fled. Her face was pallid, sickening under straight blond hair which fell as straight as a whisk broom below her earlobes.

As the uniformed guards closed in on her she began to whimper. The sound was like the frightened whine of a little puppy. For a moment she was hidden from sight, and as the executioner stood warily watching the keepers at work she began to whisper aloud:

"Father forgive them for they don't know what they are doing," she said over and over until the leather chin strap stopped forever the voice of the woman who had been the siren that led Judd Gray to destruction. . . .

In a little alcove across the room stood Robert G. Elliott, state executioner. Suddenly he threw the switch. It was exactly 11:01 o'clock.

Ruth's body straightened up within its confining gyves, writhed horribly for a fleeting moment and then was arched forward, rigid and still but, in its death throes, tugging vibrantly against her bonds.

In the void of quietness there was a curious humming sound, a whine that rose to a low, ominous pitch and held that note until it seemed as reverberating and ear rending and hypnotically terrifying as a siren sounding the millenium, worked by a madman in hell. . . .[1]

When the *News* was launched in 1919, no American paper had ever achieved a daily circulation of one million. The largest morning papers in New York were Hearst's *New York American* and the *New York Times*, both under 400,000, and the largest evening paper was Hearst's *Evening Journal* at just under 700,000.

The *News*, an A.M. paper, reached a circulation of 100,000 less than six months after its birth. In less than two years, it became the largest morning paper in Manhattan. Within four years it was the largest paper in America, surpassing the *Evening Journal*. In a little over five years it passed the one million mark. At its peak in 1947, Sunday circulation was 4.7 million, with daily at 2.5 million.

Under the energetic Patterson, the *News* was as innovative in every aspect of the "business side" of newspapering—production, circulation, and advertising—as it was editorially. Through its Pacific and Atlantic syndicate the *News* not only led in the use of wire-transmitted photos but helped develop the process. Patterson's paper pioneered the use of color photos. The *News* also changed the until then rather primitive circulation techniques used in the New York newspaper market, building the city's first independent distribution system.

And to offset the *News*'s biggest handicap, the conviction of advertisers that *News* readers were too downmarket to be worth reaching, the *News* created one of the best merchandising and market research departments in the nation. The *News*'s research into "downmarket" neighborhoods such as Manhattan's Lower East Side completely changed the conventional view of this market not only among marketers and advertisers but even in contemporary academic literature.

Patterson, whose grandfather had helped make Lincoln president, had inscribed over the entrance to the *News* headquarters on 42nd Street the phrase "He made so many," a fragment of a longer Lincoln quote,

"The Lord must have loved the common people; he made so many." The *News*'s pathbreaking market studies vindicated an often ignored truism of economics: the poor have more money than the rich, because He made so many.

There was real grinding poverty in *News* neighborhoods, but it was the poverty of the working poor in intact families, poverty inexorably beaten back by brutally hard work, family cooperation, and fanatical thrift. Tenements, the *News* researchers discovered, concealed working families who had managed to accumulate bank accounts of tens and even hundreds of thousands of dollars. The advertiser who could reach those people and get them to spend a bit of their newfound wealth, the *News* marketing staff argued, would have broken into a rich market indeed. And no paper served or knew that market as well as the *News*.

In its first full year the *News* had carried only 61,000 lines of advertising. By 1929 it was carrying more than 12 million lines a year. Eventually, the advertising makeup manager, a man named Emmett Gordon, was turning away enough advertising every day to support another large newspaper, a duty that earned him the nickname "Omit" Gordon and immortality of a sort:

> There was a man in our town
> And he was wondrous wise.
> He had some goods he couldn't sell
> Said he "I'll advertise.
>
> A column in the Daily News
> Will move them without doubt."
> He got his copy in, in time
> But Gordon left it out.[2]

None of the gaggle of tabloids launched in the wake of the *News*, almost all vulgar imitations that pandered and condescended to the readers Patterson loved and respected, ever truly rivaled the *News* in either circulation or advertising. But Patterson died in 1946, just as the one-two punch of television and Levittown was about to hit the urban newspaper market. A few years later, his cousin and co-heir to the Tribune Company, Colonel Robert R. McCormick, who had managed the Chicago wing of the business, also died, tying up the company stock in a trustee arrangement that deprived the papers of vigorous management for the next twenty years—the most devastating twenty years in the history of the industry.

In 1925, New York had nineteen daily newspapers with a total circulation exceeding the population of the city. By the end of World War II, half those papers were gone, but circulation was even higher. By 1966, there were only three papers left and circulation was in precipitous decline, especially inside the city limits. Paradoxically and perversely in this era of dying newspapers the unions struck again and again, not only winning enormously rich contracts and padded payrolls but wresting control of the plant floor from besieged and often (as in the *News*'s case) increasingly demoralized and apathetic managements.

As New York's economy contracted through the late 1960s and 1970s, the city lost a million residents. And though the endless strikes had helped kill off all the *News*'s tabloid rivals except the *Post*, the *News*'s once healthy profit margins shrank rapidly. By the late 1960s and early 1970s, says Jim Longson, one of the chief strategists in Hoge's efforts to rebuild the *News*, the *News*'s own management questioned "whether it made sense to continue to invest in what looked like a mature and maybe dying industry" and began to divert the *News*'s lackluster profits into such misguided ventures as an effort to diversify into commercial printing (in New York at least another dying business), while its suburban competitors such as Long Island's *Newsday* (founded in 1940 by Patterson's daughter Alicia, to whom he refused to leave the *News*) poured money into new technology and city-suburban border wars for circulation. These decisions, he says, "institutionalized the *News*'s decline. . . . We had shown our own lack of faith in the business," inspiring "a malaise that overtook employees and the management alike."

Then came what *News* executives call "the years of disaster," 1978 through 1984.

In 1978 an eighty-eight-day strike cost the *News* $20 million, 200,000 in Sunday circulation and 300,000 daily. Though the numbers fluctuated, from then on the *News* was really never much better than a breakeven business waiting for the bottom to drop out.

In 1982 new publisher Bob Hunt launched a P.M. edition of the *News*, called "The Tonight Edition," an upmarket product with glittery pretensions, more in the tradition of the ever lamented *New York Herald Tribune* than the *News*. Like the long years of disinvestment, "Tonight" seemed like another repudiation of the *News* by those who were supposed to protect it, as if the corner bar crowd had suddenly been told that nobody could make a buck on Bud anymore and from now on they would sip brandy Alexanders and like it. It failed with the public and lost enormous amounts of money.

In 1975 the McCormick-Patterson trust had expired; slowly the somnolent Tribune empire awakened from its twenty-year slumber. There was turnover in management and talk of going public. In the short term, however, this was more bad news. With the *Chicago Tribune* also stumbling and the Tribune Company newsprint plants losing money, the company was skeptical of its ability to fix all three properties at once.

Discouraged by the 1978 strike, and newly exposed to the short-term performance pressures on a public company, the Tribune Company put the *News* up for sale in 1982. The company offered both *Washington Star* publisher Joseph Albritton and New York real estate developer Donald Trump $100 million to take the *News* off its hands. Neither was able to get the union concessions they felt necessary. Both declined.

By the time Hoge got to New York, *News* managers and workers alike were convinced they worked for a paper nobody wanted, even if it was still the largest urban daily in the United States. So Hoge planned and talked and cajoled for the next five years. He brought in consultants, opened the *News*'s books to the unions. He wrote editorial manifestos, and produced a polished several-hundred-page "turnaround business plan." He held those quarterly meetings, and chat sessions with a couple dozen workers every two weeks. In 1987 he had achieved what he thought was the best labor agreement in the history of the company, based on the first stage of his turnaround business plan. He thought the agreement was the first step in a joint labor-management effort to save the paper.

Now it seemed he had been kidding himself.

Hoge is not an impulsive man. His avocation has always been foreign policy. After the strike was all over and lost and he left the *News* he launched a vigorous and successful campaign to become editor of the prestigious and influential journal *Foreign Affairs*. He thinks about conflicts in highly logical, grand strategic, and even military terms.

He was not asking the unions for merely economic concessions. The *News* would need not only a whole new plant but a new work culture. The unions, which had effectively controlled the shop floor for decades, would have to give up much of their power. He was proposing, in fact, a "wholesale shift of power from unions who effectively run the paper" to corporate management. Under the circumstances what he had on his hands was "a brawl—people do not give up power voluntarily." The unions, he now believed, would never give him the authority he needed to save the company, not without a fight.

He thought things over for a few days. He talked out the situation with Longson and others from the new management team he had been building. Though that final (as it would turn out to be) quarterly meeting with the union presidents was for Hoge a conversion experience, it was not entirely unexpected. For some time most of the management team had been agreed that the company should take a tougher stand in the upcoming labor negotiations than it had in 1987. Cronin had been right. There had been some serious discussion of bringing in a new, tougher labor relations team. But now finally Hoge decided to go to war. This decision took the immediate form of calling Charlie Brumback.

That same month, Brumback had become chief operating officer of the Tribune Company, owner of the *News* and of the *Chicago Tribune*, as well as a cluster of other media properties around the country—newspapers, radio, TV, and a TV production company—plus paper mills, a company that supplies TV guide data to hundreds of newspapers around the country, and partial ownership in a number of other high-tech information companies. It all added up to one of the largest media conglomerates in the country.

Brumback comes originally from Ohio, but his career and his understanding of the newspaper business were forged by the twenty-four years he spent at the Orlando, Florida, *Sentinel,* first as comptroller and then as CEO. The *Sentinel* was acquired by the Tribune Company in 1965. He came north in 1981 to serve as publisher of the company's flagship paper, the *Chicago Tribune*.

There are three important things about the *Sentinel*. First, it is a nonunion paper and always has been. So in 1976 when Brumback became CEO there were no unions to stop him from taking full advantage of the radical changes in newspaper technology that were just beginning to be made possible by computers.

Second, he did take advantage. Helped by the boom Disney World created in Orlando, Brumback brought the *Sentinel* into the future with a vengeance, building a paper that was not only state-of-the-art technologically but also a highly profitable jewel in the Tribune crown. This was not an accident, or the result of Brumback simply picking up the phone and telling the computer department to do what needed to be done. The *Sentinel*, and later the *Chicago Tribune*, and the Tribune Company itself, became successful information-age companies because the top man himself was a buff, someone willing to "listen to the technology," as Carver Mead, the great prophet of microchip technology, would say. Unusually for a man of his generation, Brumback has been a computer enthusiast for decades. He bought one of the very first Apples. Even now, he says, his chief hobby is to "spend a good bit of time at home with my PC." Unlike many newspapermen, he sees with perfect clarity that the Tribune Company is not selling newspapers, or space on the electromagnetic spectrum, but information. He looks forward happily to the day when newspapers are no longer confined to newsprint. The Tribune Company has invested, with Knight Ridder, in a small company developing "flat panel" technology that will allow daily newspapers to be downloaded into a small electronic box, 9 inches by 12 inches by ½ inch, weighing about a pound, and with a screen as easy on the eyes as a well-printed page. The investment is not motivated by any desire "to sell flat panels," he explains, but by the need to stay in touch with the technology, so that when the box is ready "we'll be ready to fit our information into it."

The Tribune Company, long considered a tired and backward firm, is now acknowledged as one of the most technologically aggressive in the industry. Most of the *Tribune*'s brief "mission statement" refers to the company's commitment to exploit technological opportunities to the fullest benefit of its stockholders. Brumback is the man who forged that commitment.

Finally, when the Tribune Company awoke from its slumbers determined to forge a new identity as a modern, profit-driven public company, it looked to Brumback and his team from Orlando to do much of the work. The Chicago-based company was soon to be run largely by men from Florida. Ask a Tribune Company executive for the story of his success, and the phrase that you are most likely to hear is "I spent some time with Charlie in Orlando."

A *News* editor once described Brumback as "the only man in history to walk out of the second act of *Cats* because he thought it was dirty." Brumback, a former accountant, inevitably is derided by critics as a "bean counter," but the *Cats* crack (while not actually true, it was *Glengarry Glenn Ross* and it was the first act) is more revealing. More than a bean counter Brumback is a straight arrow, a remarkably tough leader with enormous moral confidence and an almost religious reverence for business efficiency. A practicing Presbyterian who gives out copies of Ayn Rand's *The Fountainhead* to friends and co-workers, Brumback is utterly immune to the working-class romanticism that is so crucial to union solidarity, as well as union PR and political power, in Catholic and Jewish New York. He is that most terrifying of persons, the man with a clear conscience. While union solidarity requires businesses to share the wealth with their employees without paying too strict attention to their individual productivity, Brumback comes from an older American tradition that regards such blind beneficence as actually corrupt, a form of theft, a violation of the sacred rites of work and self-reliance whereby grace is manifest in the world. While in the last few generations many Americans have adopted at least in theory a social measure of morality, under which justice has come to mean a rough-and-ready, practical American approximation of Marx's "from each according to his ability, to each according to his needs," for Brumback justice and honesty are still simple, straightforward individual obligations laid out perfectly clearly in the Commandments: don't steal, don't lie.

His own inability to tell a deliberate mistruth is both one of his strengths and one of his failings as a leader. According to some of his colleagues he found it nearly impossible during the fight for the *News* to bring himself to employ ringing rhetoric or even conventional hyperbole to rally his own troops. He is a man incapable of saying "darn it we are going to save this newspaper" without qualifying it by saying "provided we can do it without compromising our fiduciary responsibilities to produce a reasonable rate of return to our stockholders," apparently for fear that in his enthusiasm he might be making a pledge he could not keep. As for justice, a man doing less than a full day's work for a full day's pay is simply stealing and it inspires in him a true moral horror. He regarded the unworked overtime and overmanning in the *News* plants as a moral outrage (whereas the union guys, free marketers down to their toes, simply regarded it as part of the freely negotiated price of labor) and saw its elimination not only as a bottom-line necessity but a moral obligation. Brumback's puritanical outlook is easy to deride as suicidally narrow-minded. A less honest or rigid man might not have lost the *News*. But there is something magnificent and pure about it, as if a man had reduced the beatific vision to an SEC filing.

Hoge knew that Brumback was "an anti-union manager" who was "convinced there was no way to pleasantly or reasonably negotiate with the unions the kind of agreement we needed." In 1985, as publisher of the *Tribune*, Brumback had broken several of the paper's unions in a lengthy strike because he believed the unions' stubbornness was keeping the paper's new state-of-the-art automated "Freedom Center" printing plant from fulfilling its potential. "I have trouble with managers who want to make the environment comfortable for marginal people who are not performing," he says. "I don't waste a lot of time on underperformers."

After Freedom Center was opened, he explains, "we had a terrible time getting the old pressmen" to give up their old ways and adjust to the new technology. But when recruiting potential "replacement workers" to put out the paper in the event of a strike, he discovered "you could take people off the street and if they were reasonably bright and were physically adept and—this is very important—comfortable with digital technology—you could put them in a classroom and then out on the floor and within a few weeks they would be competent pressmen."

Some say Brumback got lucky in Chicago, and that his luck made him underestimate the unions in New York. The *Tribune* is trucked by Teamsters who unexpectedly honored a no-strike clause in their contract. Since Freedom Center's technology had made it especially easy to print the paper with replacement workers, only the drivers could have made the strike work. Without them it collapsed. New York would be a tougher nut to crack.

Brumback would say he had no choice but to try. He is not a sentimental man and he would not keep the *News* alive just because it was an old family property. The *News* "was a financial basket case." It "would make a little money one year then lose a lot the next," and a close look would show "even the little profit they made was the result of bookkeeping adjustments." It had to be fixed or gotten rid of. He "didn't want it sitting out there for five or ten years as a bleeding ulcer."

Hoge knew that when he called Brumback to tell him cooperation was off and he wanted to make a fight of it, the Tribune Company would be anything but reluctant. As Hoge expected, Brumback encouraged him to act swiftly on his new conviction. "If you are going in a different direction," he told Hoge, "get into first gear. Now you are in idle."

To get into first gear Hoge turned to a man he knew Brumback trusted, Robert Ballow, possibly the most loathed and admired, respected and hated labor lawyer in the United States. Ballow has made a specialty of fighting newspaper unions, hard.

Ballow is a stocky, six-foot, dark-haired, deep-voiced, slow-talking, story-telling Tennessean, a newspaperman first who came to the law in middle age. He started working in the circulation department of the *Nashville Banner* in 1942 when he was eleven, and became circulation director before he was thirty. As an executive, he began sitting in on labor negotiations. Soon he realized most labor lawyers did not understand newspapers very well. He did some reading in the law and decided what most of them knew about labor law wasn't all that impressive either. He could not afford to leave his job, so he signed up for night classes at the Nashville YMCA School of Law, and got his degree in 1963, just a few years before computer technology would begin to revolutionize the newspaper industry.

The *News*'s choice of Ballow as labor counsel had a certain inevitability: as one *News* executive put it, for a battle that by newspaper industry standards promised to be "the Super Bowl of labor relations," who else would you call? There is no other firm in the industry like King & Ballow. They represent over 300 American newspapers, including some of the most important media groups in the country, such as Capital Cities, owners of ABC. They have handled more than 2,000 newspaper union negotiations. A significant number of these have ended with unions being effectively broken—if not actually decertified, then forced to accept contracts that make a mockery of union power.

Wherever Ballow goes now he is preceded by the myth of his own ruthlessness and invincibility. AFL-CIO president Lane Kirkland once alleged in a letter that simply hiring Ballow amounted to an unfair labor practice, prima facie evidence of intent to bust the unions. He not only infuriates unions, he mystifies and terrifies them. For what Ballow does, according to the myth, is make unions destroy themselves.

In the most common form of the myth, Ballow comes into town and proposes a contract designed to be rejected, a contract not only unacceptable but insulting, even emasculating. When he gets to the table, he tells you: This contract is the way it's going to be and that's that. "Better make the best deal you can, boys, because if you don't we are going to wear you down so low, you'll wish to have this day back so you could leap across the table and sign."

He'll never give an inch, he'll let negotiations run on and on for months or years after the contract expires. He'll stop company contributions to the union health and welfare funds, which he can do legally once the contracts expire because they are not "mandatory subjects of collective bargaining." He'll stop the union dues checkoff. He'll launch innumerable "unfair labor practice" actions against the union before the National Labor Relations Board, which he can afford to press and unions can't afford to defend. He'll annoy workers at the job site, says the myth, by bringing in armed guards to watch them all the time. He'll make sure that management disciplines workers for the slightest infringement of the rules, with firings whenever possible.

And he'll do all this for one reason: like the outlaw gunfighter played by Jack Palance in *Shane*, he wants to manipulate the unions into "drawing" on him, so he can shoot 'em down dead. The way the union "draws" is to strike (or do something that Ballow can through his mastery of labor law make to look like a strike). That's right, says the myth, Ballow is doing all this because he *wants* unions to strike. Once they do, he can bring in "permanent replacements" to do their jobs, run the newspaper without them, and decertify the union.

There is some truth to this scenario. "Ballow's negotiating style is," as Hoge wryly puts it, "arresting." Ballow clients prepare—visibly—to publish during a strike. He will negotiate for years if necessary. Many Ballow clients do bring in lots of security early on, step up employee discipline, and apply other of the tactics to which the myth alludes.

Yet the notion of Ballow as trickster who forces unions to strike against their will is flawed. For the unions it can also be self-deluding. For one thing, few Ballow negotiations end in strikes. More often the unions surrender at the negotiating table. Ballow's contracts usually include generous pay increases. For members who have not had raises for months or years and have lived all that time under the threat of a legal lockout and the loss of their jobs, the enticement can prove irresistible. Exhausted union members often force the leadership to concede defeat or face decertification.

The myth is self-deluding because Ballow is *more* dangerous than the myth implies. He is something much worse for the unions than a legal trickster. He is, like Brumback, a man who has listened to the machines. And what the machines tell him is that with their new brains they no longer need union craftsmen with years of experience to run them, and so the men who own newspapers never have to worry about the unions again.

Ballow's contract proposals are blunt and his follow-up is uncompromising. But he wins not by provoking unions to anger or to strike but by evoking despair. He makes unions contemplate their powerlessness. Sugar-coating the message would only perpetuate their illusions. Ballow wins by making his adversaries look reality in the face.

All of Ballow's tactics demoralize the enemy. The guards make the union men feel helpless, isolated, powerless. But so they are. It had been the market power of their specialized skills that once gave newspaper unions control of the plant floor. Now that power is gone.

The training of managers and replacement workers to print a paper has the practical purpose of keeping it on the street and in business during a strike. But since most of his confrontations do not end in the strikes, the real purpose of training a strike-breaking work force is to send the message, through deeds not words, that the unions' skills have lost their value.

Ballow's willingness to negotiate indefinitely also reveals the unions' helplessness. The law requires only that parties negotiate, not that they agree. The union cannot force him to move. And while negotiations drag on, Ballow demonstrates, day in and day out, to the union's members how powerless the union is: powerless to keep up the health and welfare fund to which the company has stopped contributing; powerless to keep the company from asserting its power on the plant floor because the union, afraid of giving Ballow an excuse for a lockout, will tell workers to yield to managers rather than provoke an incident; powerless to call a slowdown to protest layoffs or a disciplinary action, because a slowdown would also justify a lockout and "permanent replacement" of the work force.

In most Ballow campaigns, there are no tricks, no Nashville, Tennessee, YMCA night law school pied piper leading unions on to self-destruction. Rather a simple message is relentlessly hammered home: the unions are already dead. Sure they are still standing, still collecting dues, still negotiating. But they are husks, sheared of all power by technological and managerial changes that started more than two decades ago.

Some newspaper managements do not know this yet, so they still cower before their unions. Some of the unions do not know this yet; so they still go about acting as if they were alive and strong. Ballow is a dark messenger, come to quiet the unrestful dead.

CHAPTER 3

Deus ex Machina

This peculiar idea ... of one's duty in a calling, is what is most characteristic of the social ethic of a capitalist culture, and is in a sense the fundamental basis of it.
Max Weber, *The Protestant Ethic and the Spirit of Capitalism*

THE *New York Daily News* was founded by men from Chicago. Now men from Chicago had decided that the *News* had to change. Their determination to insist on change started the war that nearly destroyed the paper. So it is a natural first step to go to Chicago.

The Tribune Company is a notoriously taciturn organization. But it turns out that all these busy executives want nothing more than to talk to you. A year after the strike they still burn with the tragic light of loss, and ache to speak of what might have been. They do not talk in the way we expect businessmen to talk, like accountants. They talk like proselytizers and poets.

What the men want to talk about is the machines. Not the machines in New York, but the machines here in Chicago. Every conversation starts the same way: "Has anyone taken you out to see the plant yet?"

The plant is called Freedom Center, and the men who want to show it to you are not just being polite. They believe it is the heart of the story. After the *Daily News* strike the Tribune Company commissioned reporter Kathleen Hale to write a 600-page history of the strike for the company archives. The title? "They Could Have Had That in New York." "That" means Freedom Center. The *Daily News* is not mentioned until the subtitle.

Freedom Center, the newspaper plant that revived the faltering *Chicago Tribune,* the company's flagship property, became operational, as HAL would say, in 1983. It cost $180 million and was then the most advanced newspaper production plant in the United States.

Freedom Center did not really come to life, however, until 1985, when the *Tribune*'s three largest production unions went on strike and more than a thousand seasoned workers left the plant, most never to return.

They are not missed. The workers lost their life's work, a craft, and a career, and with it their place in the American middle class. No one at the *Tribune* seems entirely comfortable with this result. Nevertheless they are not missed. Freedom Center could not, say the men who run it, have come to life under the old rules and customs, the jealousies and prerogatives of nine different craft unions in the same shop, the relentless hostility between worker and manager, the endless work rules devised in a day when newspaper plants were just places to print newspapers.

Today, Freedom Center prints money, or at least it might as well. Here and in increasing numbers of plants around the country the newspaper is being transformed into an immensely profitable communications and advertising medium that in many ways makes broadcast television look primitive. In the 1970s and early 1980s the *Chicago Tribune* produced a bare annual profit of 6 to 8 percent of operating costs, less than the company could have gotten by locking its money up in government bonds. Since Freedom Center came to life in the mid-1980s the *Tribune* has consistently been the most profitable large metropolitan daily newspaper in the United States, repeatedly producing profits of 20 to 25 percent. To put it another way, if you drop a dollar in one end of Freedom Center, it will come out the other end $1.25.

Go inside. If you like machines at all you will begin to feel a bit of the thrill and a bit of the reverence you hear in the men's voices when they talk about it. There are computers of course, huge computers of a speed, complexity, and capacity that rival anything outside the best university research centers or the greatest temples of the Defense Advanced Research Projects Agency. But the thing about computers, of course, is that they are a little dull, at least to look at.

Computers are like brains. They have (almost) no moving parts. They are all but noiseless and do not require regular lubrication or rust preventative. Like brains, computers are almost impenetrable black boxes. The action of an automatic rifle or a garage door opener thrills because we can see it work, and almost understand the magic of metal moving like fingers, arms, and legs, dexterous and full of purpose. One could peer at the motionless insides of a PC all day and not feel the same thrill. But then we wonder, since PCs after all do amazing things, if we will ever be thrilled by technology again.

Yes. Here. For here are computers linked to machines, big, heavy, fast, monstrous metal machines. Most of them have that old brunt brutal look of the industrial age, analogs of freight trains, earth movers, pile drivers, wonders of might and motion, huge hunks of metal straight out of Socialist Realism or a Popeye cartoon, but one supposes dumb wonders after all.

But no—that is what is so unnerving. Not dumb. Huge hunks of metal with brains.

A full roll of newsprint is fifty-five inches high and forty-five inches wide, and it weighs 1,700 pounds. The *Chicago Tribune* uses between four and five thousand such rolls a week. For all their bulk the rolls are quite fragile. At standard cruising speed of 60,000 papers an hour, the paper rolls through the presses at twenty-one miles per hour. A crease in any part of the paper, a thumbnail incautiously traced across the surface, even insufficient humidity in the air, can cause a tear (called a web break) that will shut down the entire nine-roll press for precious minutes, or for much longer if the shredding paper fouls the works.

Web breaks are expensive and reducing them is a top priority. Delay shreds profits. Newspapers are more perishable than milk. Late newsstand delivery will mean lost sales that very day. Late home delivery means subscription complaints and cancellations and fewer total readers delivered to advertisers. Web breaks also waste newsprint, which is expensive, accounting for 20 percent of the *Tribune*'s production budget. So significant is newsprint waste for the bottom line that the Freedom Center employee bonus plan started as a newsprint waste reduction effort.

These huge rolls of newsprint perfectly symbolize the paradoxes of newspaper production. Newspapers are "heavy" industries, but they use delicate materials. Their production runs are huge, but they are completed, down to door-to-door distribution, within hours. Quality—especially for papers with color ads—is crucial and takes great technological sophistication and attention to detail; but twenty-four hours after delivery the product becomes a bulk commodity worth pennies a pound. Newspapers have traditionally been organized by craft rather than industrial unions; for the skills required were long among the most considerable in the blue-collar world. But as technology improves, the old skill requirements decline, stranding the craft unions in a new post-industrial world. With the advent of CAM, Computer Assisted Manufacturing, newspaper plants are becoming post-industrial paradigms, enormous structures of steel and stone held up by a few feathery wafers of silicon. Newspaper mass production is among the oldest of American industries, older by far than the automobile industry, or even the steel industry. Yet today newspapers are leaders in the current renaissance in American manufacturing.

The production process in Freedom Center starts in a cavernous, 4.5 million-cubic-foot newsprint warehouse. Seventy-five feet high, the warehouse can hold 25,000 rolls of paper. The rolls are stacked vertically, so the room looks like a forest of great and ancient trees, but without branches. Overhead is a huge, bright yellow crane, capable of moving to any Cartesian point above the floor, like a Skycam on steroids. Its eight suction lifts can move up to sixteen rolls of paper at a time. The lifts have to use suction because anything else might crease the paper.

The crane deposits the rolls on a conveyor that snakes into the bottom story of the main plant, where repose the nether regions of the three-story-high presses. About twenty yards in, the roll hits a "layover" machine that ever so gently lays it on its side, after which it is conveyed to a stripping station where, in the last vestige of brute manual labor in the entire plant, its protective wrapping is stripped by men wielding large butcher knives—very well.

From there the computer takes over. The roll is automatically logged into the plant computer system by a visual scanner, giving it, like all the several hundred rolls of paper moving around the plant floor or through the presses, a unique identity. From now on it will be addressed and directed by the computer "by name" until it has been used.

The *Tribune* uses ten presses, each of which has nine "units," each of which runs one roll of paper. Each press unit has three giant spools, called "reel spiders," one that holds the running roll, one that holds the roll that is ready to run, and one empty and ready to receive a roll.

The presses, like every other moving object in the plant—except for the butcher knives—are hooked into the computer. When a press nears the end of a running roll, it tells the computer. The computer selects a roll and releases it to . . . the "ghost train."

Snaking past every unit of every press is a sort of monorail track along which ride dozens of yellow carts, like the little trains that run through coal mines, except that instead of sidewalls they each bear a shallow cradle in which rests a roll of newsprint. It is a bizarre and unearthly sight. The carts are not linked. Each moves independently, starting and stopping unattended, going where the computer tells it to go. Everywhere these great rolls of newsprint in their little cars snake silently along the track, mostly parallel to the great press arrays. Then suddenly one of the carts will make a sharp turn to deliver a fresh roll to a unit, as if it has just noticed a press in need. It is hard to overcome the impression of metal come to life.

When the roll arrives it is automatically transferred to the waiting reel. A pressman is there to superintend adjustments but the machines do the work.

The ghost train has three goals: to reduce manpower (at many newspapers around the country, including the *Daily News,* men still push 1,700-pound rolls of newspaper around the pressroom floor); to avoid damage and waste; and to keep the system moving. If one unit has to slow down because its roll is late, the whole press slows down.

The paper unrolls upward; a press unit is a vertical three-story array rising through the floor of Freedom Center's second story and on up to a mezzanine level above. The actual printing and folding is done on these upper levels. Here also the computers rule.

On the main pressroom floor—the second—sit five glass-walled "quiet rooms," one for every two presses. About sixteen feet wide and sixty-four feet long, running most of the length of the presses, they are called quiet rooms because they are a place of refuge from the ninety-decibel noise of ten presses running flat out. But noise control is not their main function. They are high-tech control rooms, taken up mostly with computer consoles that regulate paper speed and "color registration," i.e., putting the right amount of ink of the right color in the right place for every roll of the press.

Color registration—the term applies even to black-and-white runs, where black is the only "color"—is, along with avoiding web breaks, the crucial art of the pressman. It is especially crucial to the full-color photographs and illustrations that can bring in tens of millions of dollars of extra ad revenue. Full-, or four-color, means printing the same page four times, once each for black, blue, yellow, and red, which makes getting the page right much more than four times as challenging. A little too much black on a black-and-white page makes a page look a little too dark. But a little too much yellow on a color page makes it look awful. Advertisers love color, but they hate bad color.

Good color is an art and requires artists, which the pressmen are. The computer is their medium. The computer "pre-sets" the ink flows, usually getting pretty close to an acceptable result. But the pressmen must be there to check sample papers and turn approximation into art.

In the quiet room of press No. 1 the crew chief, Lou, an hourly employee, but the leader of a squad that works together every night, stands by the conveyor that carries fresh papers off the press and up to the packaging and shipping levels above. Every few minutes he pulls out a paper and starts . . . reading it, or so it seems. But he's not reading really, he is checking every page: for the quality of color registration, for ink volume, even for typos in the headlines, though strictly speaking what the words say or how they are spelled is not his department. It has to be done because as good as computers are, computers are not artists. And even after the settings are right they drift, or a new paper roll will vary slightly in how it absorbs ink, or any other of dozens of factors affecting quality will change.

Here is one of the paradoxes of the new machines and their new men: the new presses are much simpler to run than the old preautomated presses they replaced. There is less "craft" involved. What was once achieved by dozens of mechanical adjustments on each unit of a press array spread almost one hundred feet across the pressroom floor is now done at a single computer console. On the old machines a pressman needed a feel for the eccentricities of every unit. But it is always and everywhere the mark of digital technology to eliminate eccentricities. The old analog world of craft, custom, and experience, years and years of experience, fades away. Computers are complicated—on the inside—but they make our machines more simple and consistent.

Thus in the traditional sense of the word the "skill" levels of the men who run the new machines have dropped. Pulling papers out of a conveyor is not a skill; even checking a paper for defects does not require much technical skill, though your eyes do get better, and your standards, if you care, do get higher over time. The "skill" that is important here is a "moral skill": the commitment to pulling a paper every two minutes rather than every ten even though there is no management supervisor watching you, the commitment to hold yourself and the crew to high standards. It is the skill of giving a darn; taking the trouble to make the necessary adjustments not just when gross defects show up but whenever a page falls short of the highest standard of quality. And for the pressmen it is trouble. It means a night of constant vigilance, rather than gossip, smokes, and the break room.

It is the machines that make these moral skills *relevant*, by making high quality *possible*. With the old black-and-white "letterpress" presses, like the fifty-year-old monsters still used at the *Daily News*, the payback for diligence was modest. Yes, a good press crew would produce a significantly better paper than a bad crew. But the gap between the results of good work and outstanding work was narrow, and the payoff in increased ad dollars was small. The four-color "offset" process has a far higher quality upside than black-and-white, an upside that can only be achieved with computer control (without which it would be impractical to fine-tune the presses constantly) *and* moral commitment (without which the fine tuning would not happen).

The computer allows the pressman to raise his sights, to become not just an artist but a renaissance artist, part of the current rebirth of American industry.

The essence of a successful business is not saving money but making it. You can cut waste but you cannot, consistently, cut your way to a profit. Businesses that consistently talk more about cutting costs than raising revenues die.

Much of what goes on in Freedom Center is about cutting costs: the huge automated paper warehouse and the ghost train, even the new presses, reduce man-hours. At the presses, however, the drive to cut costs is overtaken by the drive to improve quality, please the customer, expand the market, and make money.

Then, on the top two floors of the plant, Freedom Center becomes a money machine.

The great advantage of newspapers as an advertising vehicle has been their mass appeal. That has been their great disadvantage as well: advertisers who buy ads in the 700,000 circulation (1.1 million on Sunday) *Chicago Tribune* inevitably pay for the physical delivery of a piece of paper to hundreds of thousands of readers who have no interest whatsoever in their products. Broadcast television of course has some of the same disadvantages, but for most purposes it is the more powerful mass-market medium. To compete, newspapers must offer more than their traditional mass-market reach.

The answer, in theory, has always been "zoning": don't send the same paper to everyone, put some ads in some editions but not others, and make sure the editions with the right ads get to the right customers. A good theory, but since a daily newspaper must be produced and distributed to several hundred thousand or a million readers in six to ten hours it remained not much more than a theory for many years.

Today the *Tribune* has ninety-five different advertising zones; meaning as regards advertisements, ninety-five different versions of the paper go out every day. An advertiser can buy as little as one ninety-fifth of the *Tribune* market. Local stores that would never have dreamed of taking daily newspaper ads a few years ago can now advertise just to their neighborhood by having inserts placed into the papers destined for their zones. An upscale clothing chain with customers scattered through the Chicago area but clustered in pricey zip codes can pick a dozen or two dozen zones in which to place its ads.

In the Chicago area the *Tribune* has a breadth and depth of circulation that almost rivals broadcast television, but can fine-tune its ad delivery with a precision that rivals cable TV. In a few years, the *Tribune* will have true zip-code zoning—almost 400 zones. In less than ten years it may have house-to-house zoning. With the recent addition of Americomm, a direct mail firm, to fill the gaps in the *Tribune*'s circulation, the *Trib* will have become for most purposes a second Chicago post office.

Most zoning is done by inserts slipped into the paper; though there are also thirteen different editions of the main body of the paper itself printed most nights. Inserts once counted for a relatively small fraction of the paper's revenue. Today they account for more than one-third of total operating revenues and the figure is growing fast. During the 1991–1992 recession, in a severely depressed advertising market, the *Tribune* kept setting new all-time monthly advertising revenue records even in traditionally slow months. Zoned inserts were the reason.

The money machine is driven by the computer, but as on the first floor it is the combination of electronics with mechanics that amazes. The challenge of zoning is not to divide 700,000 papers into ninety-five zones, but to print, insert, pack, load, and ship them to the right place in six to ten hours. The computer knows which presses are running which of the thirteen editorial editions, and therefore which conveyor they are on. The conveyors carry the papers to one of several "inserters," which look something like giant roulette wheels. Each of the twenty-one positions on the inserter can place a different insert or package of inserts into the finished paper, depending on its zone. The computer keeps track of every paper, as zoned, as they are carried by conveyor from the inserter to the bundling machines, which count out the papers, thirty, forty, or fifty to a bundle, place an outer protective sheet on the bundle, and then wrap it up tight with a heavy-duty plastic tie. The bundler spits the bundle out onto another conveyor, moving very fast. The bundles race along, but where the conveyor ends the bundles keep going, arching through the air into the "traymatic." The traymatic is another ghost train, but this one has much higher spirits.

Waiting for the traymatic five floors below at the twenty-eight-bay loading dock are the drivers and their trucks. At many American newspapers, including the *News*, the loading dock is an arena of chaos and confusion—and product "shrinkage"—as drivers rush to claim what seem like the appropriate numbers of the right bundles and move them into their trucks. At the *News*, 20,000 to 80,000 papers a night disappeared from the loading and packaging area, most of them appropriated for a multi-million-dollar-a-year, citywide newspaper bootlegging operation. Theft aside, the *News*'s haphazard loading system would never work for a paper running dozens or hundreds of advertising zones. There would have been a riot every night as drivers scrambled to get the right numbers of the right bundles into their trucks on schedule.

At the *Chicago Tribune* the drivers never enter the plant. They back their trucks up to a loading bay, and punch their individual route codes into a keypad on the outer wall of the bay. The computer and the traymatic do the rest.

The traymatic consists of hundreds of shallow yellow bins fixed to a swiftly moving conveyor belt. The computer knows at all times which bundle of papers is in each of the trays, it knows what inserts are in the bundles and what zone they are going to. It knows which trucks are at which bays, which zones each truck serves and how many papers the truck needs on this particular day. As a tray whips around to the correct bay, it ejects the bundle onto a steep metal chute that carries the paper into the truck, where it is stacked by the waiting trucker and his helper. To keep the trucker from being overwhelmed, the computer even knows not to toss a bundle to a particular bay more quickly than the trucker can load them. If it happens to have the right bundle in the right place at the wrong time it will either pass it to another truck that needs the same sort of bundle or hold the bundle in the traymatic for another revolution.

*   *   *

Computer Assisted Manufacturing, CAM, unlike earlier baby steps toward newspaper automation such as electronic typesetting, is much more than a labor-saving device. When in the early 1970s computer screens replaced typewriters and Linotype machines, the primary effect was to make obsolete tens of thousands of American printers (as the typesetters were called; the men who run printing presses are "pressmen"). But the departure of Linotype yielded little more than a one-time permanent reduction in payroll. Customers noticed little change in the newspaper as a product. It was a budget-cutting, not a market-expanding change.

The prime purpose of Computer Assisted Manufacturing is to find new customers and new ways to please old customers. "Close to the customer" is the great slogan of the post-industrial renaissance. Getting close to the customer means shifting away from purely internal standards of quality and efficiency and instead finding out what your customers really want from you. CAM makes this possible by transforming traditional mass-production enterprises into flexible manufacturers of diversified products—such as zoned newspapers.

The industrial age thrived on economies of scale, on transforming all markets as much as possible into mass markets, even to Ford's extreme of transforming the market of car buyers into the market of buyers of black cars. For preautomated industrial age machinery, so difficult to adjust and retool, the goal was always to make everything alike, again and again and again, preferably by men using the "one best method" of efficiency expert Frederick Taylor and his heirs. Innovation, at least at the tactical level of the shop floor, could actually be the enemy of productivity. Productivity's great allies were uniformity and regulation.

The goal of computer-assisted plants is just the opposite: to raise the value of products by differentiating them for different customers. Computer-assisted plants are so potentially adept at modifying the products they make, even in the middle of a run, that we now have factories—huge mass-production plants—for which a run is fifty items or less. If the *Tribune* ever achieves house-to-house zoning—and finds a market for it—a "run" will be one item.

There is no point in getting close to customers and finding out what they want unless you can give it to them. Without the technology you are better off sticking with industrial age business strategies, giving it "to 'em in any color they want as long as it's black," and taking care of the bottom line by shaving costs. Getting close to the customer is an idea whose time has come, but its time could not have come before the microchip.

Yet though the potential arises out of the technology it is fulfilled in people. The new technology requires managers committed to finding and fulfilling its potential. That may require overcoming their training, habits, and even their sense of status. Workers may have to accept a completely new way of thinking not only about their jobs, but also about the institutions and managers they work for and their unions, if any. They must become willing and eager members of a team devoted to continuously exploring the potential of the machines. The challenge can be severe and painful.

A new $180 million ($300 million today) automated newspaper printing plant does not start paying for itself the first day. Printing nearly 700,000 papers a night, sorting them into ninety-five advertising zones, with perfect four-color reproductions on newsprint, and doing it on time, to specs, at an affordable price is the result of thousands of decisions made right. It is the end product of thousands of insights into the technology and marginal process improvements, years of work to reduce web breaks, cut paper waste in half, surpass industry standards for color reproduction, shave seconds off a process here that unclogs a pipeline there, capturing minutes in this stage of production, and hours in the course of the night. Precisely because the plant is designed to be flexible, to "grow" as its potential is discovered, it will never pay for itself unless the men who use it dedicate themselves to discovering that potential. Following the lead of the machines, the men must become acolytes of continuous change; dedicated to continuous improvements in quality and therefore to continuous personal self-improvement.

This is the real meaning of another catch phrase of the post-industrial renaissance, Total Quality Management, the now famous brainchild of W. Edwards Deming, the man who brought quality control to Japan. A great deal of nonsense gets talked about TQM, even by Deming himself, who has a tendency to obscure his very sensible insights in a fog of high-sounding, New Age, Zen of Technology blather. Many of his admirers and interpreters are even worse, and unfortunately many companies that declare themselves for TQM never get beyond the silly slogans.

The Tribune Company does not have much use for the slogans. To the extent it adopted them and became self-consciously a TQM company (which not everyone in the company agrees it is or thinks it should be), it did so only after it had already put Deming's essential insights into effect. For whether they use the slogans or not, all successful post-industrial companies that rely on their workers to evoke the best from technology are using Deming's principles, because those principles arise naturally from the technology.

Scott Sherman, an ordained deacon, was (until his departure for academia) by acclamation and his own admission the Tribune Company's chief zealot and leading evangelist ("I hope you don't mind biblical analogies," he says) for TQM. He likes to explain TQM by using Deming's analogy of a toaster, not least because it affords Sherman nearly endless opportunities for unbearable puns. ("If we do this right we make lots of extra dough, but you gotta know which side your bread is buttered on," etc. ad nauseam.)

The toaster is the technology, toasting is the process, toast is the product. The customer doesn't want burnt toast. As a manager you have two choices: The first is to give the toaster operator the simple directive to make as much toast as he can as fast as he can, hope most of the pieces come out unburnt, put an inspector at the end of the line and have him pull burnt pieces off the line, and hire scrapers to salvage them. It's expensive, because you have to pay for the inspector and scrapers, and it can lose customers, because people don't really like scraped toast. But it can work. It is called quality by inspection and American industry got by that way for years.

There is not much of a learning curve on such a system, because the quality control effort (the inspector and scrapers) is devoted to catching errors, not to improving the process. The process might continue for years without fundamental change, which means that the toast makers will make toast for years without producing any new insights into the true potential of the toaster. There is no progress built into the system.

But suppose you do away with the inspectors and scrapers, put their salaries in a bonus fund, and tell the toast makers their job is no longer just to make a lot of toast but to figure out why so many doggone (Sherman says things like "doggone") pieces keep getting burned. Now you have a bunch of guys who, instead of just dropping bread in slots, are thinking about toasters all day, figuring out how they work, how they might work better, and how we can squeeze new products out of them. Soon the guys running the toaster will know it a lot better than the managers of the toast plant and maybe even better than the toaster makers. Now we have a learning curve. The process isn't fixed; it is in constant flux. If a customer comes by and says, "Hey, do you think we could get a toasted bagel out of that thing?" you, or your workers, will know, or find out.

This is *Total* Quality Management, says Sherman, because *everybody* in the plant is now jointly responsible for quality. It is by making everyone jointly responsible, by breaking down the distinction between worker and manager, that you create the learning curve.

For years, the *Orlando Sentinel*'s Sunday magazine was losing money: "a lot of money," says Sherman. Sherman and some other *Sentinel* execs met with advertisers and found out what the problem was. There were not enough color pages available and those there were did not fall where advertisers wanted them. A few years ago, Sherman explains, we might have more or less assumed that the problem was insoluble. After all, "the presses cost a zillion dollars, so however much color we were getting must be pretty good relative to what was available elsewhere."

Instead, he explains, the *Sentinel* told the advertisers, "Let's have another meeting, we'll bring in some guys from the pressroom, you tell them the problem." The pressroom guys—hourly workers—heard about the problem not from a manager but from customers. They liked being treated as important members of the team. Over the course of the next few weeks they spent a lot of time fooling with the press. They found out that by making the magazine page just slightly smaller—too small a difference to be noticed by most readers—and making a few other technical adjustments, they could fit two plates on a roller rather than one, effectively doubling the number of color pages, a far greater improvement than anyone had thought possible. The Sunday magazine became profitable, largely because of the insight of a few hourly employees. As Sherman points out, no senior or even middle manager was going to solve that problem: they weren't close enough to the machines. And before TQM no pressman was going to know there was a problem: they weren't close enough to the customer.

For Henry Ford the manufacturing process determined the company's relationship with his customer. It is true of course that Ford's assembly line was originally inspired by a new idea about car customers, that cars need not be playthings of the rich but tools for "any man of good salary." But once that original insight built the assembly line, the assembly line, so difficult and expensive to retool, called the shots. Customers coped with the results.

The same might easily be said of the large urban daily newspaper, circa 1970. What newspapers could be was more or less a given: any color you like as long as it's black-and-white, any news or advertisement you wanted as long as it was the same everyone else wanted. The newspaper was a majestically unresponsive product, and the rest of the company—the marketers, the circulation and ad sales guys, and the editorial departments—had to cope with it.

At Freedom Center the newspaper has become a flexible part of a flexible system, not only a way of satisfying customers' current needs, but a challenge to the rest of the system to come up with new needs to fill. To do this workers must be devoted, personally, emotionally, financially, not to what they did yesterday, or how they have been doing it for twenty years, or to the codicil to the contract they won five contracts ago, or the ancient rights of pressmen going back to their grandfather's day (for at the *News* as at the old *Tribune* and many other Northeastern papers, news production jobs were handed down as a family legacy), but to the needs of the customer as relayed back by the system.

This requires really quite a remarkable change from the industrial work force. The new skills that make Freedom Center run are not printing, or paper-handling. Team spirit, enthusiasm, diligence, a personal commitment to quality and to serving the customer, these are now more important than a good ear for a troubled press or a good eye for ink. Not that the new employees at Freedom Center are ignorant of their craft. They know the new technology and processes well and pressmen still get ink on their hands. But technical skills pale in importance compared to the psychological and indeed moral qualities of a good team member.

The moral litany of how these qualities are built—by sharing information with the workers, breaking down artificial status barriers between workers and managers, extending psychological "ownership" of the plant to its employees, raising morale and self-respect, encouraging suggestions and participation in plant decisions, and giving employees very substantial financial rewards for quality improvements—is now so familiar, and so optimistic in its implicit view of human nature, that some critics are dismissing the litany even before American business has learned to implement it. Yet if Freedom Center and the Tribune Company's other post-industrial plants are any indication, the litany works.

The first thing that strikes one on walking into the plant—and employees will point it out—is how fanatically clean the place is. One would think that newspapers had ceased to use paper and ink. The constant cleaning costs money, but the cleanliness is a deliberate reflection of the order and purposefulness of the place. It tells employees that this is an important and good place to be treated with respect and that they are important and good and should respect themselves.

That at least is how a management consultant would explain it. A Sunday school teacher would use fewer words: "cleanliness is next to Godliness." The Sunday school teacher would add that "idle hands are the devil's plaything." The constant cleaning is part of the frantic—albeit cheerful and orderly—level of activity of the place. For Freedom Center is at all times a place of work. One never sees groups of employees lolling around despite natural slack times in the nightly cycle of production. Slack times are used for preparation, cleaning, maintenance, training, and so forth. This is simultaneously a cause and an effect of the moral enthusiasm of the work force. Every moment of the workday has purpose and meaning. As more than one pressman told me, the night goes by quickly.

Artificial status distinctions are minimal. Walking around the plant floor one is struck by all the unprompted first-naming going on between VP-level managers and plant employees. One manager I walked around with was greeted by a bunch of guys who shouted "Thanks for the tickets, great game." Bulls vs. Knicks. The tickets are an executive perk, but it is expected here that executives will spend those perks on good workers. Executives and hourly employees share the same cafeteria and it is first-rate.

The great leveler, however, is information. The information flow to hourly employees is heavy and constant. At a regular meeting of line supervisors, who are hourly employees, an inserter crew chief asks why the Tribune Company has purchased Americomm, a direct mail firm that delivers some of the same ads by mail that the *Tribune* carries. Isn't that cutting into our business? Is this going to mean layoffs and lost overtime?

Jim O'Dell, the man who runs Freedom Center, launches into a five-minute talk about the insert business, how profitable it has been, how fast it is growing, and how great the guys on the inserters have been at handling the increased volume. But the way this business works, he tells them, is that advertisers want to be guaranteed a level of "penetration" (the percentage of potential customers in a given area who actually see the ad) higher than the *Trib* can provide in some areas. Americomm lets them fill in the gaps. That means more insert advertisers, not fewer. The crew chief is asked to explain this to the guys on the crew, so they understand their work is getting more important to the company, not less.

The *Tribune*'s bonus system for employees who make suggestions for improving quality and efficiency has produced 800 individual approved changes so far. Employee teams crossing department, job, and union lines (for there are some union members left) are charged with getting the most out of the new technology and planning and integrating new acquisitions.

The rewards for high performance must be more than psychological. Bonuses paid for "Quality Points" now make up a substantial part of the compensation of Freedom Center hourly employees. One of the biggest targets of the bonus system was newsprint waste, which was reduced from 5.5 percent of the paper run to 3 percent, compared to an industry average of 4.5. That added up to a saving of about $3.5 million in 1993, much of which went into the bonus account. Quality points are also awarded for on-time, on-spec performance at every stage in production, and nearly every stage in production has improved to industry-leading levels. Industry analysts call the *Tribune* the most productive major-market paper in the country.

Freedom Center is in many ways a profoundly inspiring place, a Utopia of work. But Utopia means "no place," and there was no place here for 1,000 union men who believed they were the heart and soul of the *Chicago Tribune*. Though *Tribune* executives say the remaining union workers here fit into the new culture, many of those same executives are convinced that you cannot build a truly post-industrial enterprise with unions, at least as we have known them.

It is hard enough to build a post-industrial company with industrial unions, which for decades used Taylorism for their own purposes. If there was "one best method" to do the one simple job assigned an industrial worker on an assembly line, then the unions' reaction was: "Very well, the contract will define the performance of that one job in that one manner, no more or less, better or worse, as the worker's responsibility." That transformed contracts into hundred- or thousand-page minutely detailed work agreements utterly incompatible with flexible automated systems.

Many unionized newspapers, however, are burdened not only with the customs of industrial unionism but with those of an older union tradition as well. For newspapers have traditionally been organized not by industrial unions but by craft unions. At older papers especially the production workers are represented not by one union as in most industrial shops, but several, each representing a different craft or skill. At the *Daily News* there are ten, eight of which are production unions that work primarily inside the printing plants.

While the organizational principle of industrial unionism is "one shop, one union," for craft unionism it is "one craft, one union." Practically speaking, all members of the craft in a given city are members of the same local, no matter who employs them. The craft union member's primary *employment* relationship is to the union, not his employer. The union, in negotiation with all employers (simultaneously or separately), sets work rules, and standards of skill and effort. The union through the hiring hall provides workers to employers, rather than employers carrying full-time exclusive employees trained to their own standards and practices. The union will guarantee that every brick mason, or carpenter, or plumber, or every printer, or printing pressman, or paperhandler is a skilled practitioner of a standardized craft.

To this day in New York a pressman, in principle, may work at the *Times* two days a week, the *New York Post* another, and the *News* two more. The union is even responsible for keeping seniority records, except that unions call it priority and may use other criteria in addition to duration of service to decide who gets it.

In practice the newspaper unions modify some craft customs because newspapermen, unlike carpenters and bricklayers, work in an industrial plant and choose among not thousands of contractors but a few employers. Nevertheless the principle holds true: The craft unionist supplies a single highly defined type of skilled labor to whoever contracts for his services; his loyalty is to the craft and the union, not the enterprise or the shop.

Even with the best will in the world, this arrangement is fundamentally incompatible with post-industrialism. TQM requires commitment to the company, unionized or not. It requires a sort of employee patriotism, even chauvinism. The goal cannot be to give the company the exact same level of performance everyone else in the trade gives to their employers. You have to want to work harder and be better, because this is your company.

Teamwork goes out the window when eight different unions, jealous of their jurisdictions, vie for power on the plant floor. Yet a post-industrial plant pursuing Continuous Process Improvement must frequently shift personnel around on the floor, running the paper with, say, fewer pressmen and more inserters. All the process improvement committees cut across the old jurisdictional lines. Pressmen, mechanics, electricians, paperhandlers, and mailers all work together and all have to know each other's jobs. Try that sort of thing in an old-fashioned craft-union shop and there will be endless wrangles and even legal arbitration over whether, horror of horrors, a new procedure shifts work from one union to another.

A craft union regime subverts teamwork even at the micro level, within, say, a press crew, because under the hiring hall system the same people may not be there two nights in a row. Crew pride is high at Freedom Center in part because crews earn bonuses and compete for awards as a unit—impossible under craft rules.

Craft unions are deeply traditional organizations with roots in medieval guilds. Their moral and spiritual heritage is to preserve the craft, not to innovate. It is a great mistake to assume that this heritage is irrelevant and that unions care only about dollars and cents. Craft pride, and the belief that those who practiced the craft always have controlled and always should control the work and the workplace, was one of the most powerful motives in the *News* war.

In the newspaper industry, moreover, all this hoary traditionalism was combined with dirigiste industrial union contracts: the newspaper unions work, after all, in an industrial environment under quasi-assembly line conditions. Whereas most craft union contracts, for carpenters or bricklayers, for example, are short and simple, allowing the skills of the workers to define the work, the newspaper unions in both Chicago and New York had adopted the Taylorist approach and had hugely detailed contracts with voluminous work rules and side agreements.

This indictment of the unions all makes perfect sense. Its unions busted, Freedom Center makes enormous profits. And the men who run the Tribune Company are enormously proud of that.

But there is more going on here than making dollars or making sense. The men in Chicago were and are on a mission. The first thing that strikes one, talking to them, is their fierce idealism. Bill Reel, the *News*'s (now *Newsday*'s) staunchly conservative columnist, described them as "religious zealots," men "with a gleam in their eyes." Don Singleton, a *News* reporter originally skeptical of the strike who went on to become a militant, calls them fanatics. James Grottola, the printers union president; Jack Kennedy, president of the pressmen; and other union leaders dismiss them with one of the most contemptuous terms known to practical men: "ideologues."

Aren't businessmen supposed to be relentlessly pragmatic? These men shimmer with ruthless idealism as they take you out on the plant floor of Freedom Center and say in effect, "This is good, this is right, this is the best we can do, and that means this is what we should do."

Listening to these men talk more than a year later about "the plant," dream about what they could have done in New York, listening to them marvel at how the work force in New York could have let salvation slip away, one is tempted to say that Freedom Center has become an icon of what the Tribune Company understands itself to be.

But of course that is the wrong term entirely: wrong religion, wrong century. Freedom Center is not an icon, but, like the Tribune Company's healthy bottom line, a visible manifestation of grace, the outward sign of men who do God's work in the world.

No one at the Tribune Company would describe it that way. True, Brumback is a Presbyterian. But the Presbyterian church is not reliably Calvinist anymore, and the people around Brumback certainly do not think of him as a deeply religious man. Neither do most of the other men from Chicago think of themselves that way. If you ask them, "What was the role of religion in this story?" they will look blank or get embarrassed, because they are practical men.

Nevertheless the Protestant ethic to which Max Weber credited the spirit of capitalism is the heart of the post-industrial renaissance, the soul of the new management, never mind that Deming or Tom Peters and the other apostles never mention it, or that Deming sometimes seemed to believe he had discovered an entirely new religion, the "religion of quality" as Deming apologist Mary Walton calls it. No, that Freedom Center both evokes and depends upon a revival of an older and far more powerful spiritual impulse is made all too clear by the moral enthusiasm of the men who run it, and by their deep conviction that in creating a realm of economic order and rational productivity they have created a morally superior environment for their workers as well.

For Weber's "worldly ascetics," grace was exhibited in two ways: by their deep inner confidence of justification, and by the objective results of their work in the world. In Freedom Center both are abundant. The inner confidence of justification is found not only among the executives who believe they have made something good but in the purposefulness and confidence of the employees and their conviction that what they are doing makes sense as part of a larger enterprise. As for the objective results, God's universe is purposeful and well ordered, and for that reason good works are bountiful. Works, and therefore the inner virtue of those who work, can be judged by their fruits. The divine order, like Freedom Center, produces just results for diligence and sloth, for faith and despair, commitment and compromise, steadiness and folly. Freedom Center is a paragon of order, and creativity within order is good.

For the most part the Catholic tradition (at least outside the monasteries, where *ora et labora* prevailed) praised individual works only insofar as their fruits reflected the glories of God and his creation. But for Calvin and his followers, work was almost a good in itself. The glory of God could be served by work of any kind as long as it was systematic, diligently pursued, and materially productive. The fundamental ethic of a capitalist culture, Weber tells us, "is an obligation which the individual . . . does feel toward the content of his professional activity, *no matter in what it consists. . . .*"[1] This is what the new management wants from its new employees: a commitment to work itself in all its constantly changing forms, and a commitment to the enterprise, the larger work, regardless of its changing needs. It is not looking for men who find their fulfillment in the traditions of their craft, or who jealously guard their hours, their efforts, their loyalties, their very selves, holding them aloof from the enterprise, doling them out in strict accordance with elaborate agreements that exist to remind employers that their workers work to live, not live to work.

In the post-industrial factory, "labour must be performed," as Weber said, "as if it were an absolute end in itself, a calling."[2] Above all else the new managers want men who will fit themselves into the enterprise as an enterprise, who will join in a corporate effort and devote themselves to it wholeheartedly, seeing their employers not as natural enemies but as brethren. Weber knew that the Catholic craft guildsman, the progenitor of the craft unionist, despite all the guilds' communal traditions, was the intractable individualist unwilling to sacrifice the habits of a lifetime to every twitch in consumer demand, to conform his entire life to the pleasure of those who may advance his prosperity. It was Calvin—and later John Wesley and others—who forged communes of capitalist effort from men willing to submit themselves to a productive enterprise, to become "worldly ascetics" persuaded of the moral value of productivity itself, quite aside from the enjoyment of its fruits. TQM depends on the same sort of moral commitment.

Weber writes that "the great religious ethic of the seventeenth century bequeathed to its utilitarian successors . . . an amazingly good, we may even say pharasaically good conscience in the acquisition of money, so long as it took place legally."[3] The consciences of the men who run the Tribune Company, men who fought ruthlessly not one but several of the toughest strikes the American newspaper industry has seen in recent decades, who employed the most notorious union-busting law firm in the United States to run the strike in New York, who shut the door in Chicago on a thousand men who had made their careers with the *Tribune,* who were denounced in America's two most important Catholic cities by princes of the Catholic church, who were condemned by opinion managers and politicians and social activists of every stripe as arrogant, fanatical, cruel, and dangerous ideologues, who in New York were shunned by even business leaders who might have been expected to support them, the consciences of these men ring as clear as a bell.

The sentimental rhetoric of unionism touches them not at all. They are sure in their minds that productivity, and efficiency, and quality, and getting the most out of the technology, and workers who work as if work were a good in itself, men with the capacity to lose themselves in the productive enterprise, that all this and 25 percent operating margins are obvious moral goods and that the pursuit of them is right.

They have no doubts about the righteousness of Freedom Center, and of the Orlando plant and the Fort Lauderdale plant and the plant they would have built in New York—and this certainty forged their strategy. For the Tribune men not only believed that what they were doing, what they would build was right, but believed—oh how fatally—that all honest men would see that they were right.

CHAPTER 4

Fall from Grace

*A man does not "by nature" wish to earn more and more money, but
simply to live as he is accustomed to live and to earn as much as is
necessary . . . with a maximum of comfort and a minimum of effort.*
Max Weber, *The Protestant Ethic and the Spirit of Capitalism*

UNLESS you work on an airport runway, it is probably the loudest sustained noise you will ever hear. It makes a rock concert sound like a tea dance. Everywhere on the pressroom floor it is loud, and over time the noise is maddening, disorienting, and isolating. But this close to the presses, where the pressmen work, noise becomes the only reality, hearing seems to become the only sense, sound overwhelms the nervous system.

George Kennedy, the "chapel chairman" (union shop steward), who is not showing off the sound but trying to explain the machines, is yelling about some technical point. He might as well be screaming in space. So he bends close, while you cover up your other ear, and with his lips about an inch from your lobe he shouts as loud as he can about this important technical point. Nothing. Not one syllable. You are alone in the noise, buried in the sound.

Generations of pressmen had no choice but to live with this noise, but today the noise is supposed to be obsolete. The presses in the *News*'s Brooklyn plant, which prints, packs, and ships more than 80 percent of the paper's daily run, almost a million papers a night before the strike, are letterpress rather than offset presses like the ones used at the *Chicago Tribune* and most other papers today. Offset printing plates are completely flat. The printing portions of the plate—the letters and pictures that show up in the newspaper—pick up ink because they are electrochemically treated to do so, while the rest of the plate remains clean. But on letterpress plates, as on Gutenberg's, the printing portions of the plate are raised, the impression is made by "pressing" the ink onto the paper. It is a lot louder. Also a paper of the *News*'s size cannot do four-color printing with letterpress; everything is black or white. The Brooklyn presses are fifty years old. They are antiques, but not even valuable antiques. When the Tribune Company was forced to sell the paper after losing the strike, the value assigned to the presses was near zero, useless except as scrap. They are still in use.

Unlike in Freedom Center, there are no quiet rooms in the Brooklyn plant. All the work of adjusting the presses, pulling sample papers from the folder, setting the color, is done out on the pressroom floor by the men buried in the noise. There is a break room, where men can go to hide from the noise, and there is Freddy's bar, just outside the plant, where some of the men spend hours hiding from the noise, but you can't run the presses from either place.

Being buried in the noise is unpleasant for the worker. But that is not the only drawback. Machines and men make each other what they are and these machines make these men—alone. Back in Chicago, where the presses are not as loud and where the press crew spends much of its time working together in the quiet room, all that TQM talk about teamwork seems realistic. The press crew is a team: they can hear each other talk, not just on break but while they are working on the press; they can laugh and joke, not just in the break room but here at work on the floor. But in Brooklyn, buried in the noise, you are always alone. Human discourse has to take place somewhere else—somewhere away from the work, like the break room.

There must be enough light to check the paper by, because we do that: George shows me a column of gray on a tabloid page of black-and-white and twists the manual control valve to adjust the flow of ink to the relevant few square inches of the roller. Nevertheless the pervasive impression is of darkness, in part because everything is black with ink. The plant is filthy; ink and paper dust cover everything, especially the floors, which are terrifyingly slick, considering how dangerously close together the machines are. Where Freedom Center has broad bright avenues between the presses, in Brooklyn there are only dark and dangerous alleys.

All these things are isolating too: because the room is crowded people go about Indian file. In the slick-floored dark and narrow allies, the dangerous footing and the sheer effort of getting from place to place safely absorbs most of one's attention, not to mention making you very much want to be somewhere else. It is a relentlessly hostile environment. Just being there makes men edgy and irritable. There are no bright optimistic post-industrial visions here; they are all absorbed in the pervasive gloom.

Continuous Process Improvement? By all means. Call in the scrap man tomorrow.

The press floor of the Brooklyn plant is a room full of angry and suspicious men. It is more than a year after the strike, but Mike Tachi, Ken MacAvoy, Ray Walsh, all supervisors and all union members, and George Kennedy are all still in a shouting rage about it. Walsh's son is also a pressman. Walsh tells me he was arrested during the strike for robbery and assault, a charge Walsh calls "bullshit." But they were angry before the strike. Some of them appear to have been angry for decades. They are angry that this place has never been modernized. In their view the Tribune Company made a solemn promise to do so in exchange for contract concessions the unions made in 1984 and 1987. But they are angry also because anger has become part of their job. Bad labor relations on an epic scale have become a tradition at New York City newspapers.

Here, there is no casual first-naming between managers and workers, no Knicks vs. Bulls tickets being handed around. For one thing there are no managers here tonight. There are no managers here most hours of most nights. The unions control the plant. They discourage too many managers from making too many appearances on the floor.

Mike Maloney, the plant manager who looks like Stacy Keach, is not technically management: he still carries a union card. He came up from the ranks starting as an apprentice pressman, or "flyboy," thirty-one years ago. Everyone agrees that Mike has to represent the interests of the company, not the union, and Mike does not go to most union meetings. But dropping his union card would make his job harder and less pleasant, so he keeps it. As a supervisor he has a legal right to leave the union, but the company, eager not to violate the etiquette of power, does not insist he do so.

Getting onto the plant floor is not easy. Unlike the *Chicago Tribune* or most newspapers the *News* offers no public tour of its production facilities. The VP who finally arranged my tour told me he'd better not come to the plant that night: the tour would go a lot better, he said, if I was not seen with a manager.

Instead I go with George Kennedy, who, as chapel chairman of the pressmen, is the ranking union official in the pressroom that night. Throughout the night I tour plant provinces controlled by different unions—the mailers, the paperhandlers, the pressmen, printers, and stereotypers. At one point I walk a few feet away from George to a dolly carrying a roll of newsprint and gesture at him to come over and show me something. He won't. He walks about two steps toward me and points at a line on the floor. I don't cross that line, he explains. I stay on this side and the paperhandlers stay on that side.

The fact that my tour has been officially approved by the current CEO of the *News* does not necessarily mean I will be allowed to take it. At each checkpoint one union official hands me over to his counterpart in the next province, asking permission for me to come through. In some places, such as the composing room, the domain of the few remaining printers, nobody particularly cares whether I cross the line. But the bigger, tougher provinces, like the paperhandlers' or the mailers', take their borders very seriously. At the checkpoint leading into the mailers' territory—where the papers are bundled and packaged—there is an extended negotiation with the union supervisor, who at first flatly refuses me passage. I never get to tour the drivers' area because the mailers, who share a border with the drivers, and now have custody of me, don't like to talk to the drivers. The mailers are afraid of the drivers and are also afraid the drivers will make a bad impression on me and make the unions look bad in my book. At no point during the night do I even see a manager.

"The unions killed the papers." That's what almost any New Yorker old enough to remember the days when the city had more papers than the American League had teams will tell you. They say it because most of the papers died from strikes, like most AIDS patients die from pneumonia or some other opportunistic infection. It was TV and the flight to the suburbs, however, that created the immune deficiency in the newspaper business. The odd thing was that the weaker the industry got, the more powerful the unions became, even as they were losing thousands of jobs.

Because a day-old newspaper is worthless, a day's production lost to a strike can never be made up. If a rival continues publishing in the meantime, so much the worse: if the *Mirror* is struck and shuts down while the *News* keeps publishing, *Mirror* readers and advertisers who sample the *News* may never come back. In a shrinking newspaper market full of pessimistic publishers who sense TV cameras pointed right between their eyes, this suggests a simple equation: if a certain number of papers are going to die, and if being shut down while your competitors publish is the most common cause of death, then the obvious business strategy is to pay almost any price to avoid strikes or slowdowns. At all costs stay on the street until the market or the unions cut down your competitors. Publishing through a strike was not an option; in those precomputer days, newspaper production workers, especially the all-important printers (the typesetters), were highly skilled and irreplaceable in the short term.

Following this logic New York papers repeatedly yielded to union demands at the negotiating table and granted wage, manning, and work-rule concessions that they would have otherwise rejected as unsustainable. The theory, especially popular at powerful papers like the *News* and the *Times*, was that there would be time to do something about the contracts when the market stabilized, i.e., after their competitors died. The papers that were still standing when the carnage stopped were left with labor agreements management found intolerable *and* unpleasant labor relations to boot. For, inevitably, the "give till it hurts" strategy had its limits, and even the richest papers eventually found themselves saying no and taking a number of long and bitter strikes.

News management, under a revived Tribune Company, began fighting for givebacks in the early 1980s. But going into the 1990 negotiations, the *News* labor agreements, in management's view, were still intolerable: roughly 48 percent of its revenues went to employee compensation, compared to the industry (and Tribune Company) average of about 25 percent. (Quality papers in the Northeast generally pay around 35 percent.)

Much of this added expense stemmed from manning rules. The pressmen's contracts, for instance, required eleven to fourteen men to run presses that management believed could be run by six or seven. Five to eight allegedly superfluous pressmen earning more than $20 an hour added up to huge labor costs and a structural reduction in competitiveness. Overmanning, in management's view, was not confined to the presses. In a plant like Freedom Center, much of the work of the paperhandlers, for example, would have been obsolete, divided between the pressmen and the machines. The "Kearny retie" provision in the drivers' contract provided that when the *News*'s Sunday color inserts, printed and packaged by an outside contractor, were delivered to the

News's Kearny, New Jersey, satellite plant, a crew of drivers would off-load the bundles and add a second plastic tie to them, a maneuver management claimed was completely unnecessary, but the drivers insisted kept the bundles from falling apart during delivery. The retie added nearly fifty jobs and cost the *News* more than $3 million a year.

At one time the *News* shipped tens of thousands of copies of the so-called country edition to upstate and Connecticut towns on the commuter trains running out of Grand Central Terminal. By 1990, says management, only seven bundles a day, totaling a few hundred papers, went to the station. Under the contract, those seven bundles had to be carried by five drivers, each of whom was paid a full day's wage.

The costs of what management considered overmanning were compounded by rules guaranteeing huge payments in "static" overtime, that is, overtime paid whether it was worked or not. The *News*, for instance, was required to pay paperhandlers, whose base pay going into the 1990 negotiations was $18.42, overtime to strip damaged rolls of newsprint off their reusable cores even if the work was done in the course of the regular workday. Junior pressmen or flyboys who did pre-press work in the plate room had to be paid one and a half hours of overtime even though they worked only an eight-hour day.

Some of the static overtime actually resulted from management's early attempts to win concessions at the bargaining table. The unions would give ground at the table. But when the contracts were implemented the unions would say they were unworkable—that the only way to get the work done would be to make up some of the concessions and givebacks with static overtime for certain employees. The static overtime agreements became codicils to the contract. In top management's view this was no more than extortion, and a particularly obnoxious form of it since it established officially the notion that some men had a right to be paid without working. But in the view of union veterans like George McDonald these givebacks of givebacks made a lot of sense. It was like having an informal bonus system, a way to reward key employees without disturbing the whole wage structure. McDonald thought management should be grateful for a system that gave them the kind of discretion they were always saying they wanted.

Actually the practice left both sides dissatisfied; union members kept making concessions that did not pay off for the *News;* and the *News* kept coming back for more, thus persuading the average union member the company was both insatiable and untrustworthy. Moreover, even if the side agreements did originally amount to discretion for management, managers complained they quickly became just another set of calcified work rules, inherited privileges divorced from any special effort that had originally justified a "bonus."

The drivers enjoyed some of what management regarded as the most extravagant overtime provisions. Certain highly prized delivery routes carried so much built-in overtime they could double or triple a driver's pay. The Montauk route, carrying the *News* to the tip of Long Island, carried four and a half hours of overtime every day, a provision written into the contract before the Island's country roads were replaced by the Long Island Expressway, and before the *News* built a satellite production facility in Garden City on Long Island, making it possible to do the route in less than seven hours. Nearly every delivery route was defined as taking a minimum of seven hours, regardless of its actual length. So favored drivers who got cushy runs like the one to Newark Airport (two hours) could be paid for two (and in a few cases three) shifts in a day, the additional shifts paid at the overtime rate though all were worked in less than eight hours. Drivers who delivered country editions were paid to show up at the plant at least an hour before they were needed. Some of these favored routes, according to both management and law enforcement officials, were allegedly assigned by the drivers union leadership to favored members in return for political support and illegal kickbacks.

Inside the plant, work rules not only defined how work would be done, but limited how much of it could be done. Under the pressmen's contract one junior pressman was assigned to the cleaning of every five press units, a job that should take only five hours according to management. After completing the task he could go home and would be paid a full shift no matter how long he worked. Maintenance crews charged with such jobs as installing and removing of "press blankets," a regular maintenance task, were limited to ten "moves" (an installation or removal) per day, after which they could go home. Management's view was that workers should do as much maintenance as they could squeeze into a day, rather than working on what effectively was a piece-rate system. Piecework meant there was often neither time nor room in the budget for more serious long-term maintenance. Delays from equipment breakdowns were epidemic.

Cleanliness and maintenance can raise morale, letting them slide breeds discouragement, hostility—and blurry newspapers. During the strike, Dick Casson, a production manager imported from the *Chicago*

Tribune, could not figure out why the Brooklyn presses even after numerous adjustments were still laying down spotty, uneven impressions. After ordering a complete breakdown and cleaning he discovered remnants of old rags in the inkwells—the fibers from the rags were fouling the ink. The wells apparently had not been cleaned for years. The paper immediately looked better.

Under the system prevailing at the *News,* management could not even control who showed up for work on a given night. In most departments, production workers had nearly an unlimited right to call in absent immediately before a shift. They would not be paid of course, but they would not be fired either, and replacements would have to be found. In theory, absentees could be disciplined but the realpolitik of the work floor dictated otherwise. Even union foremen complained that on high absentee nights, like Fridays or holidays, they could end up with crews drawn largely from the "shape" list, inexperienced apprentices who were trying to build enough seniority to become regulars. One or two per crew would not matter, they could watch and learn, but many more than that and the night would turn into a nightmare of baby-sitting, constant web breaks, and missed deadlines.

As harmful as this practice was, it was a logical extension of traditional craft union prerogatives. Though the *Daily News* plants were complex interactive systems in which hundreds of men at a time worked toward a single end, the *News* had no right to interview, evaluate, or select prospective employees for most of its blue-collar jobs. The union ran the shape, the equivalent of a hiring hall, from which new employees came. Management had little contact with its blue-collar employees and barely knew who they were.

Bizarre work rules, lax management, and gross overmanning destroyed not only productivity but morale, and turned workers into scam artists.

It is a simple problem really: If the paperhandlers or the pressmen or the mailers cannot be assigned extra work, say cleaning or maintenance, during their natural slack time, what do they do? If you need only six or seven men to run a press and you have twelve, thirteen, or fourteen, where do the others go? Do they just stand around on the pressroom floor drowning in the noise? Do they hover around the press trying to look busy? It is hard to imagine fourteen men per press safely hovering in those narrow alleys.

At the *News* they went to the break room, or else they just went. The break rooms, say both *News* managers and some union men, were demoralization made visible: crowded with men and beer—the soda machines were stocked with it and the break rooms stank of it. There were TV sets and VCRs surrounded by crowds of drinking men—bored irritated angry drinking men, stuck somewhere between guilt and denial, and between a determination not to do more than their share and a hatred for the noise. The demoralization of the break room led directly to the scams: the beatout, the buddy system, and the marriage.

The beatout is just what it sounds like: come in, sign up for work, put in an hour or so, and beat it on out of there. Just a few steps from the Dean Street entrance to the Brooklyn plant lies the most popular place to beat it to: a bar called Freddy's. At Freddy's draft beer is ninety cents, a short one is sixty-five. Or you can cut right to the chase and order the thirty-two-ounce mug, one quart of beer, for three bucks.

Freddy's is a workingman's bar and looks it. The decor is 1950s dumpy: you can sit at the bar or at a folding table. The main decorations are a cheap plaster bust of a cop hauling off a drunk and one of those mini–bowling alley games, which nobody ever plays. There are no customers from the neighborhood and in fact no neighborhood. Everyone who drinks here works in the plant: mostly pressmen and paperhandlers.

Take a seat at the bar and listen. No matter how they begin, the men eventually end up talking about one thing: what they are doing right now—beating out. You might think that men would get tired of beating out just to talk about beating out, but it seems to fascinate them endlessly.

A youngish man with brown hair and glasses, about five ten, say thirty-five, walks up the bar and downs a couple of quick ones. Then he gets up to go. "You leaving, B——?" a fellow drinker shouts. "What are you doing, working or drinking?"

B. ostentatiously leaves money on the bar. "I'll be back in ten minutes," he says. "I've got work to do." Actually work takes about thirty minutes. Then he resumes drinking.

Not all of the talk is approving. Much conversation is devoted to condemning those who beat out too much or too blatantly: "slobs" or "pigs" who don't even wait until the shift gets decently started so the supervisors—some of whom are here now, beating out—can properly record them as present. "I told the slob to be here at ten-thirty so I can make up the sheet and he shows up a fuckin' hour late and he expects me to write him in. It's fuckin' too much." Another unacceptable abuse is taking off without telling anybody where to find you in case things get hot or some less relaxed supervisor calls the roll.

The barmaid is Sally,* a cute, very busty, but otherwise tomboyish blonde. Sally has one unbreakable rule, she explains to me, serious and unsmiling: no empty glasses on the bar. "I assume you are here to drink. If there is money on the bar and the glass is empty it gets filled, I don't ask first."

With her barside manner she might as well be a drug dealer. The men at the bar may be lackadaisical workers, but the woman who serves them is on a mission: she stands behind the bar like a hawk looking for that empty and swooping down to refill it. For some guys, the fast drinkers, she stays a shot ahead: one in the glass, one on the bar, when the glass empties, Sally swoops by, dumps the shot and the mixer, pours another shot for the on-deck circle, pulls out the two bucks and resumes her perch, hawk eyes all over the bar. Maybe ten seconds, max. The bar is littered with drunks in the late stages, not only of this night, but of their lives.

At midnight, half a dozen paperhandlers enter the bar. One of them, fairly young, good-looking, a joker but also clearly somebody the other guys like and respect, sits next to me. He is drinking vodka, with orange and cranberry juices and a splash of soda. He does them very fast, keeping Sally on her feet. By the time I am impressed enough to start counting, it is 12:30. In the next hour he has nine more, so figure at least a dozen in ninety minutes.

At 1:30 A.M. another paperhandler bangs on the door, then leans into the bar and shouts that a load of paper has come in. All six, including the one with a dozen drinks in him, and four others who were keeping him fairly good company, and one who is on the wagon and stuck to Diet Coke, go back to the plant to play around with 1700-pound rolls of newsprint. That's the beatout, and if it beats working you never want that job.

The buddy system is a refinement of the beatout: a two-man working partnership under which both guys sign in but one takes off and the other covers both their job responsibilities. If a supervisor calls roll, the one who stays behind says his buddy is in the bathroom or running some work-related errand. If things get serious the word goes out that guys better get back.

---

* Not her real name.

Before the strike at least, the most extreme form of the buddy system was the marriage; two pressmen would work roughly half the days for which they were paid, permanently covering for each other on alternate shifts. Marriages were most popular among pressmen who lived in distant Suffolk County: a three-hour roundtrip commute to work began to seem intolerable to men who knew they were not needed anyway.

With fewer men on a press since the strike, there is somewhat less of this stuff than there was. And even before the strike not everyone did these things, certainly not blatantly and constantly. The most extreme abuses were neither admitted to nor condoned by either the union leadership or many of the men. More than one former union member told me that the pressmen's new president, Jack Kennedy, made a serious effort to get his men to tone down the worst abuses.

Sit down one of the union leaders and read him a litany of management's complaints and he will dispute the details and call even the valid complaints exaggerated. Most important, he will argue that the contract gave management the power to eliminate abuses, so the company had only itself to blame if it didn't.

There is more than a little truth to these rejoinders. The labor agreements were so riddled with codicils and side agreements, coffee-stained memos and references to oral agreements that most questions about the contract had at least two answers. On paper, management could come up with legal grounds for eliminating some abuses. After all, beating out was against the rules. The real problem, say managers, was that down on the shop floor the threat of a two-hour delay or a sudden epidemic of web breaks to take revenge for a management crackdown would almost guarantee a union victory in any dispute. Challenged on the floor, line managers had little choice but to give in unless top management was ready to go to war, not a sporadic, cold war of attrition—the unions would always win on those terms—but a war for, as Hoge might call it, a fundamental and permanent shift of power. And that was just what management had not been willing to do for decades.

"Look I am going to give you five minutes to call me back and tell me you have resolved this situation and the man is back to work. If you don't I'm gonna get out of bed. Then I'm gonna put on my pants. Then I'm gonna get in my car and drive down to the plant. Figure an hour and a half, hour forty-five minutes. And until I get there, not a single paper is gonna leave that plant. So take your choice."

The speaker is former drivers union president Jerry Cronin explaining how he used to settle the middle-of-the-night labor disputes that were an almost daily part of his job. *News* management, he says, would hear that threat of losing that precious hour or two and they would just fold. He must have used that line about my pants "fifty times," he says, and it worked every time.

"They never challenged me," he explains, even though they had every legal right in the world to do so, since the drivers had a no-strike clause in their contract. "They had no leadership at the *News*." To call his bluff, he says, "all the manager had to say was 'I tell you what, you tell these guys to get back to work or I am going right down the line and asking them if they are going to work. If they say no, I'm going to fire them one at a time and lock the doors behind them. And then I'll see you in court at nine o'clock tomorrow morning. Have your pants on by then.'"

If they had done that even once, he says, "I wouldn't have known whether to shit or wind my watch." Cronin says it used to drive him nuts that the *News* would not fight back, because he could see it was killing the paper and would end with management going to the other extreme and trying to kill the unions. Eventually the suicide pact forged by *News* management and unions together became too much for him to take. "One time I was sitting with my wife and I said, 'If I threaten to turn one more place into a bowling alley'—meaning I'm going to march my guys out and leave it empty—'I'm going to go crazy.'" Soon after, he decided to step down as president.

"We got away with so much crap," he says, that it bred "a malignant collective ego" among the drivers. They began to believe they could get away with anything, and felt obliged to prove it. One consequence was that Cronin's primary job as president became bludgeoning the company into reinstating men fired, suspended, or disciplined for what Cronin says were often outrageous abuses. "If you couldn't get a guy back to work in a few days, even after he slugged a foreman, you just weren't doing something right." Once Cronin had to talk a member at the *Post* into unloading the gun with which he had been threatening to kill large numbers of people, including a *Post* circulation manager. Cronin succeeded in persuading the man to unload. But as soon as the bullets were out, the manager told the member, "You're fired," at which the member started screaming, "You can't fire me, you bastard, I emptied the gun!"

*   *   *

The union work force intentionally sacrifices the potential rewards of individual competition for the security of solidarity. It is an attractive idea especially as men grow older and are less fit for competition, but it demands a strict and precarious ethic: to work hard and honestly not in order to get ahead but because it would be unfair to one's fellows to shirk. When the workplace is deluged with opportunities to shirk, this delicate ethic is inexorably corrupted. No one wants to be the chump who does all the work. Soon people are trying to excel in the only field open for achievement: "getting over." Eventually, for all too many people, the goal of work becomes not working.

Managements that tolerate this, far from being valued by their employees, wind up being hated and loathed. People who know they are doing wrong often hate those to whom they do it. One longtime union supervisor who came up from the ranks told me the reason the production workers acted so hostile to any "shirt and tie" on the floor was exactly because every minute of the normal workday was a scam: "Anybody walking by could see there were not fourteen men on the press." The very presence of a suit made the pressmen feel "like kids with their hands caught in the cookie jar."

In such a system the interests of workers and managers really are in conflict. Every attempt to make the workplace a place of work runs head on into the interests of the worker who lives by the buddy system and the beatout. The workers' larger, longer-term interest in being part of an expanding productive enterprise seems ever more farfetched and less relevant. The plant becomes the very picture of a zero sum society: all gain is another's loss, anything given to the company is lost forever. Despair rules; no one really believes in the future.

When workers produce less than they consume, management ceases to think of them as assets and begins to think of them exclusively as costs. Companies begin to speak the language of those doomed businesses that believe they can cut their way to profitability. Thinking of workers only as costs to be cut, they begin to give up on the idea that they are men to be led. Workers, equally persuaded that their gain is the company's loss and vice versa, act as if they and the enterprises to which they have devoted their working lives really are natural enemies.

At the *News* this cycle had been accelerating for years until men on both sides seemed to forget it could be any other way. To the unions every management move seemed like a trick, all talk of increasing productivity sounded like an enemy plan for taking away some natural right. To management, leading such a work force back from lassitude, despair, and anger to teamwork, self-respect, and productivity seemed an ever more Sisyphean task. You could push and push that boulder up the hill and then, just a few steps from the summit, there was Lenny Higgins shouting at you and banging on that damn table. Perhaps, really, it was not worth the effort.

It is possible to rationally enumerate the forces that forged this labor-management suicide pact: the economics of newspapers, lax management, the disincentives written into the contract. But in the plant, talking to the men, hearing their anger, one begins to feel deeper motives at work.

Most of the production unions have been Irish fiefdoms for as long as anyone can remember. It is said that at one time you could tell which part of the plant a man worked in simply by asking from which of the thirty-two counties his people came. It is not popular today to say that ethnicity affects character. But if this is a story, as I partly believe it to be, of a resurgent Protestant business culture going to war with a decaying Catholic one, then we cannot entirely ignore these questions. The Brooklyn plant would probably be a dark, angry place no matter who worked in it, but there is no denying that the anger is of a particularly Gaelic hue, and that is dark indeed.

The plant itself has much in common with the Irish plantation under the penal laws that did so much to forge modern Irish identity. Irish-Catholic tenant farmers and laborers reaped few rewards for industriousness, since any improvements they made in the land reverted almost entirely to the benefit of the landlord. And scamming the landlord, like beating out to Freddy's, brought little reward beyond the pleasures of vengeance, since a decline in productivity would only make it harder to pay the rent. It was a system under which work was little more than an unavoidable evil necessary to achieve a bare subsistence. As in the Brooklyn plant, it was above all a system in which the interests of bosses and bossed were utterly at odds, in which blind hatred and Gaelic fatalism combined to make revenge and rebellion and a fearsome need to assert one's ultimate—even if secret—independence the prime motives of some men's lives.

Ethnic explanations may be fanciful or unfair, but there is no doubt that solidarity, secrecy, rebellion, and the sense of work as at best a necessary evil were essential to the culture of the plants. As Bill Reel, the *News*'s populist conservative columnist, who wrote mostly about the working-class neighborhoods of Brooklyn and Queens and strongly supported the strike, told me, for generations union "strategy" could really be summed up in one simple, favored phrase: "fuck the bosses."

The anger in the plants was Gaelic also in its constraint; the men brooding, resentful, but disciplined and deeply loyal to the union. During the *News* war, the union leaders worried constantly that the drivers, mostly Italian and Jewish, who worked outside, away from the bosses, in jobs inherently more self-directed and even entrepreneurial, would lose their tempers and start a strike by accident, maybe by punching a couple of supervisors and walking out in a huff. No one ever feared that the pressman, mailers, or paperhandlers would do that. Blood and history have bequeathed them great discipline in all matters political, and the mastery of silent anger. They would never take a swing at a manager walking through the plant, but if he looked over his shoulder he might find his trail covered in spit.

This discipline, this solidarity, however, did not bring order to the men's lives. Instead, directed as it was against the place where a man made his living and spent much of his life, the anger divided a man against himself.

For Calvin one of the great virtues of work was the order it imposed on the lives of those who were faithful to it. Constancy of devotion to work was a great sign of salvation. As Weber wrote, "The God of Calvinism demanded of his believers not single good works but a life of good works combined into a unified system. There was no place for the very human Catholic cycle of sin, repentance, atonement, release, followed by renewed sin. . . . The moral character of the average man was thus deprived of its planless and unsystematic character and subjected to a consistent method for conduct as a whole."[1] This steady, constant, devoted state of mind is crucial to the new post-industrial factory.

The idea of losing oneself in one's job, especially a factory job, is a bit creepy. The TQM culture smacks of fanaticism, of subsuming the self, and of company songs—sung in Japanese. It does, however, require the practice of personal virtues like self-control, self-directedness, teamwork, duty, and the ability to carry through on commitments. Weber wrote that "the Puritan like every rational type of asceticism tried to enable a man to maintain and act upon his constant motives, especially those which it taught him itself, against the emotions. In this formal psychological sense of the term it tried to make him into a personality."[2] By joining a larger order the self orders itself. If that is so, it has got to be better than Freddy's.

At Freedom Center the pace of work is frantic, but the place is not. Freedom Center is supremely orderly, and it is productive—and, as workplaces go, happy—because the people share the order and purpose of the place. The pace in Brooklyn, even today, two owners and one bankruptcy after Jim Hoge decided to go to war, is leisurely. But it is a place of economic and moral chaos.

Freedom Center is in one very important sense an autocracy. The men there are almost all "at-will" employees. They could lose their jobs tomorrow at the whim of management. Their insecurity is terrifying, conjuring up the possibility of a nation where workers can drop out of the middle class in the blink of an eye. And yet in its day-to-day character Freedom Center seems a republic of virtue, genuinely egalitarian, free of the old Taylorist hierarchies, a place where men are self-motivated, who give more than they are asked at work, who view themselves as equal members of the enterprise.

In Brooklyn the men had far more "constitutional" power. Not only could they not easily be dismissed or even disciplined, they had effectively seized control of the shop floor from management. Yet for all their power, the men seemed to regard themselves not as equals or team members but eternal victims. They were bored and angry, they talked endlessly of perceived petty injustices, and obsessed over the dread possibility they might give more than the minimum due. They wanted change, but were frightened of it. Soon they would be more frightened still.

There was, however, one very special union at the *News* whose members were not accustomed to thinking of themselves as victims, or to being afraid.

CHAPTER 5

They Drive by Night

IN the early 1920s Joseph Medill Patterson sent a telegram to Max Annenberg, his chief of circulation for both the *News* and the *Chicago Tribune*, with a series of instructions about current business. The final order in the list was "No more killing."[1]

The warning was no joke. Annenberg, the founder of the great Annenberg publishing fortune, was a killer and a boss of killers. It was killing that had brought the two men together. In 1905, the idealistic young Patterson, who was alienated from his family and had temporarily left the newspaper business for politics, was serving a term as Chicago's director of public works. He was a hard-charging reformer and something of a Socialist. Annenberg, a Chicago mobster, was circulation director for Hearst's *Chicago American*. There was nothing unusual in that. In those days in Chicago, even more than in New York, the most important men in newspaper circulation were toughs whose job it was to persuade newsstand dealers to display prominently the newspapers published by the toughs' employers and hide or lose competing papers. Hearst right then was in a circulation war with the old *Chicago Daily News* and Annenberg was his field general.

The war got out of hand. One *Daily News* tough was shot. Patterson stepped in with a typically straightforward solution: he mobilized a battalion of street cleaners, ordered them to seize the newspaper stands that were the objects of the war, load them into Department of Public Works wagons, and haul them to the city dump to be burned. Annenberg, furious, showed up at Patterson's office the next day and made threats. Patterson stood his ground. Annenberg backed off, the violence abated, the newsstands were returned, and two of the toughest men in Chicago became deep, lifelong friends.

Annenberg did not become a saint. Within a few months he and his Hearst thugs were going after the *Chicago Tribune*, Patterson's family's paper, trying to push it off the stands to the benefit of Hearst's morning paper, the *Examiner*. The *Tribune* publisher at the time was one James Keeley, also a straightforward man. His solution to the Annenberg problem was to hire Annenberg away from Hearst. He did. Soon both the *Tribune*'s and the *Examiner*'s circulation staffs were stocked with future stars of the Chicago gang wars, including, on the *Examiner* side, future mob boss Dion "Deanie" O'Banion. The ensuing violence was even worse than usual. Dealers who refused to take extra *Tribunes* were terrorized; the Chicago River was the final resting place for tons of *Examiners*; newsboys were beaten so badly they had to be hospitalized; there were several murders. Mossie Enright, a *Tribune* man and future mob big, put six .44-caliber slugs in the chest of one Dutch Gentleman, a Hearst thug. Annenberg was suspected by the police of at least two murders and tried for one. He got off. The *Tribune* won the circulation war. Patterson returned to the paper in 1912 when the war was at its height; he did nothing we know of to stop it.

Annenberg never entirely reformed. But he had real talents as a "legitimate businessman." His destiny lay outside the rackets as the founder of a great publishing empire of his own. Fanatically loyal to Patterson, he came to New York to help launch the *News*. In New York the violence never reached the Chicago scale; the *News* won the circulation wars in New York more with marketing and editorial innovation than gunplay. But with nineteen papers competing for space on newsstands the old ways did not die out entirely. A good proportion of *News* drivers and deliverymen were Annenberg toughs, and in New York as in Chicago carloads of them would visit uncooperative newsstand dealers, some of the toughs rearranging unsatisfactory displays while others looked threateningly.

Annenberg's men and the city's other circulation toughs eventually found a home in the Newspaper and Mail Deliverers Union of New York and Vicinity, or NMDU, the drivers union, formed at the turn of the century. The union has had Mafia ties since the 1940s, especially to the Lucchese and Bonanno crime families, though other families have been active as well. The families seem to have originally gained influence through bookmaking and loansharking operations that catered to the drivers, drawing men who had debts they could not pay into mob activities.

In the past fifteen years two NMDU presidents and numerous other union officials have gone to jail for racketeering. Mike Alvino, who became president in spring 1989, had helped put union president Douglas LaChance in jail by confessing he had collected bribes for LaChance from employers who wanted the union's permission to eliminate jobs. In 1984, the federal National Labor Relations Board officially designated the drivers union as an organization with "a proclivity to violate the law."

It was on November 23, 1992, however, long after the strike was over, that the NMDU really made history. After bringing a series of corruption and organized crime indictments against NMDU members, on that day New York City District Attorney Robert Morgenthau announced that the union itself had been indicted for "enterprise corruption." This marked the first time in American history that a union was accused of being not merely the victim or tool of organized crime, but a criminal enterprise in its own right. According to Morgenthau, for more than a decade a criminal racket within the NMDU had "a stranglehold on the distribution of magazines and newspapers in New York." The corruption was "so pervasive that it was necessary to take the extraordinary step of charging the union itself."

At the heart of the corruption, alleged the DA, was the "Newspaper Delivery Mob," a multifaceted criminal conspiracy directed by members and associates of New York's crime families and officers and members of the NMDU, some of whom were themselves "made" members or associates of the families and were also made newspaper executives. At least one union supervisor, alleged the indictment, was a capo in the Bonanno family. Alvino was named an unindicted co-conspirator.

According to the indictment, the Newspaper Delivery Mob effectively controlled the union. The indictment suggests that the union made millions of dollars a year through a variety of corrupt activities. The core of the conspiracy was a newspaper-bootlegging operation. Members of the drivers union stole tens of thousands of newspapers a night from the *News,* the *Post,* and the *Times,* usually reselling them to nonunion distribution ("bootleg") companies, some of them controlled by union members. The bootleg papers may have brought in at least $2 million and perhaps well over $10 million a year.[2]

In addition, according to the indictment, the Newspaper Delivery Mob allegedly collected bribes from wholesale newspaper distribution companies in exchange for allowing them to operate as nonunion shops.

The mob, according to the DA, sold NMDU union cards "to people . . . who were not qualified to receive those cards" with the knowledge and approval of the union's executive council. They stole seniority rights from legitimate NMDU members and transferred them to drivers affiliated with the Newspaper Delivery Mob, with the cooperation of union business agents. This way mob affiliates were protected from layoffs, and could secure favored jobs with lots of overtime, or even no-show jobs. The mob extorted no-show jobs and phony overtime from management, or created ghost employees, with threats of work stoppages, or violence, or through bribes paid to middle managers. The money from the no-shows would be divided among members and associates of the mob, say law enforcement officials. The mob also accepted or extorted bribes, usually from the wholesalers, for lax enforcement of union contracts. They also stole money from the newspapers by inflating the figures for "returns," the unsold newspapers returned by newsstands. Since drivers, at least at the *News*, made their collections in cash, this could be a lucrative way of effectively stealing thousands of additional papers a night.

The mob allegedly intimidated nonmob NMDU drivers or members of other unions (such as the mailers) who refused to cooperate in or protested these schemes, by threatening to use the union's power to take away their jobs, and by "repeatedly and publicly stating that they were associated with La Cosa Nostra . . . creating an atmosphere of fear through repeated assaults" and "sabotaging employers' property when those employers threatened their schemes," according to the Morgenthau indictment.

The Morgenthau investigation even uncovered a major heroin-smuggling ring. Joseph Taglianetti, a captain in the Bonanno crime family and a member of the Delivery Mob, was a key figure, along with other members of the Bonanno and Genovese families, in an operation that smuggled large quantities of heroin in from Europe. Taglianetti pleaded guilty to possession within a week of his arrest.

It is also widely believed that the mob was running loansharking, prostitution, and drug-dealing operations at several newspaper plants, including the *News*'s Brooklyn plant, and that some NMDU drivers used their trucks to move contraband such as untaxed cigarettes and candy and magazines stolen from some newsstand dealers and resold to others, and to run numbers, though Morgenthau brought no indictments for these offenses.

Mike Diana, who at the time of the strike was a business agent of the *News*, a power within the NMDU, and according to the indictment an associate of the Bonanno crime family, allegedly stole some $25,000 from a union hardship fund set up to help union families through the strike. He gave the money, the indictment said, to fellow mob members and to his girlfriend.

Because the *News* was on strike during much of the investigation leading to the indictments, most of the specific acts cited in the indictments occurred at other papers or periodical wholesalers. Nevertheless law enforcement officials say these practices were pervasive throughout the city, including at the *News*. The drivers' scams not only cost the *News* money but corrupted its efforts to serve its customers. The amount of money moved by the Delivery Mob virtually guaranteed that corruption would seep upward even beyond the unionized supervisors to middle managers, most of whom had come up from the ranks. Bill Deering, the *News*'s director of distribution, and later of circulation sales, came to the *News* in 1989 from UPS, where he had supervised a Teamster work force. He was shocked when he encountered the men of the NMDU. "It was a given that everyone was on the take," he says. "Envelopes were passed all over the place, even among management. There was some surprise when I wouldn't take."[3]

Both law enforcement officials and *News* VP for planning Jim Longson confirmed that some *News* middle managers are believed to have been involved in the corruption: Longson says this was an open secret in the company and that from a business standpoint the real problem was not just that some supervisors, both union and management, were getting some stolen money, but that men implicated in the scheme were in no position to give the distribution department the aggressive management it sorely needed.

The Morgenthau indictments seemed to confirm what many observers of the NMDU had long suspected and *News* management had long claimed: the union was a creature of La Cosa Nostra. Former union president Jerry Cronin, himself named in the indictments as an unindicted co-conspirator (he denies involvement in any corrupt activities), disagrees. There are one or two mafiosi and a clutch of Mafia "associates" in the union, he says, and a good deal of corruption, though not quite as much now as in the early 1970s. But, he says, the Mafia never controlled the union or even came close. The real source of the union's mobbed-up image is a myth deliberately fostered by the members, many of whom not only would want other people to believe they are "connected" but would dearly like to believe it themselves.

"The whole mob thing," he says, "is an image perpetuated at all levels at the NMDU." It starts with the fact that the drivers are all men, lots of them Italians, who work "mostly at night, usually in tough neighborhoods." Then when *The Godfather* came out in the 1970s, he says, a lot of the members were "really taken with the glorious image portrayed by Brando" so much that it actually "changed how people talked." Soon it became a point of pride for members to hint that they had "connections" too. In the higher levels of the union the mythology of being connected took on real political importance because "if you view a guy as half as strong a power broker as he wants it to seem, he is still going to get power from that." In some cases that power could intimidate others into going along with a corrupt scheme or scare them into remaining silent.

New president Mike Alvino, says Cronin, "catered to the tough-guy routine. He carried himself in such a way that even if he denied being connected, he did it with a big smile on his face. He was always talking about 'his people' as in 'I don't want to have to go see my people about this.' " On occasion, says Cronin, "I even did it myself, just because I was so fed up with the bullshit. I'd have some guy in my office talking about how if I didn't do right by him he'd have to go see 'his friends.' So I'd tell him, 'Go ahead, and I'll go see my friends and we'll see what happens.' " It even worked, he says, and "in a way it was true." After all, he remarks, smiling, "I do have friends. It's just that none of them are in the Mafia."

The "wannabes," says Cronin, far outnumbered the real bad guys, and some of them convinced themselves they were as tough as they acted. When the strike came, they would convince other people as well.

CHAPTER 6

Broken Covenant

THAT day in January, Higgins and McDonald and Barry Lipton and others felt not just angry but betrayed. Hoge, whom McDonald would ultimately decide was "a nothing," had started so strong. He seemed to recognize that his job was deeper than simply making a few technological updates or cost cutting. He had to convince all parties—Tribune Company, local *News* management, and the unions—of three things: that the *News* could be saved; that the sacrifices and investments required to save it would pay off for all three parties; and finally all three had to be convinced the others were committed. There had been a time when it looked as though he might do it.

The union leaders believed that Chicago would be the most difficult party to convince. The men in Chicago *knew* they would be the most difficult to convince. To the Tribune Company, as Jim Longson explains, the *News* was a franchise that by long custom the parent company had left alone and "therefore did not understand too well, where things kept going from bad to worse and it looked like there was nothing anybody could do about it." CEO Stanton Cook, a man almost universally well liked and described by union leaders as "decent," was deeply committed to saving the *News*. But Cook's patience was not infinite; he had decided to try to sell the paper in 1982. He might do so again. Chief Financial Officer Scott Smith, on the other hand, was a skeptic, fearing the Tribune Company might keep throwing good money after bad. Charles Brumback's views lay somewhere in the middle. He believed that the *Daily News*, brought in to the modern era, could yet become hugely profitable, a half-billion-dollar property or better. On the other hand, he had been hearing horror stories about the *News* since the day he joined the Tribune Company. Could the company justify investing several hundred million dollars of shareholders' money to build a modern newspaper? And could they do this in the face of the Times Mirror Company's apparent willingness to spend at least that much building up its new entrant into the market, *New York Newsday*, launched in the early 1980s when Tribune confirmed the *News*'s troubles by trying to sell it? Treading water and accumulating the annual losses was not an option for a now-public company. The *Tribune* and *News* relationship was no longer a familial one. Brumback briskly concludes: "We had to fix it or get rid of it."

"Our people in New York didn't believe in themselves or the franchise and what they could do with it," says Longson. "So when they came to the Tribune Company for money it was always, 'You owe it to us; we need it to keep going.' That's not the way most public companies make investments." Yet the Tribune Company, despite its reputation for fiscal conservatism, had "never been reluctant to put really big dollars on a conviction," Longson points out. The company had staked hundreds of millions to revive the newsprint business in the late 1970s, and done the same to build, in Freedom Center, one of the most expensive—and profitable—newspaper plants in the world. But whenever the Tribune Company had bet large sums on future profits, "somebody provided the conviction." In New York that was Hoge's mission. He was sent to New York by the men from Chicago to create for the *News* a business rationale the men from Chicago could accept. He would have to convince them, the *News* management team, and the unions to think of the *News* not as a charity case, but as a big important opportunity in the New York market.

On the editorial side, Hoge moved quickly and decisively. Rejecting the notion of his predecessor, Bob Hunt, that the *News*'s traditional audience could no longer support a paper, Hoge in an "editorial manifesto" promised to revive the *News*'s glory years, recapturing its unique voice: "muscular," "vernacular," but "in its own terms ... very elegant."[1] He promised to reestablish the paper's "emotional connection" to its readers. Thinking perhaps of Patterson he told his staff, "We don't want newspapers only for elites. We want to address broader audiences and that means [re]discovering ... our own forms of journalistic elegance—tight editing, personal approaches to the news, forthright editorials, tough social commentary."

To fix the *News*'s production and business systems, however, Hoge needed expert advice. He brought in McKinsey & Co., which he had used to do a turnaround plan for the *Sun-Times*. McKinsey's assessment of the *News*'s financial condition was bracing at best. In its first major report in 1986, the consultants predicted the *News* could be losing as much as $54 million a year by 1990. By the end of the century, it said, there would be room for only one tabloid in New York. The *Daily News* would not be that tabloid unless it fundamentally overhauled its systems, especially its classified advertising and circulation, built new color plants with high-tech zoning technology, and solved the paper's labor problems. The *News*'s labor contracts, according to McKinsey, amounted to "slow suicide." The overmanning, phony overtime, and decades of accumulated work rules would have to go, as part of a plan to cut labor costs by more than $50 million a year.

Hoge used the McKinsey report as the basis for his own turnaround business plan and took it to the men in Chicago. They were impressed. Receiving a serious comprehensive business plan from a *Daily News* publisher was a new experience for them. Though skeptics remained, the majority view was that Hoge's plan was credible: the company would invest in the *News*—if Hoge could get the unions to accept the plan and make the necessary concessions.

Hoge mounted an all-fronts campaign to make the turnaround business plan the basis of the 1987 round of labor negotiations. The McKinsey report gave Hoge credibility with the unions, especially because it placed most of the blame for the paper's current conditions—including the labor contracts—on management, where it belonged. Hoge says, "Workers thought the place was making lots of money and that there were double books, etc." So Hoge opened the *News*'s books to the unions. The company's figures were verified by the unions' auditors at Peat Marwick, and McDonald announced he was convinced the *News* needed substantial relief.

As part of the campaign Hoge met with hundreds of *News* workers in small groups. A series of letters addressed to "Dear Daily News Employee and Family" carefully explained his plans for the paper, including new plants, financed by company investments and union concessions. It was all meant to display a level of communicativeness, concern, and energy that most *News* employees had never seen from management. And it succeeded. From the beginning the union negotiators worked off Hoge's carefully prepared agenda. Eventually the two sides incorporated the first stage of his turnaround business plan into a sort of nonbinding treaty called the "Mutual Investment Program," MIP.

The day it was signed the MIP seemed to Hoge like an enormous triumph, the first step in a new era of labor-management cooperation. The MIP said that in return for some $30 million in union concessions over the next three years, the *News* would invest $60 million toward upgrading or replacing its production facilities. That was not nearly enough to build a state-of-the-art newspaper plant, or even buy new presses. And the union concessions were neither enough to dig the *News* out of the red or change the balance of power at the plant. They were not nearly enough to bring Freedom Center, or its culture, to New York. But Hoge believed a pattern had been established. The two sides had taken "the first bite of the apple," he said, and there was no reason they could not finish the job next time.

In fact, the MIP was flawed at birth. The union leaders, to whom the personal touch and the personal commitment were always immensely important, refused to sign until Stanton Cook brought them to Chicago for a meeting in his office. There he pledged—not for the first time—to do everything he could to bring the paper back. There was a discussion about the new $150 to $300 million plant the *News* needed, and the union leaders who were there say that Cook made an absolute verbal commitment to build the plant.

Cook denies this. But in the minds of McDonald and the other leaders, the MIP that day became not just a written commitment to invest $60 million but an irrevocable moral commitment by the company to build a new plant. McDonald concedes there was no firm promise to do it all in three years and that the unions realized they might have to make additional concessions to accommodate new technology once it arrived. But in principle, the union leaders believed, the thing was settled.

The Tribune Company believed no such thing. Cook and company were encouraged by Hoge's progress but they would not invest $300 million in a new plant unless the unions had already made the concessions that would make the plant profitable. Otherwise the Tribune Company would be held hostage in some future negotiation by a $300 million investment, useless without union concessions. In the next two years this misunderstanding festered until it had more than destroyed all the progress Hoge had made in the first three.

Part of the problem seems to have been that for very different reasons neither Hoge nor his executive team seemed to want to confront the misunderstanding directly. According to Longson, Hoge seemed almost as disappointed as the unions to discover, in the months after the MIP had been signed, how skeptical Chicago continued to be. The Tribune Company would stick to the letter of the deal, eventually spending some of the $60 million on new plant sites, but clearly Chicago was still not ready to commit absolutely to the bright future Hoge saw for the *News*. The gap between Chicago's demands and the unions' expectations, and the difficulty of getting either to move first on the "second bite of the apple" remained daunting. Hoge began to seem less energetic and even a bit depressed as it sank in that the immense efforts of the previous three years were only a first step. Some union leaders also say he became a less forceful communicator. Some colleagues say he stopped pushing quite so hard in Chicago for investments the Tribune Company was reluctant to make. And in the quarterly meetings, according to union leaders, Hoge kept talking about the new plant but was less frank and forceful about the need for more concessions. Hoge's vagueness, they claim, reinforced the leaders' own belief that the MIP had guaranteed the new plant, no strings attached.

Meanwhile Hoge's planning team, headed by Longson, was euphoric. Prior to the MIP agreement, the company had planned to spend roughly $150 million to upgrade the existing plants, adding a few Flexographic printing units, a then new technology heralded as being a low-cost way to add color to an existing letterpress array. Now the Flexographic plan was dropped, partly because of technological problems but mostly because short-term solutions seemed beside the point. The MIP had convinced Hoge's planning team that the *News*'s labor difficulties would be overcome somehow: "It was just something we [now] assumed we could get past," says Longson. With that dark cloud cleared from their radar screens they became convinced that "rather than spend $150 million on printing equipment it made much more sense to spend the $300 million" to build a completely automated plant, like Freedom Center, says Longson.

Perversely, the decision by Hoge's planning team to go all the way only worsened the unions' suspicions about whether the company would stick to the deal—or stick with the *News*. After abandoning the Flexographic idea, *News* management did little to improve the Brooklyn presses, though it spent some money improving the plant in other ways.

Instead the team embarked on what turned out to be a frustratingly long search for sites suitable for a new post-industrial plant.

Jim O'Dell, the manager of Freedom Center, came in to aid the search, and two different consulting firms specializing in newspaper plant engineering and design were brought in to evaluate proposed sites. These proved difficult to find, at least in New York City. Modern newspaper plants are huge, the presses must be set on bedrock or enormous foundations, and the *News* plants had to be near main transportation arteries if the paper was to be a serious player in the suburbs. Suitable sites were not located and purchased until the eve of the 1990 negotiations. By then the *News* and its unions were on a war footing.

The union leaders found the company's slow pace maddening. It seemed that all Hoge's guys ever did was tinker with their plans. And though Hoge kept the union presidents informed, no senior union people were ever seriously brought into the planning group. From the time of the MIP on, says McDonald, the unions met with Hoge repeatedly "about getting sites but they just were not getting it together." Jack Kennedy, Lenny Higgins's successor as president of the pressmen, says Hoge "would say how wonderful things were. But nothing ever happened."

McDonald complains that Hoge refused to compensate for his inexperience on the business side by bringing in "a general manager who could get things done," leaving that slot vacant his entire time. "They did not have hands-on management for years. You need a ramrod to kick asses," while the executives "go to lunch," says McDonald. To make matters worse McKinsey did a follow-up report strongly criticizing the company's slow pace. The unions, having been persuaded by the company to take McKinsey seriously, became even more suspicious.

In January 1989, Brumback became chief operating officer of the Tribune Company, which all the unions took as a bad sign. The *News*'s unions had followed closely the 1985 Chicago strike, in which Brumback had broken the *Chicago Tribune*'s largest unions, some of which were in the same internationals as the *News* production unions. Brumback, says McDonald, who had met him several times, "had a whole different attitude from Cook ... he hated unions. He is the one that brought King & Ballow into Chicago and they beat the shit out of the unions."

As Hoge's carefully constructed "pattern" of labor conciliation was collapsing, so was the New York economy. This came as a surprise to

Hoge's team, despite the 1987 stock market crash. The *News*'s economic consultants had been painting a fairly rosy picture of the city's economic future, even as the city was about to plunge into a local recession far deeper than the national slowdown. The *News*'s losses accelerated in 1988, as revenues fell much more dramatically than expected. The collapse in revenues weakened the *News*'s and Hoge's position in Chicago, and—rather suddenly, some of the leaders thought—hardened his stance toward the unions. If he had heretofore sidestepped the two sides' differences in interpreting the MIP, the collapse in *News* revenues allowed for no more vagueness: he told the union leaders flat out that only major union concessions would convince Chicago to move forward, or even continue to support the paper. The unions, predictably, regarded this as a new position equivalent to reneging. Hoge got blasted.

For both sides the MIP had turned into a disaster of self-delusion. In hindsight this seemed almost inevitable. In the language of the agreement, and in the way of thinking that it inspired, union cuts and concessions on the one hand and company investments on the other seemed not a united coherent game plan to revive a newspaper, but a cold trade-off, men for machines, in which the most important goal of both sides was not to get ripped off by being the first to give.

The MIP had made something enormously complex seem falsely simple. The *News* needed not only an exchange of men for machines, it needed a change in how men and machines worked together. As Longson said, the MIP encouraged management to believe it could "get past" its labor difficulties and to think instead about technology. But without a dramatic change in the culture of the workplace, a change for which management should have been the evangelist, the technology would not work.

The MIP encouraged the unions to obsess on the goal of getting precisely what the Tribune Company would not give: an absolute commitment to build the new plant before the unions would agree to change. As the unions fixated on the Tribune's unwillingness to "go first" and began to clamor, insistently now, for a commitment to the technology, they lost sight of the fact that it was precisely the technology that would require not only dollars-and-cents union "concessions" but a complete change in the culture and governance of the plant floor, a change utterly disruptive to union traditions.

To make the post-industrial transition, two warring camps (one of which contained many different tribes) had to become one willing team. The MIP did nothing more than make them, for a while, somewhat more peaceable adversaries, still on opposite sides of a transaction rather than on the same side in a revolution. It encouraged both sides to underestimate the job ahead. Management, instead of involving the unions in the process of change, hoarded its knowledge and its vision for the future; a reflexive impulse in any adversarial situation. And the unions, given little food for thought by management, never faced up to how destructive their behavior had become, or allowed themselves to imagine how much better the post-industrial future might be. Kept out of the loop by management, convinced that delay meant betrayal and the eventual closing of the paper, the unions came to see concessions not as prerequisite for a vibrant renaissance but as a grim human sacrifice calculated to coax a few more good harvests from a dying business.

If Jim Hoge viewed his "blasting" at the January 1989 quarterly meeting as a declaration of war, the unions felt the same way about the hiring of Bob Ballow. The manner of Ballow's hiring, in March of 1989, added insult to injury. It was announced not in private to the union leaders but in the pages of the *News*. Hoge claims that by announcing Ballow's hiring in the paper he was keeping a promise to the unions never to hold back any information about the company's plans. He says he had no intention to "rub their noses in it" or take them by surprise. But to McDonald and Kennedy and the others, that is exactly how it felt.

McDonald and several of the other leaders went to see Hoge for lunch almost immediately. McDonald told Hoge that he had embarrassed him, and demanded that he get rid of Ballow. If he is still the *News*'s lawyer by the time the next quarterly comes around, McDonald told Hoge, we're not coming. We can't pretend that you guys have done anything but declare war on the *News*'s workers.

Hoge told them not to be "ridiculous," that they were overreacting and did not understand Ballow. "Sure he is tough and he is pro-management. What do you expect from a management lawyer? But he only has a handful of strikes in over a thousand settlements; we should be able to reach agreement." The union leaders left before lunch was served. There were no more quarterly meetings.

McDonald spent the next month trying to get Hoge to reverse the decision. He wrote a series of letters in which he tried to convince Hoge how serious and potentially disastrous a step he had taken in hiring a "notorious union busting law firm." Engaging King & Ballow, he said, was an ungrateful slap in the face to unions whose sacrifices just a few years before had "made it possible for the Tribune Company to go public" so that its "stockholders and executives [could] realize huge profits." Now the company was taking steps that would convince the unions they had been betrayed. "Your decision to retain King & Ballow has unfortunately caused us to suspect that the Trib Co has changed its mind about financing a new plant and is planning to offer the *News* for sale after extracting more concessions from us."[2]

Hoge, who always disliked the unions' tendency to recount in sentimental terms the "favors" they had done the company, brusquely replied that McDonald was ignoring the very substantial raises and buyouts the company had given in return. The *News* was poised to spend millions on the plants, but the unions had to make more concessions.[3]

McDonald didn't buy it. It did not matter what the *News* was "poised" to do. The question was whether the Tribune Company was similarly "poised." "Retaining King & Ballow forces us to assume the answer is no." McDonald told Hoge the unions believed he had brought in King & Ballow "specifically to distance yourself from Stanton Cook's commitment to build new plants."[4]

Knowing themselves to be committed to rebuilding the *News*, Hoge and his team tended to discount the unions' skepticism as a negotiating or public relations ploy. Later they would discount the unions' loud complaints about Ballow's tactics as mere playacting, intended to distract management and win public sympathy. The more the unions protested, the more management would become convinced the unions were acting in bad faith. Hoge and the team missed the genuine rage that was building in the ranks.

McDonald warned Hoge that if Ballow stayed, the unions would take it as a declaration of war. When Hoge would not back down, McDonald decided finally that war was what the company wanted. But before deciding what to do about that, he would do what he had done for years whenever he faced a major decision. He would call Ted Kheel.

CHAPTER 7

What Kheel Knew

BALLOW came aboard in March of 1989. Negotiations did not begin until almost a year later. But long before the two sides sat down at the table, the unions had developed a theory of the conflict. The theory was inspired by Bob Ballow, but it was crafted by a man named Theodore Kheel.

Ted Kheel had been advising the city's newspaper unions since 1963, when Mayor Robert F. Wagner asked him to help mediate a citywide newspaper strike that shut down most of the city's eight papers for almost four months. Kheel was instrumental in brokering a solution. For the next thirty years he played a major role in the resolution of nearly every important newspaper labor dispute in the city.

Although 1963 was Kheel's first newspaper strike, Mayor Wagner's choice was a natural one. In 1963 American labor law was, practically speaking, less than a generation old and Kheel had been involved almost from the beginning. He joined the New York bar in 1937, the year the National Labor Relations Act, passed two years earlier, took effect. He joined the National Labor Relations Board established by the act as a review attorney in 1939. He served through the war, during which it was called the National War Labor Board and "our procedure for settling strikes was that we called up people and told them, 'You have a patriotic duty not to strike,' which pretty much worked." By 1945 he was the board's executive director. After the war Kheel resisted becoming a conventional labor lawyer. He disliked the idea of representing either labor or management. He preferred to work as an arbitrator or mediator, a role he performed for several mayors of New York and at least once for a president of the United States—when Lyndon Johnson called him in to be one of two mediators of the 1964 national railroad strike.

The 1963 strike made newspapers a lifetime passion for Kheel. He started off as an impartial mediator, but over the years he evolved into what might best be called an "interested" mediator on the union side. He always carefully identified himself as an "unpaid advisor" to the unions, and in particular to the Allied Printing Trades Council, but he never accepted a position as their legal representative. He saw himself as a voice of reason who could protect the unions from the hazards of a shrinking industry and sometimes from their own folly. There was no doubt whose side he was on, but he played, quite genuinely, the role of peacekeeper.

Kheel had a remarkable ability to shift the terms of a negotiation, finding not just middle grounds but "third ways," which both sides found surprisingly appealing. He mediated the famous 1974 automation agreement, which allowed New York's three remaining newspapers to introduce electronic typesetting, while giving lifetime job guarantees to thousands of printers made obsolete by that technology. The agreement set the pattern for similar deals all over the country, paving the way for unionized newspapers to take their first steps into the electronic age. As late as August 1990, even while embroiled in the escalating conflict at the *News*, Kheel was instrumental in negotiating a deal to keep the *New York Post* alive after *Post* owner Peter Kalikow suddenly announced he had lost $80 million in the last two years and was going to put the paper out of its misery if the unions did not immediately make fresh concessions. Kalikow had been able to reach agreement with every union but the Newspaper Guild (representing reporters and other white-collar workers), which balked in part because many Guild members preferred to take the substantial severance pay they would get from a shutdown. Kheel saw that the *Post* might be killed by reporters who had no intention of even staying at the paper. He suggested Kalikow give them the severance pay even if they resigned voluntarily, taking away their incentive to kill the *Post*. Kalikow did, and the *Post* for the time was saved.

Kheel was particularly close to George McDonald. McDonald had long been accustomed to consulting him on major strategic decisions, and often passed important letters or statements by Kheel before releasing them. When important matters came up it was not unusual for the two men to speak on the phone several times a day. In the spring of 1989, when it became clear Hoge would not fire Ballow, the Allied

Council began to meet every two weeks to plot strategy. Kheel attended nearly every meeting. Kheel was not as close to any of the other principal leaders: Jack Kennedy, who succeed Lenny Higgins as president of the pressmen, was a newcomer. And the pressmen used Michael Connery, from the high-powered New York law firm Skadden, Arps, as counsel. The drivers, who until recently had not been members of the council, had their own methods of securing concessions from management and little need of Kheel's gentler arts. But though Kheel was not particularly close to some of the other leaders, he influenced them all. He had become, or made himself, the historical memory of the unions in their struggles with the Tribune Company. He had a theory of that struggle and his theory became the unions' principal interpretive tool in deciphering the company's intentions, strategies, and even tactics. Ask the union leaders what the strike was all about and most of them will echo the Kheel theory with uncanny fidelity.

The Kheel theory arose out of the Tribune Company's 1981 attempt to sell the *News*. That attempt foundered on the issue of the *News*'s "shutdown liabilities." Kheel's version of the story, which most of the union leaders came to share, goes roughly like this:

When the Tribune Company decided to unload the *Daily News* in 1981, it quickly realized it would have to pay someone to take it. Not only was the paper poised to lose big money, but the new owner might be acquiring as much as $400 million in shutdown liabilities that might have to be paid out by the *News*'s owner if the paper went out of business. The potential shutdown liabilities included roughly $25 million in severance payments, mostly to Guild members, at least $75 million in unfunded pension liabilities, and most seriously, as much as $300 million in prospective payments to the printers and stereotypers who had been given lifetime job guarantees in 1974.

Washington Star publisher Joseph Albritton, the most serious prospective buyer, was willing to accept the liabilities only if he got major concessions from the unions. He asked and received from the Tribune Company an option to buy the paper contingent on obtaining such concessions. The unions balked. So Albritton, seeking negotiating leverage, asked the Tribune Company to tell the unions it would shut the *News* down if the unions did not give Albritton what he needed.

At that point, the Tribune Company's lawyers made a ruling that effectively scotched the deal. The 1974 automation agreement, they pointed out, was an agreement for the lifetime of *either* party. If the *News* died a natural death before all the printers and stereotypers died their own natural deaths, the lifetime job guarantees would end. The Tribune Company would not be responsible for continuing payments to the surviving workers, eliminating three-fourths of the total shutdown liabilities. This was welcome news in itself. But it raised a key question: What would constitute a natural death for the *News?* Anything that smacked of corporate suicide, the lawyers ruled, might simply *confirm* the *News*'s parent company's responsibility for the lifetime guarantees. As Kheel explains it, an announcement that the *News* would be shut down if the *News* unions did not cave in to Albritton might prompt the courts to later rule the *News*'s death had been contrived, leaving the Tribune Company legally responsible for the $300 million in guarantees. (It would probably be liable for the $25 million in severance and the $75 million in unfunded pension liabilities in any event.)

The lawyers' finding, says Kheel, meant any "give us concessions or we will kill the *News*" declaration was useless as a negotiating device: the unions would know the Tribune Company could not do it and they would call its bluff. The deal with Albritton fell through.

The collapse of the Albritton deal, paradoxically, might seem to have opened up the path for the company to kill off the *News* and get out of the guarantees. If no buyer could be found, then maybe the paper was already brain-dead and the Tribune Company could safely pull the plug. Instead, with Albritton out and no other serious buyers on the horizon, the company canceled plans for the sale. The Tribune obtained $50 million in givebacks from the *Daily News*'s unions, and made the most of those concessions in its prospectus for the company's transition to becoming a publicly held firm.

Nevertheless the failure of the 1981 sale attempt seemed to Kheel to yield at least one clear moral: the *News* might be worth more dead than alive—if the death could be arranged convincingly.

By the late 1980s the *News* was the single biggest drag on the profitability and stock price of the Tribune Company. In the spring of 1990, one industry analyst, Robert Wiley of Furman, Selz, Inc., estimated that Tribune Company earnings could rise by almost 50 percent if the *Daily News* problem was resolved, even by a shutdown of the paper. A few months later, during the *News* strike, Wiley argued that the Tribune Company's stock price would double if the *News* died, though he believed the stock would rise even more if the company won the strike and turned the *News* into a profitable modern operation.

Kheel had been skeptical of the Tribune Company's commitment to the *News* ever since the attempted sale. When the MIP went awry, Brumback became president, and Hoge hired Ballow, Kheel became even more suspicious. He calls Brumback a devious accountant with macho fantasies derived from his memories of his days on Princeton's football squad. He became convinced that Brumback and Ballow were as happy to kill the paper as save it, that in fact they had launched a devious plot to lure the *News* into an apparently natural death in a strike, wiping the ailing paper off the Tribune Company's balance sheet and legally shedding most of the shutdown liabilities.

As Kheel tells the story, and as he told it to the unions, Brumback faced three conventional options to solve the problem of the *News*, but found all three unacceptable. The first was simply to go after more concessions in the context of an ordinary negotiation. This Brumback could not do, believes Kheel, because it would spotlight the *News*'s failure to build the $300 million plant verbally promised by Cook at the end of the 1987 talks. The unions would not agree to more cuts without an irrevocable commitment to build the new plant, a commitment Brumback would not give.

Brumback's second option was to shut down the paper *voluntarily*. But the shutdown liabilities, though much reduced through the death or retirement of many of the printers and stereotypers and the strong performance of the pension funds in the 1980s, made voluntary shutdown an expensive choice. Kheel estimates the liabilities in 1990 at about $100 million. Tribune Company executives give various estimates, ranging from $75 to $150 million.

The third option was to sell. But Kheel believes that sale, like shutdown, was unacceptable not only because of the financial implications—the Tribune still would have had to pay someone to take the paper off its hands—but because of corporate pride. "They should have said we will put it up for sale and if we can't get a buyer we will shut it down," says Kheel. But, he believes, "the Tribune Company, a great media conglomerate, did not want to tell the public they could not operate a newspaper in New York City." Crucially, Kheel dismisses the notion that Brumback wanted to hold on to the *News* because he thought he could turn it around. The Kheel theory, and much of the behavior of the unions throughout the conflict, absolutely depends on the premise that the Tribune Company under Brumback had little interest in holding on to the *News* over the long term.

To avoid embarrassment, says Kheel, Brumback found a fourth, more sinister, option: if the paper died as the result of a strike, the death would be ruled natural. If the unions struck and thereby *forced* the paper out of business, the shutdown would be *involuntary* and, in Kheel's view, most of the lifetime guarantees, the largest shutdown liabilities, might be legally dissolved. "Being devoid of interest in the *News* or its employees," says Kheel, Brumback decided to use Ballow "to force the unions to strike."

Kheel at various times seems to have given either more nuanced or more sensationalist versions of the alleged Brumback plot: in the sensationalist version, which Kheel sometimes slipped into before and during the strike, and of which he seems perhaps inadvertently to have convinced some of the union leaders, Brumback, with the secret collusion of Ballow, set out deviously, conspiratorially, viciously to force the unions to strike so as to deliberately destroy the *Daily News*, thereby wiping the paper off the Tribune Company's balance sheet. In this sensationalist version, Chicago actually preferred destroying the *News* to winning the strike. A shutdown would drive the Tribune Company's stock up, Kheel argued. Whereas, he says, if the company won the strike, the *News* would still require hundreds of millions in investments, and Tribune would be stuck with the opprobrium of running a scab paper in New York, which might prove difficult as well as unpleasant. The death of the *News* would be a much cleaner resolution.

In the more nuanced version, which he holds today, Kheel says Brumback was not necessarily absolutely determined to destroy the paper. Forcing a strike, crushing the unions, and then selling a few years later, Kheel concedes, would have been acceptable. But, Kheel says, Brumback still behaved deviously and viciously because he was willing to risk destroying the paper in order to avoid the embarrassment of doing "the only logical thing, which was to put the newspaper up for sale and then close if they could not find a buyer."

So says Kheel, Brumback decided to "try this strategy under which if they got what they wanted they could have a hell of deal and if not and the paper went under the stock would go up anyway." Brumback, he says, thought he had come up with "a heads I win tails you lose situation. Either they got what they wanted or the unions shut the paper down. . . . They thought this was cute. It was. It was too cute and it blew up in their faces." But of one thing Kheel was sure: Brumback and company "obviously had no interest in staying with the newspaper, otherwise they would not have engaged in this tortuous program that was doomed to failure." Failure, Kheel was convinced, was the company's goal.

In every version of the Kheel theory Brumback and Ballow set out to *force* a strike—not merely to risk a strike by making stiff demands, but to *force* a strike. They would do this by making inflexible demands they knew the unions could never accept. Win or lose, the company would profit: win and the company would have an effectively nonunion shop, lose and the *News* would die a natural death, and the perennial drain on the Tribune balance sheet would end. Ballow's strategy, Kheel believed, made "a traditional labor-management relationship out of the question." Before negotiations even began, the unions' most senior advisor became convinced they were pointless.

Although most important union leaders eventually accepted the Kheel theory, some union advisors dissented or even regarded it as "ridiculous." For one thing, the numbers did not work. Kheel before and during the strike put great emphasis on Brumback's desire to escape the *News*'s shutdown liabilities. But as Kheel himself notes, those liabilities had been reduced by more than half during the eighties and were probably down to around $100 million, only about $75 million of which was accounted for by the lifetime job guarantees that *might* be canceled if the *News* died in a strike. Moreover, if Brumback's alleged devious—and illegal—plot were discovered, the courts would not only force the company to pay the guarantees, but assess huge penalties for the very serious labor-law violation of conspiring to force a strike. The penalties could total tens or hundreds of millions of dollars.

Moreover, just as Kheel was selling his theory to the unions, the company was very visibly spending millions of dollars (eventually more than $40 million on prestrike preparation alone) getting ready to publish through a strike. This expense would make little sense if the company's goal was to get the unions to kill off the paper. Why spend millions to publish through the strike if the company viewed winning the strike as at most marginally preferable to losing it? The strike ended up costing the Tribune Company somewhere between $140 and $200 million. And in the end the company had to pay British publishing baron and embezzler Robert Maxwell $60 million to take the *News* off its hands. All told, it cost the Tribune at least $200 million to dump a liability much smaller than that.

Because the numbers fail to add up, Kheel today emphasizes the psychological aspect of Brumback's motivation, his embarrassment at admitting defeat in New York, which made him unwilling simply to unload the paper without the Sturm und Drang of a strike to excuse his failure. But this explanation appears to misread the motivating psychology of Brumback and the Tribune Company, men who deeply believed that what they wanted to build in New York was right and good. Brumback is a man who passionately believes it is "human nature to want to accomplish things, to truly achieve and be productive, not to play-act at make-work," a man who judges a plant floor by walking in and trying to make eye contact with the men because "in a well-managed shop where workers are working hard and well and are proud of what they are doing they look you in the eye." Men like Brumback commit sins of pride, megalomania, or intolerance. But deceitfully engaging in a venal conspiracy to murder a great newspaper because he can't run it himself seems totally out of character for a latter-day Calvinist cum Randian. That is the sort of thing a Rand *villain* would do.

If Kheel's theory was psychologically inept in its assessment of the company, it was psychologically destructive for the unions.

For the unions, the difference between a Brumback willing to play hardball, including taking a strike, to build the plant he wants, and on the other hand, a Brumback deviously determined to simply rid himself of a problem by forcing a strike, might seem small operationally. But psychologically the chasm is as great as that between a game of chicken, and a game of chicken in which one driver is convinced the other driver wants to die. In the first case you assume the other fellow values his life. There is some point to playing that game—you can win it. But if your opponent prefers death there is no way to win.

Kheel's great discovery, he thought, was that the Tribune Company had welded its steering wheel in place and bolted the pedal to the floor. Believing that, the unions lost their incentive to play at the negotiating table. Of course the talks went on anyway and were in some ways more substantive than might have been expected. But the Kheel theory would be almost as destructive to the negotiations as Ballow's uncompromising, point-blank negotiating style and his infuriating psycho-legal gamesmanship.

Kheel's theory also encouraged union denial about what had gone wrong with the *News*. The notion that Brumback was simply an eccentric monster willing to plot a newspaper's death in order to raise the

Tribune Company's stock price, or save his own name, gave the unions moral succor. If Brumback was a monster, then there was no need to contemplate the ugly reality that no sensible person would want to own a newspaper the unions controlled. If Brumback was a sort of mad criminal embarked on a "devious plot," then there was not quite as much reason to face the new post-industrial reality. If Brumback and Ballow were not the harsh heralds of an inexorable new order but merely criminal kooks, then some other owner not as criminal or as kooky could be found. As long as the unions could dismiss Brumback and Ballow as devious, mad, or fanatical, they could comfort themselves—as they did constantly—with the thought that the Tribune execs were behaving this way because they hated New York, or the workingman, or the *News*, but never because the old union culture was obsolete.

Kheel's rhetoric, unsurprisingly, downplayed any union responsibility for the *News*'s plight. His explanations for the paper's troubles focused either on economic abstractions beyond the *News*'s control such as inflation, or on management's failure to invest in new facilities even as it sold off old assets such as the *News* building, the *News*'s commercial printing operations, and the *News*'s own truck fleets.

A few days before the strike, Kheel gave a speech at a *New York Post* "Labor-Management Breakfast" at the Plaza Hotel, contrasting two different "styles of labor-management relations" pursued by the *Post* and the *News*. Both papers, he explained, needed concessions from their unions, but they had gone about getting them in very different ways. The *Post*, he said, did it right. Peter Kalikow, the owner of the *Post*, "eschewed advance publicity." When he did speak about the *Post*'s problems either in public or to the employees, "Kalikow blamed the economy and not the unions" for the paper's difficulties. He never seemed to challenge the notion that "the employment practices in the newspaper industry were the product of agreements negotiated by the publishers and the unions." Most important, the *Post* asked for concessions without asking for a workplace revolution that would violate long-established traditions of the industry: "The *Post* confined its demands to labor cost reductions that would not destabilize the structure of labor-management relations established in the newspaper industry through years of bargaining," Kheel said.

On almost every point the *News* did the opposite, argued Kheel. It wanted revolutionary changes. It sought publicity. It refused to say the paper's problems arose from a declining economy. And most important of all, "far in advance of contract negotiations, the *Daily News* publicity accused the unions of 'featherbedding and other flagrant labor abuses.' " By contrast, he pointed out, Kalikow did not offend the unions. He went to them in a spirit of cooperation, said Kheel, and got what he needed. The *News* would get nowhere because its behavior was so offensive.

The problem with this reasoning was that under Kheel's rules of engagement management could never tell the unions the truth, which was that the established traditions of the industry, including "the structure of labor-management relations," would no longer work. Playing by Kheel's rules, the concessions Kalikow obtained were cuts in the most literal sense. Most of the savings came by reducing the number of days or hours in the workweek. The *Post*, the day after the agreement, was not in any sense a better paper or more productive company; it was simply a slightly cheaper company to run. The workers were costs and costs were reduced; Kalikow paid less and he got less in return. Both sides made "shared sacrifices" as if the *Post* were just another mismanaged government agency with not quite enough taxpayer money to distribute to its clients. The newspaper's real need—to be able to produce a better, more competitive product, rather than simply lose less money—was not part of the equation.

When Kheel mediated the 1974 automation agreement, the technology in question was meant not to transform the work force but replace it. Electronic typesetting is no more than the direct transmission of reporters' stories from word processor to typesetting machines without retyping by printers. It does not require the printers to become a post-industrial work force; it requires them to go away. As epochal as the 1974 automation agreement was, it was far more simple and less psychologically traumatic than the changes the *News* now needed. In 1974 power over the workplace was not at issue because most printers would not be in the workplace anymore, except in admittedly make-work jobs, at which they showed up only to collect on their lifetime guarantees.

In mediating the 1974 agreement Kheel never had to confront the need to change the culture of the workplace and replace the bickering fiefdoms of the unions with a single unified companywide, post-industrial team. Although Kheel brilliantly steered the printers through a traumatic confrontation with technology twenty years ago, Kheel today seems unable to comprehend the much more profound changes required by computer-assisted production. Like the unions he advised, he was convinced that this new dispute also should be settled by the numbers: bring in so many new machines, eliminate so many old jobs, and come up with so much for "buyouts" to compensate departing workers. He apparently did not grasp, and could not help the unions to grasp, the nature of the technological revolution at hand in the industry.

Kheel was like Ballow's photographic negative. Kheel was always benevolent to the unions; but rather than helping them see reality he helped them avoid it. While Ballow was preparing to deliver his message in as stark, brutal, and infuriating a fashion as possible, Kheel was telling the unions that Ballow's very willingness to offend them was proof his message was insincere. Where Ballow would try to shock the unions into a recognition of the new balance of power, Kheel insisted that the company's lack of reverence for the past rendered its claims morally illegitimate.

Meanwhile, the company was doing everything in its power to persuade the unions the Kheel theory was right.

CHAPTER 8

War Games

It is held to be an absolute duty to consider oneself chosen, and to combat all doubts as temptations of the devil, since lack of self-confidence is the result of insufficient faith, hence of imperfect grace.
Max Weber, *The Protestant Ethic and the Spirit of Capitalism*

FROM the day Ballow came aboard, it seemed that almost everything the company did could be used to confirm the Kheel theory. Every display of the company's power and its resolve to fix the *News* right now could as easily be taken as evidence of the company's utter indifference to the *News*'s continued survival, as proof that Brumback's pride and Ballow's blood lust had overridden all more rational business considerations.

The company began to "arm" for the negotiations almost immediately after hiring Ballow. The core of Ballow's approach is to be visibly prepared to publish through a strike, and so not have to do so. Soon after his arrival the labor situation was transformed from "something we would get past," in Longson's phrase, into the cause of a massive, almost military, campaign of contingency planning and preparation. The top Tribune and *News* execs strenuously deny it was their intention to provoke a strike. But they did not have much hope for a peaceful settlement, and as they prepared for war they began to talk and act as if war were inevitable. From there it was but a short jump for many of those around them, either lower down in the management hierarchy or in the unions, to the conclusion that provoking a strike was company policy.

No one now remembers exactly when it was decided that no expense would be spared, no possible advantage overlooked, no contingency left unprepared for. But from the first there was a thrill in the air. The negotiations were almost a year away—but that seemed only to increase the urgency. Unlike most labor actions this one could be planned in every detail. The Tribune Company was rich, Ballow was the best, Brumback and Hoge were committed. As Ed Gold, the young Ballow protégé brought in to be the *News*'s new director of labor relations, says, "This was the fight to be in, it was going to be the Super Bowl of labor relations."

Most of all, the technology was on the Tribune's side. Strictly speaking, the technology had been on their side since 1974, when the printers union stepped aside and allowed electronic typesetting into New York's newspapers. The men in the seven other production unions—the pressmen, the paperhandlers, the mailers, and the rest—were all skilled laborers. But only the printers had a skill that practically speaking was irreplaceable over the relatively short course of a strike. For decades the other production unions had all depended on the power of the printers, who had led nearly every important strike. When the printers were replaced, the pressmen became the dominant production union. They were the largest union after the printers, and running a press was the most demanding remaining skill. The pressmen, however, were not irreplaceable and so could never frighten employers the way the printers had. A craft union coalition led by the pressmen would be much weaker than the old printer-led coalition. And with new technology waiting in the wings, their power was even less. The company might after all prefer to have new blood throughout the plant, men more amenable to change. If the unions refused to change and struck, management might just say good riddance, bring in permanent replacements, as federal law allows, and go forward without its old workers.

This was the new balance of power. Of course it was not apparent immediately. The New York unions had struck successfully in 1978, for eighty-eight days, in part because management at the *News*, *Times*, and *Post*, not having adjusted to their new strength, did not lay serious plans to publish when struck. The *News* made a last-minute, halfhearted attempt to do so, but swiftly gave it up when the drivers, not originally expected to join that strike, did so, a contingency for which the company had no plans.

Though the new balance of power may not have been immediately apparent in New York, it had long been crystal clear to Ballow. This reputed fox of labor law is actually a hedgehog. He knows one thing: traditional newspaper craft unionism has become impotent. Knowing that one thing has made him a rich man and something of a legend. His strategy is simply to force the unions to recognize their weakness.

Actually both Ballow and his protégés dislike the term "strategy." They talk more simply of pursuing the "process"—that is, relentlessly delivering the message that the unions have no choice but to settle on the company's terms. Ballow's job is to supply information, albeit often quite vividly. It is the unions' job to decide how to react, to write the script for the last act, to decide whether to make a deal or die on the battlefield.

Ballow wins simply because he is a tough and unsentimental man who delivers his message as "arrestingly" as possible, banging it home in so many different ways, so relentlessly and convincingly that eventually the unions believe it and succumb. In short Ballow's goal is not to provoke a fight but to evoke despair. Ballow and Brumback are very different men, but Ballow has something like Brumback's stunning moral confidence, though the tone is different, more Marxist than Christian. Ballow and his people talk like men who believe they are on the side of history.

Soon after Ballow arrived the unions began to hear about strange things. In early spring the company brought in a team of psychologists to administer evaluations to *News* executives to determine who would make good strike leaders. As Hoge put it, the tests were used as "a screening tool, to get a management cadre" temperamentally capable of handling a difficult confrontation. The test was graded not A, B, C, but red, green, or yellow. Those who scored as good war leaders got green lights; others suddenly found their careers stalled by red signals. There was a flurry of personnel changes as men the company felt were not up to the coming challenge, or men who wanted no part of it, were eased out or left and more militant men like Ed Gold and John Sloan, the new head of human resources, were brought in.

Pressmen president Jack Kennedy thought the changes guaranteed trouble. When Ballow "comes in [he] literally takes over the labor relations department; there is virtually nobody in the building we know. . . . It was like an inverse lawyer-client relationship. The people in the labor department were working for Ballow rather than the other way around." As for the people he did bring in like Gold and Sloan, "Our research turned up that they were bad guys too, real hardliners who don't like unions."

Ed Gold would be proud to hear himself described as a younger, thinner, Jewish, Southeastern Seaboard version of Ballow. Like Ballow, in fact at Ballow's prompting, he made a midcareer decision to attend law school, and actually joined the bar only a few months before taking the job at the *News*. Though actually a doctor's son, Gold looks at first glance like a Marine brat. Hawk-nosed, he has the wiry twice-as-strong-as-he-looks build and erect bearing that shout "drill instructor," along with (by his own admission) a comically compulsive lust for organization. Pressed for details on, say, a negotiating session, even some union leaders referred me to Gold on the usually correct assumption that he would have the most complete and reliable notes. No event in Gold's life ever occurs at noon or a quarter to two; somehow everything contrives to happen at 11:57 or 1:43.

Like Ballow, Gold is tough but usually good-humored, a professional soldier who relishes his role and frankly disdains opponents who "take things personally." At a negotiation he is a needler, ridiculing union positions to get the other side to react emotionally and make a mistake. But what Gold would consider his best qualities, his professionalism, his aggressiveness, his ability to treat a labor negotiation as a sort of war game, infuriated the labor leaders, who variously describe him as "arrogant," "hostile," "sarcastic," "hotheaded," "a law thug," or "a punk." Perhaps the last was the most relevant. Gold was thirty-two years old, a hired gun assigned to decimate the jobs of men in their fifties who would never make the kind of money he did, and he treated the whole thing, they thought, as if it were just some big game. And there were chinks in that professional armor. Try though he might to emulate the usually cool-headed Ballow, Gold by his own admission has a terrific temper. He does not stand up well to the kind of needling he dishes out.

All that spring and summer of 1989, long before the formal opening of negotiations the following January, the company engaged in a largely symbolic two-sided psychological campaign, aimed simultaneously at impressing the unions with the company's resolve, and building morale among its own executives. Hoge flew a team of executives to London to visit Rupert Murdoch's "Fortress Wapping," the heavily secured high-tech newspaper plant that Murdoch had used to smash the power of British newspaper unions in 1985. Ostensibly the goal was to see how it was done, but just as important was to convince the *News* team that it could be done: the tour also included visits to the clutch of new newspaper plants that had opened in the wake of Murdoch's victory.

For similar reasons the company sent about ninety nonunion and management employees in three different groups to the Tribune Company's old Fort Lauderdale *Sun Sentinel* plant to learn how to run the

News's presses. As it happens, no *News* manager from outside a production department ever ran a press during the strike, but some managers do say these two-week "strike schools" were great morale builders, instilling a sense of team spirit among managers who had barely known one another before. But Brumback, who visited the sessions, made a bad impression on some of the mid- and lower-level managers who thought him severe, cold, and uninspiring. According to Terry Teachout, a longtime *News* editorial writer who attended one of the strike schools, Brumback at a dinner and "pep rally" for Teachout's class told a group of managers that he was fully committed to saving the *News* but only "provided it could be done in a way consistent with our fiduciary obligations to Tribune stockholders." "Of course strictly speaking he was correct," comments Teachout, "but this was supposed to be a big-game locker-room speech. These were people he was asking to go out into the line of fire. They needed to hear that he was committed to the bitter end, not that he was a responsible fiduciary."

Longson, a rock-ribbed Brumback loyalist, says Brumback's "harsh" speeches to the managers assembled at Fort Lauderdale convinced many that unquestioning militancy was the only acceptable stance for a *News* executive. "Charlie used this image of the Old West. We were the Indians and the *News* was our home and we had let the cowboys, the unions, take our home away. But now we were going to make the business work and to do that we had to take our home back." It wasn't just Brumback, Longson says. Most of the senior *News* execs "set a pretty tough line. We were going to take control of the business, come what may." The hard line had serious consequences. Brumback, Hoge, Ballow, and the rest of top management, says Longson—who finds himself guilty of the same charge—encouraged an atmosphere in which "people tried hard to come up with answers to please" so as to look like team players rather than ask tough questions about whether the company's provocative strategy made sense. In particular, says Longson, people started avoiding the most important question of all—could the company win the strike for which it was so visibly preparing?

Even as the editorial writers and ad salesmen were playing pressman, Longson, as head of the strike-planning team, was building a real and amazingly thorough contingency plan, soon to be put into action at an enormous cost. From the outset the planning team's job was defined not as determining whether the paper could publish during a strike, but how to do so. Longson was adamant that the contingency committee view its mission as operational, not strategic. "Nobody put us in a room and said, 'Decide whether or not you're going to have a strike, or whether the *News* should have a strike, or whether a strike is a good strategy, or beneficial.' " On the contrary, Longson says, it was obvious that a strike would be costly, damaging, and not necessarily successful. But that was not the contingency team's business.

The decision to give the contingency team only a tactical mission reinforced the message that the company no longer had any use for skeptics. The most prominent skeptic was Gil Spencer, the man Hoge had brought in from Philadelphia in 1985 to be editor of the *News*. He doubted the company could win a strike. And he thought massive strike preparations were the best way to provoke one. Tell people their job is to figure out how to win a strike, he says, and they will convince themselves they can win one, and then they will have one, because they will be feeling too macho to compromise at the negotiating table.

Within a few months of Ballow's arrival the *News* executive team was not really managing anymore, Spencer says, it was just responding to "Charlie's macho bullshit." Spencer thought that the Fort Lauderdale trips were an "excessive" display—contracts would not expire for almost a year. He found Ballow's rationalization (to prevent wildcat strikes) transparently, and insultingly, disingenuous. "Bullshit! The unions were not going to wildcat . . . they'd be slaughtered legally. . . . The real point of all this was to send a message that the *News* management were ready to fight. But had they asked the question could they win? That was a serious question but I don't think they ever seriously answered it."

By the fall of 1989 Spencer was gone. Ostensibly he quit over the paper's endorsement in the 1989 Democratic mayoral primary. But he had quit many times before, and Hoge had always gotten him back. This time Hoge let him stay quit, thereby depriving his management committee of its most senior and vocal dissenter from the "total war" strategy.

The exclusion of dissent led to one of the most fundamental miscalculations of the entire war. Maintaining circulation during a strike would be crucial, not only to bring in revenue, but because circulation levels would be the best way of measuring who was winning. If the *News* could hang on to most of its circulation during a strike, the unions would have no choice but to capitulate quickly while it was still possible for some of the men to get their jobs back.

At contingency planning meetings, the representatives of the circulation department were always reassuring on the key question of whether the 12,000-plus newsstand dealers who accounted for 80 percent of *Daily News* circulation would carry the paper during the strike, even in the face of harassment from the drivers. The owners were devoted to the *News* and would stay loyal, the circulation group claimed. And even if some did defect, the circulation folks repeatedly claimed they were ready to put a thousand hawkers on the street to sell papers. (In fact, little had been done to recruit the hawkers. When the strike came they were still not ready.)

Longson, and Tribune Security Chief Paul Stellato, detailed to the *News* for the duration, were skeptical of circulation's claims. As Longson remembers it the dispute "culminated in a very noisy meeting sometime in October" (1989). In that meeting Longson presented financial projections that assumed a much larger drop in circulation during the strike than the circulation people were estimating and showed poststrike circulation down to about 800,000 from more than a million. Longson's estimates would turn out to be almost exactly right. Nevertheless, he says, his projection presented "the possibility of winning the battle and losing the war" and coming "out the other side with a newspaper that wasn't viable." The meeting turned angry. Ultimately Longson's numbers were rejected, not only because the circulation group felt slighted but also because Longson's bad news flew in the face of the can-do spirit management had been carefully nurturing. It would be one of the company's most fateful mistakes.

From the very beginning the contingency group had been handed the grandest possible definition of what it meant to publish during a strike. First, foremost, and most expensive: the *News* would not miss an edition. Managers and emergency replacements would be ready to fill in for striking workers instantly. Within days of a strike the *News* would begin to replace its union work force with a full complement of permanent trained replacement workers capable of sustaining every normal operation. Not long after, the paper would be running at normal size and near normal circulation. The implications were vast. Readiness is expensive. *Instant readiness* proved not only fantastically expensive but ultimately misguided.

Every department built a crisis-operations plan detailing how it would get its job done during a strike. The plans covered prestrike readiness procedures, the immediate response in the event of a strike (or other labor actions including slowdowns, stoppages, rule violations, etc.); emergency and long-term communications procedures, including procedures for keeping nonunion and replacement employees apprised of events, a logging and reporting system for violent and criminal acts, procedures for getting in touch instantly with the legal or PR teams; protection of facilities, staffing requirements for various emergencies, transportation, housing, and protection of those who would work during a strike and, if need be, their families, and legal training to avoid unfair labor practices charges especially during the early days of a strike. Every aspect of normal operations and how to maintain them during a war was covered.

The crisis-operations plans were not just strings of ideas and suggestions. In effect they were invoices, and the bill was huge. The advertising department, for instance, based its worst-case plan on the assumption that the strike would come at 10 P.M. with work on the next day's paper not even begun. The department was to be prepared to put out immediately a forty-eight-page paper with ads, and to notify 470 key advertisers within a few hours that the *News* was still available to carry ads. The main threats to advertising were harassment of advertisers by union supporters and sabotage of the *News* telephone lines, over which ad sales and service personnel do almost all their work. So the ad department set up a system to monitor harassment through an Advertising Control Room where incidents would be reported. The Advertising Control Room would also keep *News* advertising personnel and advertisers informed of developments in the strike, special promotions, and daily circulation figures. It would also coordinate security for advertisers and ad personnel. As for the phone lines, the *News* hired Tele-Disc, a small phone services company, to install and maintain extra telephone lines, linked to one another as business lines normally are but handled directly through NYNEX facilities rather than the *News*'s own switchboard. If the *News*'s regular lines were sabotaged these would be unaffected.

For all departments the first priority was security. The first step was to boost the *News*'s own security force. Tribune Security Chief Paul Stellato increased the size of the regular force from only 45 to 160 officers, most of them younger and better trained than the men of the old force. In addition he arranged for the services, as needed, of more than 1,000 contract security personnel. An executive protection service was retained to protect top executives, including Hoge and Ballow.

The *News* brought in Richard Koehler, former head of the New York State Department of Corrections, as chief security advisor and liaison to local and federal law enforcement. To head the new security force Hoge and Stellato tapped Grover Howell, formerly the director of the Communications Division of the New York Police Department, the biggest 911 operation in the country. Previously he had served in the NYPD's detective division for twelve years, as an instructor in detective investigation at the Police Academy, and as deputy inspector and eventually inspector general for the Department of Corrections. Stellato also set up a *Daily News* detective squad, roughly fifty strong, staffed mostly by retired NYPD detectives and run by a former high-ranking NYPD detective, Al Cachie. Their mission would be to record and investigate acts of violence or harassment against company employees or customers, preparing NYPD-style investigative reports to be turned over to New York law enforcement authorities as well as to the *News*'s legal team.

The *News* recruited and trained more than one hundred emergency replacement drivers and driver's helpers, actually security personnel with strike experience, i.e., professional strikebreakers, to be on call to distribute the paper on the first night of a strike. The drivers along with a core group of replacement workers for other jobs were actually paid to show up every night for months and lodged in nearby hotels at company expense.

When most of the unions took strike-authorization votes in the early spring of 1990, the *News* advertised for real permanent replacements, ordinary New Yorkers who would consider coming to the *News* permanently in the event of a strike. Some 15,000 applicants showed up; the lines in front of the *News* building stretched around the block. More than a thousand were scheduled for possible callback and several hundred were actually trained.

The upgraded security force started showing up in the plants and even in the 42nd Street newsroom within a few months of Ballow's arrival. Hardly anything the company did outraged the unions more. The unions were convinced the security personnel were brought in to provoke incidents that could be used as a pretext for firing strong union men, or even better to provoke a union job action Ballow could call a strike and use as an excuse to replace the work force. Ballow and all the senior executives of course deny this. But there were incidents and men were fired.

The *News* set up an emergency satellite newsroom in a former Sears warehouse in North Bergen, New Jersey. From the emergency newsroom the paper could be reported, written, and edited, and pages made up, should the *News*'s 42nd Street headquarters become unusable. The emergency newsroom actually put out a mock edition, an exercise that involved some 200 employees. The *News* installed new microwave transmission systems to ship pages in electronically from even remoter sites (such as a Tribune-owned paper in Virginia) and retained a fleet of Learjets in case the microwave system failed.

Practically speaking, the expense of setting up the satellite newsroom was a complete waste. It did give the *News* some capacity to keep publishing even if the *News* building were actually captured by strikers and the police refused to remove them. But if the *News* had to physically retreat across the Hudson River in order to publish the paper, the strike would be lost anyway. In any event, reporting, writing, and printing the paper were not going to be the main problem; even in 1978 the *News* had been able to do that.

All told, the prestrike preparations cost well more than $40 million. Gold argues that a great deal of this was waste and ultimately undermined the company's willingness and capacity to withstand a lengthy strike. The directive to be able to publish through a strike, he says, became an end in itself to be pursued at any cost regardless of its effect on the larger battle. Instant readiness and the "don't miss an edition" policy, he argues, wasted millions or tens of millions of dollars. The psychological advantage of not missing an edition turned out to be negligible in a five-month strike. Moreover, the *News* got "too ready, too early." The hotels were packed with replacements on March 31, the night contracts expired, six months before the strike eventually came, though, Gold says, "we *knew* the unions were not going to strike then." Moreover, both Gold and Longson say the "don't miss an edition" policy actually failed long before the strike. By the summer of 1990, with the unions apparently determined never to strike and the readiness meter running full tilt, the *News* cut back drastically on both outside security personnel and on the number of on-call replacement workers. By then, says Longson, "We were willing to concede a day's publication" in the event of a strike, "and would have, except that the night the strike started most of the papers had already been printed."

Gold also argues the company spent too much on security early on. "Some people may say, 'Are you willing to let somebody get killed before you pull out the security?' " But, he says, "I'd like to see a little bit of threat first. In labor situations, nobody gets murdered in the Paul Castellano fashion. . . . It starts by somebody getting chased, or getting a Molotov cocktail thrown in their front yard, or their tires slashed, or their house painted. I think you absorb a little bit of that, test their firepower before you spend a zillion dollars on security—because what you are really spending is your ability to hold out in the war of attrition that most strikes turn into."

At the same time the company was preparing for a strike it was also fighting to retake control of the plants. This campaign was both parallel to and part of the strike preparations, a way of very visibly preparing to run the plants in the event of a strike, but also a way of taking advantage of the strike preparations to improve the *News* right now. Since the company was putting its cannons on the ridge to cow the unions, why not use that advantage and start to run the plant as a new plant would be run if the company prevailed?

The man chiefly in charge of this effort was Dick Malone, a thirty-five-year-old veteran production executive from the *Chicago Tribune* and previously from the Gannett chain. He came to New York originally in the fall of 1989 to head up the effort to site and design the *News*'s future production plants. But within a few months he was made the production manager for all three old *News* plants, reporting directly to Hoge but working closely with Eugene Bell, Tribune Company's corporate VP for newspaper operations and a longtime Brumback ally who had helped make Freedom Center and the Orlando plant into state-of-the-art facilities.

Malone, a studious, blond efficiency expert, had two great passions. One was running computer models of the *News*'s production system, pouring in new data from the squad of "press analysts" he had brought in to put the *News* plants and personnel under a microscope in order to figure out how they worked and where the waste was. Malone would run the models repeatedly, finding ways to squeeze out a few more inefficiencies and a few more dollars every day. His other passion was to bring order and discipline to the plant floor. Malone, accustomed to the benevolent order of Freedom Center, was appalled by conditions in the Brooklyn plant. "I had seen many newspapers," he says, "but I was really shocked. The work ethic was nonexistent." He was amazed that

News workers smoked on the floor, "which is verboten around newspapers because of the volatility" of paper dust and ink, or that men would drink on the job, surrounded by antiquated and very dangerous heavy machinery. He took an absolutely hard line not only on the beatouts and the buddy system, but on drinking, hanging out in the break room, and, for lack of a better word, deportment.

Part of the plan for retaking the plant floor had been to co-opt the unionized supervisors, gradually selling them on the company's vision of the future and eventually persuading them to drop their union cards and become real managers. Early in his tenure Malone got together with all the supervisors and tried to enlist them in an effort to enforce the rules. It was a failure. The pressmen, for example, had a practice of taping paper over the break room windows looking out on the pressroom floor, so they could not be observed while on break. Malone says he repeatedly ordered the supervisors to clear the windows but it never got done. Eventually he returned many of the unionized supervisors to the ranks and brought in more than 30 new nonunion supervisors to enforce the rules. Out of dozens of production union supervisors, only three ever dropped their cards.

Malone did, however, reestablish management control. Like his counterpart Bill Deering, the former UPS executive brought in to do the same job for the distribution department, Malone and his team of watchers concentrated on enforcing the existing contract. They were able to cut back on waste and abuse (including unnecessary overtime), raise productivity, and cut costs dramatically. In the process Malone made himself the most universally reviled member of the *News* team after Ballow and Gold. Even today you can get a rise out of just about any man at the Brooklyn plant by mentioning Malone's name.

One reason for the bitterness, say union members, is that in the months before the strike Malone disciplined and fired more plant workers than anyone can remember being fired or disciplined for years before that. Daniel McPhee, an officer in the pressmen's union and a *Daily News* employee for thirteen years, calls Malone "a goon" who would suspend men for offenses they regarded as trivial, like "walking out of the smoke room without their hearing protection on." The firings, McPhee says, were unprecedented: "Before all this happened nobody ever got fired. You could practically murder somebody and you would only get suspended or sent away to the clinic or rehab." It is one of the possibly true myths of the strike that Malone fired one worker for spitting on the floor, though Malone says it never happened and that the number of firings is exaggerated.

The new supervisors were widely regarded as spies whose prime job was to catch the men in infractions or browbeat them into provoking an incident, such as a spontaneous walkout, that the company could turn into a strike. "If there was a web break," says McPhee, Malone would have a crowd of supervisors down on the floor, surrounding the men responsible and "questioning us as to why there was a break." The "press analysts," they believed, were future scabs, there to learn how the presses worked so they could run them during the strike, and, if possible, provoke a fight.

"The pressmen," Longson comments, "have made a virtual religion of their role in the newspaper. They believe they are the soul of the newspaper," and they were deeply offended not only by the firings and the alleged scabs but by what they regarded as Malone's presumptuousness. To the pressmen, Malone was the man who wanted to bury them in the noise even when there was no good reason to be on the floor. He was the outsider who knew more about the rules than about getting a paper out; the smart aleck who scorned the wisdom of the village elders; the company man with no respect for tribal rights.

Even as relations with their own workers were deteriorating, Hoge's team launched a public relations campaign to take their case to the outside world. It worked about as well as Malone's efforts to win hearts in the pressroom.

Hoge and Ballow deeply disagreed over public relations strategy. The only audience Ballow cares about is the unions he is negotiating with; he has no interest in winning any other hearts and minds. Public opinion, he figures, can never win the game for management. Nobody ever got dewy-eyed and romantic over the hardships of capital. The best strategy is to do what you have to do without attracting much attention.

Hoge disagrees. Ballow, he says, has mostly worked in "smaller markets where you could bring in the Antichrist and no one would notice." In New York, Hoge felt, a vigorous public relations campaign was crucial.

Gold would come to feel that Hoge was obsessed with the PR side of the battle. Hoge's obsession with the media "really shook my confidence," Gold remembers. "Every single time we got together with Jim, it *appeared* that we were always playing some political angle or some PR angle. You win labor disputes in the trenches, but Jim was thrilled playing to the media. You got the impression at times he thought some newspaper article was going to win the whole labor situation. Alex Jones of the *New York Times* is going to write a piece, and we'd be declared the winner! When he did this stuff your mind would wander; you'd wonder if his heart was in the right place. Maybe it was that he wanted to be a media star, or maybe he wanted to be the Messiah—who knows?"

Nevertheless, for the most part Hoge accepted the Ballow policy, including one decision the unions would interpret as further evidence that the *News* had been hijacked by fanatics who would rather fight than win—the decision to make Jim Hoge disappear.

Shortly after Ballow brought Gold on board, the company team agreed that all direct communication to or from the unions (other than at the negotiating table) would come through Gold. There would be one company position, one voice on every issue. No union attempt to communicate directly with higher authorities, including Hoge, would be recognized. When negotiations started, Ballow would preside, and Hoge would not attend. Hoge would not speak to the press. John Sloan, the new human resources VP, would handle that.

Hoge to this day endorses the policy, arguing that the unions had a history of using meetings with top company officials to claim the company had made promises on which it later reneged, such as the MIP contretemps that came out of a meeting with CEO Stanton Cook. And Ballow does not want the unions distracted by fond hopes of escaping their fate by engaging in personal diplomacy with the CEO. Combined with the post-Ballow exodus of moderates from the executive ranks, however, the effect was to deprive the unions of contact with any senior executive with whom they had a long-term relationship. Hoge, who had undertaken a frustrating five-year campaign to establish personal relationships with the union leaders, which ended only in the embarrassing failure at the January quarterly meeting a few months before, at times seemed to welcome his new isolation. The pressmen's new president, Jack Kennedy, remembers vividly his first meeting with Hoge, which occurred just as Gold was coming aboard and the new policy was taking effect. Kennedy had been on the job (after being chosen to succeed Lenny Higgins) for less than a week when he was invited to a going-away party for Dick Jordan, the outgoing *News* chief of labor relations and one of the most prominent departing moderates. When Kennedy got to the party his first impression was that he did not see many people he knew. Eventually Hoge, whom he had never met, strode into the room. "He cruised the room for about ten minutes," says Kennedy. "Then he came up to me and somebody introduced us. He shook my hand. But he did not say anything." A few minutes later he was gone. Kennedy did not see or speak to Hoge again until more than a year and a half later, long into the strike. He found Hoge's behavior bizarre, especially when the other union leaders told him Hoge was treating everybody like that. "He had just cut everybody off."

It was not only from Hoge that they had been cut off. George Mc-Donald, who had had a working relationship with the top brass of the Tribune Company long before Hoge or anybody on his team had ever seen the inside of the *Daily News*, found himself completely unable to get through to anybody else either—except for Gold. In October 1989 McDonald wrote an anguished letter to Tribune CEO Stanton Cook, plaintively reminding him of the "new spirit of cooperation" to which Cook had committed himself just two years before, a spirit contradicted by Ballow and Brumback's behavior. He could not believe, McDonald wrote, that Cook could have changed his mind so quickly. Cook was still CEO and could still control events. And so he "respectfully" asked for a meeting with Cook and a quiet discussion "of where we are and how we got there" and how the company and the unions could get off the "collision course" they were now on.[1]

The reply, though superficially polite, could hardly have been more insulting or frustrating. It came not from Cook but from Gold, a man half McDonald's age who had been at the *News* for less than six months. Gold wrote that he was glad to hear McDonald was interested in meaningful negotiations but made it clear that certain "lines of communication" had been established and that all communications should come to him, Gold. Gold himself, however, would be happy to meet McDonald for a discussion "of where we are and how we got there."[2]

McDonald would not be allowed to talk to anyone above Gold or Ballow until much later, after it became clear the company was losing the strike. When it was all over and the Tribune had sold the paper to Robert Maxwell, McDonald met Gold coming out of Maxwell's office. He kicked him in the shins.

Despite the near blackout of Hoge, and Ballow's and Gold's preference for operating in obscurity, there was a *News* PR campaign, some of it perfectly reasonable and ordinary—like sending Hoge around to talk to business leaders. But the first big move in the PR campaign that anybody noticed was a disaster for management, a profile of Hoge published in the October 1989 *Vanity Fair*. The Edward Klein article alternated between fawning and breathless descriptions of Hoge's rich and famous lifestyle, including his million-dollar Gramercy Park apartment redecorated by his wife with help from Lee Radziwill, and a deeply partisan account of how the *News*'s workers were allegedly destroying the paper, or would unless Hoge was victorious in his coming "war" with them. Klein's account of union abuses was reasonably accurate, but the tone was credulous and propagandistic, and Klein included no specific rebuttal from the unions. The article was the brainchild of PR consultant John Scanlon, who had taken on the *News* as a client.

With friends like this, the *News* did not need media enemies. Unwittingly, the effect of the article was to paint Hoge and the *News* as the aggressors, "ready, even eager for combat." The piece carried a picture of pressmen president Jack Kennedy, a man as good-looking as Hoge, whom the caption bizarrely identified as Hoge's "nemesis," though the two had never spoken. Kennedy took the reference as more evidence that the Tribune Company had been captured by corporate ideologues cut off from reality. The juxtaposition of Hoge's luxurious lifestyle with glib talk about "an old-fashioned newspaper war" or "humbling" unions that represented men who would never be allowed to stroll across the private, iron-fenced enclave of chic Gramercy Park read like a deliberate slap in the faces of *News* workers.

Hoge and just about everyone but Scanlon almost immediately regretted the piece. Hoge particularly cringed at Klein's ham-handed attempts to psychoanalyze him. But no one in management foresaw the depth of the article's effect on the unions.

The unions felt the piece as a deep betrayal, a shock, an impious declaration of war on members of the *News*'s own family, a deliberate attempt to embarrass workingmen who had given far more to the *News*, they felt, than a Hoge ever would. McDonald wrote to Hoge that the article was "another salvo in the war of nerves you publicly declared against your employees" when the company hired King & Ballow. "We the 'tough guys' you want to bust happen to be the same unions who came to the aid of the *News* with $50 million in savings in 1983 and another $30 million in 1987." But rather than respecting the unions' past efforts, "you have embarked on a campaign to embarrass us." Perhaps most insulting of all, management now apparently so disliked talking to its employees "that information we would normally have received at the bargaining table came to us first in a magazine of fashion."[3]

News executives tended to regard the union guys' emotionalism over things like a *Vanity Fair* article or the hiring of Ballow, their lavishly displayed anger and hurt feelings, and their constant laments that the Tribune Company did not care about them and wanted to be rid of them, as not only beside the point but as affected. Crocodile tears. To management the union guys seemed not only at least as tough as the managers themselves, but almost brutes. These were the same men who had turned Hoge's last quarterly meeting into an indoor riot; men who would shut down a pressroom if management attempted to discipline even the most flagrant malingerers; men who took bribes to sell their fellow workers' jobs, or who were lifelong Mafia fellow travelers; men who seemed perfectly content to let the *News* die rather than concede the principle that a man should be paid only for productive work; men who, for that matter, were masters of verbal abuse themselves. It seemed incredible that such men could have any feelings to be hurt by articles in fashion magazines. Surely men with such a tough-guy, hard-ass, bottom-line confrontational approach to life could not be made any more hostile simply because the *News* spoke frankly about the damage they were doing to the paper? For Hoge in particular, the implication that the unions could not be expected to negotiate with the company unless the company was nice to them was "baloney." For the strategist what mattered was not "personalities" or the unions being "offended" by the company's attitude. The only thing that really bothered the unions, he believed, was "that management was . . . proposing a wholesale shift of power" that would effectively curtail "all sorts of excessive and illegal [union] activities."

Some of what Hoge calls baloney surely was playacting, aimed at a romantic press corps largely peopled by second- or third-generation immigrants still ambivalent about their own flight from the working class. If the unions could persuade the press that the *News* fight was a struggle between the *News*'s abused but faithful union children and their wicked WASP stepmother from Chicago, well and good. But Hoge and the others missed the reality that underlay the playacting. They seemed deaf to the emotional nuances of the Irish, Italian, and Jewish families that were the cultural bedrock of the *News*'s unions, unaware of the very different rules of social engagement under which their employees had grown up.

True, Italian families can be as violent in their disagreements as they are intense in their loyalties. And the Irish certainly can make war with words: Eugene O'Neill plays every night in homes throughout the boroughs, if often in a comic mode. Under ethnic rules of social engagement family members can devote a lifetime to such pursuits—but only as long as it stays within the family and in private. Under those rules, what the union leaders had done to Hoge at that final quarterly meeting was no more than an acceptable family spat. Yet however you might abuse family members, you don't just get rid of them. Family lays down intractable claims. The Tribune did not even seem aware of those claims, never mind inclined to honor them. However much the unions might have fought with or even abused management, however selfish, even suicidal their claims, it was genuinely wounding to them, outrageous to be spoken of as enemies, thrust out of the family in public among strangers. And what kind of strangers? The kind of fancy people who would read *Vanity Fair*, the kind who would regard it as a major life setback if at a cocktail party they got stuck talking to George McDonald, which of course they never would, because he would never have been invited in the first place. Imagine going to a party full of such people and talking trash about your own children.

For all the hell they put the company through, for all the decades when the unions' program could be summed up in the single ancient and revered phrase "Fuck the bosses," the union guys never thought of the company as alien or of themselves as its enemies. They were the company. And if the company was a family there was no doubt as to who were the parents and who the children. As McDonald would say, "We know we need a boss. Unions can't give five cents in wages." It is bosses, like parents, who run the show and come up with the money. Children depend on parents, but they also rebel against them. This is natural. But parents who abandon their children just because they act like children are fiendish and unnatural.

The company's cold, unnatural vices seemed to excuse the unions from self-examination or restraint. Prissy righteousness on one side and rage on the other soon overcame rational judgment, and it was rage, offended piety, and the conviction that they were facing an enemy beyond human decency that would finally be the unions' most powerful weapon.

In this happy state of mind, the two sides finally entered negotiations.

CHAPTER 9

A Modest Proposal

The sole and exclusive rights of management shall include but not be limited to the right to: hire, assign, schedule, lay-off, recall, transfer, suspend, discharge, or otherwise discipline employees; determine, establish and implement terms or conditions of employment. . . .
From the *Daily News*'s "Management Rights"
contract proposal, January 1990

"THE efficiency of an institution depends . . . on the extent to which it organizes man for his moral victory over himself."[1] Peter Drucker's insight, penned over fifty years ago, could serve as the slogan for the current renaissance of American industry. Whatever the jargon employed—Total Quality Management, Continuous Process Improvement, Close to the Customer, Theory Y—whether there are fourteen points or seven principles or 87.5 rules of thumb, and despite the insufferable New Age nonsense that some post-industrial gurus seem incapable of resisting, and the innumerable disappointments of the companies that never get beyond the buzz words, the essence of the movement is a moral revival.

In the *Daily News* war the two sides had deeply, radically different moral visions of the workplace. The *News*'s unions got their first good look at this moral chasm in January 1990, when the company presented its opening contract proposals.

Ballow had a hand, perhaps the largest hand, in drafting the contracts. The wording and certain particularly offensive anti-union provisions of the contracts were certainly meant as a weapon in the campaign of psychological warfare he intended to wage on the unions, threatening them with effective destruction if they would not agree to the company's substantive demands. But the substance of the contracts reflected a deeper vision. For men like Scott Sherman, Jim O'Dell, Dick

Malone, Gene Bell, or Brumback himself, the contracts were to be the foundation of a well-ordered, indeed—though they might blush to use the word—virtuous organization. Run through the list of the company's core demands—demands denounced by the unions as vicious, hateful, cruel, and inhuman—and these men will explain not only how each change would have made the *News* more money, but how each would have made the (remaining) workers happier, richer, and better men.

The purpose of Total Quality Management is to enable the men and women of the organization to make the enterprise better and more productive by making themselves better and more productive. It aims to do this not merely through mechanical improvements in the workplace, but by a moral improvement of the work force. Quality management seeks to raise employees' commitment to the enterprise, to make them better team players, to engage their minds in the drive to improve process and product, and to uproot the notion that those who give their all to the company are chumps.

As such TQM is a radical break with not only the technology but the philosophy of the industrial age. Like all modern materialist philosophies, Adam Smith's economic theories were inspired by Newton's mechanical universe. In the same way that Newton built a living universe of dull lifeless particles, classical economists dreamed, or seemed to, of constructing "a system so perfect no man need be good." They imagined that policy could transform the private vice of greed into the public good of productivity. Quality management, however, reaches back to an earlier Christian moral tradition that dispenses with such moral alchemy: not only does vice never yield virtue, this tradition declares, but there is no need to make it do so.

Standing behind the Protestant work ethic which declares work good for the order it imposes on men's lives, for the way in which it makes them good stewards of creation, and for the distraction it provides from vice, is an older and deeper Christian tradition. This tradition, stretching back through the Thomists even to Augustine maintains that "virtue is the fulfillment of nature"; that a creature is good when it does the things for which it was created. In this moral tradition, work is good because it is the exercise of God-given faculties. It is in the exercise of the faculties that we become most fully human, and fulfill our God-given nature. The sweat of the brow may be punishment for sin but the use of the talents was always God's will. Augustine, a far bigger fan of work than Aquinas, even argued that the afterlife would be full of work, though stripped of the pain of sin, joyful and glorious in its perfect fulfillment of our God-given abilities.

If virtue is not the renunciation but the fulfillment of nature, then in a well-ordered world the distinction between doing good and doing well tends to dissolve. In a well-ordered world (or workplace) it is not man's greed (contrary to Smith) but the exercise of his virtues that brings prosperity and true happiness. In the fallen world, of course, virtue and self-interest do not always coincide. Bad circumstances, bad leadership, or a badly ordered society can make the conflict between the two worse. The goal of quality management is to partly recover the world before the Fall by building an organization that rewards men for virtue and in which virtue is productive and personally rewarding.

The great hulking machines of the industrial era prompted both management and labor to embrace mechanical materialism, to view men, like machines, as interchangeable elements of a system whose goal was not to exercise human virtue, but to banish human error. Management wanted workers to become not more fully human but as much like machines as possible, to fill in the mechanical gaps in the assembly line—by merging with it. And labor, after some hesitation, followed along: adopting the same goal of eliminating human error—in the form of management abuses—for example by replacing managers' discretion with work rules.

This campaign to eliminate human error, to turn men into efficient machines, was not merely abstract and general. Both management and labor took aim at a particular human target: the foreman, the noncommissioned officer of industry.

Labor identified the foreman as the enemy long before management did. In the early days of mass production, foremen wielded enormous power: to hire, fire, and set work standards, often operating as almost independent middlemen between the enterprise and its workers. Often paid according to the productivity of the work force he managed, the foreman had an incentive to work employees as hard as possible and dismiss troublemakers of any sort.

The foreman's arbitrary power was one of the prime targets both of the American union movement and of Frederick Taylor's scientific management. Both management and labor, for different reasons, strove to eliminate the foreman's discretion. For decades the foreman diminished in importance, as the work rules and methods launched by Taylor to eliminate the foreman's discretion were blessed and adopted by unions, which saw in them a way to codify the upper limits of effort that could be extracted from workers. By the 1950s Drucker lamented that the American foreman had been so emasculated by middle and upper management as to make him logically a wage worker, with less and less reason to think of himself as management or to stay out of the union.

Now that the post-industrial revolution is putting mind into machines, creating systems that can change and improve, but only if men exercise discretion and choice, the foreman is on the rise again. Automation and the pursuit of quality have revived him.

The goal of the post-industrial company is not to avoid human error but to capture human ingenuity. Unlike the Taylorism of the industrial age, quality management strikes to make factories more like men— more intelligent, more flexible, more capable of continuous change and improvement. The foreman is the small-group leader without whom the flexible factory cannot flex and without whom Continuous Process Improvement subsides into stasis. The foreman, or team leader, is the intellectual and moral center of quality management. The post-industrial factory restores the foreman's power by transforming him from an enforcer of work rules into a leader of men, evoking the creativity and commitment of the men under him. If he leads well and fairly, good workers thrive and so does the company. If not, the system becomes self-destructive.

The shocking new contracts the company handed to the unions in January 1990 hardly mentioned the new role of the foreman or front-line supervisor. Yet, true to the principles of post-industrialism, the foreman was actually the central battleground of the dispute. All the diverse changes the company demanded added up to a single coherent vision (rarely discussed during negotiating sessions) of a workplace consisting of work teams and run by team leaders. Management's goals could be summed up in one directive: recapture shop floor supervisors (from the new team leaders up through the formerly unionized plant managers, the sergeants major of the system) for the company and let them run the plant. The shop floor supervisors would decide a whole host of issues that for generations had been decided by contract, from how often the presses are cleaned to which employees get to work overtime.

To bring a post-industrial plant to life, the company believed, the supervisors had to come out of the union. Under American labor law, however, supervisors' union membership was unlikely to become a major issue in the negotiations directly: a company has a legal right to insist that the supervisors drop their union cards as long as their duties meet the definition of a supervisor under the National Labor Relations Act. The question of supervisors' union membership is classified under labor law as a "permissive," as opposed to "mandatory," subject of bargaining. The unions can try to make it a bargaining issue, and the company may consent, but the company can legally refuse to discuss the matter: it is illegal for unions to strike over permissive issues. Yet even though the union or management status of the foreman was not an issue of direct importance in the talks, the company's desire to recapture its foremen, all of whom had been union for years, was the core of its most controversial contract proposals—for instance, manning reductions.

The *News* needed to cut the size of its blue-collar work force by a third or more. That did not shock the unions: cutting jobs had been the dominant motif in newspaper negotiations for decades. But the Tribune Company wouldn't settle for the usual sort of job reductions. It wanted to abolish the entire notion of contractual manning tables specifying how many men would be used for a particular task, say running a press. Under the company's proposal, the *News*'s shop floor supervisors would have the power to decide how many men they would need. It was an especially radical proposition given the recent history of the New York newspaper unions. For two decades now the unions' most important mission had been to delay job losses and extract compensation when they came. Now the unions were told they would have no say in manning at all.

Hardly less radical was the company's position on seniority—for all practical purposes the company wanted it eliminated. Seniority is the great enemy of discretion, particularly the discretion of the shop floor supervisor: it makes his judgment of how hard or how well a worker works largely irrelevant. Scott Sherman is quite blunt on the subject. "In my view seniority is the proper way to decide one issue, vacations: it decides how much time off you get and it decides who is first on line to claim the most desired weeks for the year. In a good plant every other issue is decided on the merits"; that is, perks and promotions go to the men who, in the supervisor's judgment, earn them.

Sherman considers it absurd, for instance, to give a man overtime unless he is one of your most efficient, energetic, and productive workers. It is, he says, "a classic economic problem." If you are going to be paying a premium (i.e., overtime) wage, "you want a premium worker, somebody who can be productive beyond 7.5 hours, somebody who uses the machines well, so maybe at time and a half you are getting just as much productivity out of this guy as out of an average worker at straight time."

Sherman is no Ballow, no hard-ass, Nashville YMCA night school lawyer with a reputation for eating small unions for breakfast. He is a mild-mannered idealist, an ordained deacon of academic inclination who eventually left the Tribune Company to get a Ph.D. in management and devote his life to spreading the gospel of quality. Nevertheless even on the question of who gets called back first from layoffs (a classic case for seniority since middle-aged workers may be slowing down after years of service, but with mortgages and tuition payments can least afford to be off work), he is adamant. Workers should be called back from layoffs "based on talent and energy." "Even more obviously you promote or slot people into a particular job for those reasons." I tell Sherman that Jack Kennedy's objection to the new order is that in high-tech, quality shops with no or weak unions, "you never see any fifty-year-old pressmen," presumably because they have been worn out by taskmasters determined to use as few men as possible and keep them working all the time. Sherman dismisses the notion instantly. Not only does Kennedy have his facts wrong, he claims, but the "whole point is to work people smart not hard." (This is a favorite TQM buzz phrase.) "The job is less physically demanding all the time and should continue to be so for efficiency's sake."

At the *News*, even hiring had really been a matter of seniority controlled by the unions, through the shape, an informal union hiring hall through which a man might be hired for a night if there were not enough "regular situation holders" available to fill all the contractually allotted job slots. If a man shaped often enough he could acquire enough "priority" (seniority) to become a regular employee, more or less guaranteed steady work.

The company wanted to abolish the shape, the union priority lists, and all union control over hiring, instead hiring all personnel through the company personnel office. The company wanted the right, as Sherman puts it, to select not the workers who had shaped the longest but those "with the best aptitudes, not only knowledge of the equipment but energy, enthusiasm, cooperativeness, and an aptitude for team-work."

For the apostles of quality the notion that men should be rewarded not for how well or hard they work but for how long they have been employed is both corrupt and inefficient; indeed inefficiency and corruption are in this view much the same thing. In the new cult of quality, change is the only constant, stasis is the great enemy. To reward a man simply because he persists is wrong. The apostles of quality want the work force to be constantly challenged to improve. That is impossible unless supervisors have the power to reward good workers and punish poor ones regardless of how many years they have been on the floor.

To the unions, one of the most shocking things about the company's contracts was their brevity. Some of the old contracts were hundreds of pages long and detailed decades of hard-won privileges for workers. In most cases the substantive core of the company's new proposals took up only a few pages. With a "zipper" clause eliminating any customary procedure, codicils, or oral agreements not explicitly recorded in the new contract, and a "management rights" clause, the company would sweep away hundreds of work rules and open up the work process to constant change and innovation, led by the team leaders and, if all went well, by the teams themselves. For the apostles of quality, sweeping away decades of workers' rights was a step toward not only a more efficient factory but a more virtuous one. Ancient work rules that, to unions, were the equivalent of constitutional rights were, to management, violations of the fundamental laws of quality and justly measured rewards for work.

It is almost impossible to overstate the depth of the conflict on this point. Static work rules are not a minor inconvenience for a firm pursuing Continuous Process Improvement. The rules limiting, for instance, how much maintenance could be done on a press in a day could not be fixed simply by renegotiating the number upward. The goal of quality management is not to get the process right once and for all, or to achieve perfection at a moment in time. Deming himself argues that companies should "focus on constant improvement rather than the elusive goal of 'zero defects' " as defined by the standards of the moment. The point of Continuous Process Improvement is to raise the company's sights and generate a constant stream of improvement and innovation. Fixed work rules deny the fundamental rule that the rules must always change. In a quality factory most changes come from workers and team leaders. A work force constitutionally opposed to change outside the contract cannot be the agent of change.

The apostles of quality believe that static, rule-worshipping systems corrupt and demoralize the worker. Decades ago, Drucker, Deming's first American booster, lamented that the status and psychological rewards of the industrial worker were low, even though his pay was high, because workers played so negligible a part in designing the system that employed them. "For the great majority of automobile workers the only meaning of the job is in the paycheck, not in anything connected with the work or the product. Work appears as something unnatural, a disagreeable meaningless and stultifying condition of getting the paycheck, devoid of dignity as well as importance. No wonder this puts a premium on slovenly work, on slowdowns, and on other tricks to get the same paycheck for less work. No wonder that this results in an unhappy and discontented worker—because a paycheck is not enough to base one's self respect on."[2]

This, according to the gospel of quality, is the moral result of being part of a system in which the worker is not practically engaged in the pursuit of quality, in which all that is required of him is that he do what he is told, as if he were not a man with a mind but a machine of flesh and blood. Drucker quotes a longtime Detroit craftsman who had risen up from the line to become a well-paid supervisor but decided to leave Detroit just about the time Drucker was finishing *The Concept of the Corporation*. He was leaving, he said, because "the whole place is on relief; even if they have jobs, they still behave and act as if they were unemployed."[3] As far as management was concerned he could have been describing the *Daily News*.

Other, lesser issues in the negotiations also reflected the company's implicit conviction that efficiency and morality were inseparable. Brumback was absolutely determined to end the practice of compensating men for tough assignments by granting them static overtime, i.e., overtime pay for hours not actually worked, rather than giving them wage raises or bonuses. The unions could not comprehend the company's vehemence on the issue; it seemed a mere bookkeeping matter. To Brumback, it mattered a great deal not only because static overtime was difficult to control but because he hated the symbolism of paying a man for nonwork, or the notion that the highest aspiration of a worker could be to figure out how to get paid for nothing. The apostles of quality want every man in the work force to have a bourgeois regard for work. Men who are alienated from work or develop the habit of avoiding it become resentful proletarians no matter how well they are paid. A work force of such men cannot be the basis of post-industrial renewal.

The company also wanted a radical new pension policy. The *News* wanted to withdraw from most of the ten old union-dominated pension funds and set up fully portable, tax-free retirement accounts for each employee, "his own money, in his own account, with his own name on it," as the *News* negotiators were fond of saying. During the negotiations there were interminable and often incomprehensible (even to the negotiators) debates about the objective, bottom-line merits of the old and new pension plans. But the real issues here were of power and principle.

Under the old system, management claimed, the unions effectively dominated the joint labor-management pension boards and were able to award extra, unearned pension points to union-favored employees, endangering the system for everyone. The new system would cut the unions out of pension management, weakening their power over their members. The new individual retirement accounts management favored would also help reinforce the Tribune Company's individualist moral code. The money in the retirement account would be exactly what a man earned and invested. To provide for their retirement, men would have to look to their own efforts, not sink into the all-too-comforting abyss of union solidarity.

The Tribune Company *might* be willing to live with unions, but it was unwilling to live with union solidarity. In a quality factory workers have solidarity only with the enterprise. The heart of *union* solidarity, says Scott Sherman, is to "deny management the right to make discriminations between workers" and deny workers the right to do their best and earn appropriate individual rewards. Under the system the company hoped to install, the front-line supervisors would make management discretion work and destroy solidarity or make it irrelevant. As Sherman explains, "The job of the foreman or team leader is to translate the company's goals into the goals of the front line. Their job is to discriminate among workers, evaluate people for promotion, training, transfer, or removal." The foreman is the personification of management's reemergence on the work floor, of the replacement of negotiated rules and passive quotas and performance standards with active ingenious change, and of the work force's ascent of the learning curve, enabled and demanded by automation.

At its best it is a benevolent vision. Liberating the foreman liberates the men. Giving the team leader more power and prying him out of the union elevates the team, creating a bridge between it and upper management, putting everyone on the same larger team. "We have blind stupid rules like basing advancement on seniority," says Sherman, because the workers don't trust management was be fair. But under the old system the real power in management was far away. When the foreman or team leader has real power, he can be a tool for building trust between labor and management, especially if management picks "good supervisors and trains them how to evaluate workers, how to communicate what the company is looking for in workers and how they will be rewarded, and to make sure no reward or punishment comes as a surprise."

The theory seems to work in Chicago and Orlando and other Tribune Company papers—where either there was never a union or the unions have been crushed. But for the unions still in place at the *News*, which with every good reason had long lost all faith in management, and now had watched for months as Hoge, Ballow, and company "armed themselves," in Hoge's phrase, the notion of the company putting a core of hard-driving managers on the work floor, as many as one for every five workers, and arming them with enormous discretion and the full faith and credit of upper management, was nightmarish. Even under the old contract, Dick Malone and Bill Deering, in charge of production and distribution operations respectively, and their crews of nonunion managers were cutting huge swaths out of union power on the work floor, a condition most union men devoutly hoped would be temporary. But under management's plan, with no seniority, work rules, or manning tables, and with new, more aggressive discipline policies, the permanent nonunion supervisors would hold the working lives of the *News* employees in their hands. The company might dream of a workplace full of workers liberated to do and be their best, but in both fact and rhetoric the whole thing came down to a massive transfer of power away from the unions and to the company.

For the unions the essence of the proposed new contracts was contained in a single clause, called the management rights clause, an aggressive statement of management's determination to overthrow the "constitution" of the workplace and replace it with managerial discretion:

The union recognizes that any and all rights concerned with the management of the business and the direction of the work force are exclusively those of the Publisher. The Publisher retains all of its normal, inherent common law rights to manage the business, whether or not exercised, as such rights existed prior to the time any union became the bargaining representative of the employees covered by this Agreement. The sole and exclusive rights of management shall include but not be limited to the right to: hire, assign, schedule, lay-off, recall, transfer, suspend, discharge, or otherwise discipline employees; determine, establish and implement terms or conditions of employment; establish or continue policies, practices and procedures for the conduct of the business and, from time to time, to change or abolish such policies. . . .

Strictly speaking, there was less to the clause than there seemed to be. Attached to a contract explicitly describing management, worker, and union rights and obligations, the management rights clause was mostly boilerplate. Contrary to union fears it would not empower the company to set aside the provisions of the contract, which in any event were so pro-management the company could hardly have desired to set them aside.

Nevertheless, writing "Slavery Is Freedom" across the front of the contract could hardly have been a blunter reminder that whatever the company's broader vision, its goal at the negotiating table was to establish absolute control of the workplace. Like the company's military preparedness campaign or the *Vanity Fair* article, the clause appeared as one more proof to the unions that the company preferred total war to a negotiated vision of the future.

At the same time the company was sending out contract proposals it sent every *Daily News* employee a video titled *The Newspaper of the '90s*. The video, hosted by legendary St. John's University basketball coach Louis "Looie" Carnesecca, started out as a locker room speech, exhorting *News* workers to pull together to build the new *News*. There was lots of footage of Freedom Center and the new Fort Lauderdale plant showing how much better a modern paper would be. But as the video progressed, and other voices replaced Carnesecca's, it ceased to be a rousing speech to *News* employees and became an investigative report about them: *News* executives appeared proclaiming that the company must stop paying "those who do not work" and stop supporting "jobs that do not contribute at all." The video equated contractual extravagances such as static overtime with criminal abuses such as the buddy system in such a broadbrush way as to slander even many workers who never cheated.

Management knew that it bore much of the responsibility for allowing abuses to mount over the decades, but the video conveyed no sense of shared responsibility. It asked all Newsies to work together but blamed only union workers for the paper's difficulties. It was a management brief against its own workers—addressed to those workers. Scott Sherman, an enthusiast for the contracts, calls the company's approach to the unions a disaster. "Wretched management decisions for the previous twenty years created enormous distrust. Then these guys from Chicago want to change everything but do not give the unions any basis to trust them. You can't do it by crunching the numbers and calling people names. But that is what we did."

As appalled as the unions had been by the hiring of Ballow and the months of watching the company prepare for war, still they were astonished when they saw the contracts. Utterly unprepared for the company's proclamation of a radical new order, they kept telling Ballow and Gold they were ready to make "a good deal" to "give the company good relief," desperately trying to lure the company back into the old familiar world of trading numbers—numbers of jobs, of overtime hours, of buyouts, while maintaining their old power as long as possible. But the company did not want "relief" or a deal by the numbers. It wanted a cultural revolution on the plant floor: a technology-driven production process that could not be laid out in detail at the negotiating table because by the very principles of quality management no one could predict in advance what it would look like, except that it would involve constant change.

A favorite union phrase throughout the negotiations was "bought and paid for." *News* management would point out some static-overtime provision or work rule that violated its ruthless sense of business logic. Then McDonald or Alvino, who both loved the phrase, would explain that the disputed clause might look silly now, "but we bought and paid for that at the negotiating table," meaning they had given management something in exchange for that years before.

Management was not interested in years before. It hated the past, full of failure and frustration. Management was for revolution, the rationalist re-creation of the social order. It was the unions that were the hoary traditionalists, the conservatives, the devotees of the common law and of their treasured contracts and codicils, the bedrock of their Bleak House of ancient rights and privileges.

CHAPTER 10

Rites of Spring

The so-called issue is usually nothing but a surface phenomenon; the real issue arises very often out of a failure of management to imagine what goes on in the minds of the worker, and a failure of labor to imagine what management is after and why.
—Peter Drucker, *The Concept of the Corporation*

ABOUT three months into negotiations with the pressmen, Bob Ballow and Jack Kennedy were discussing, once again, how many men would be on a press. Kennedy was doing his best one more time to make it clear to Ballow that altogether abolishing manning tables (which specified how many men the company was obliged to put on a press in various situations) was impossible. There could be reductions but the company had to name a specific number. The membership would never accept "open manning," which would give management complete discretion.

Kennedy did not believe for one moment that he could get through to Ballow, but in one of the psychological paradoxes that abound in negotiations gone bad, he argued and explained and cajoled just as earnestly as if there were some possibility of agreement. The pressmen's negotiating strategy, by this time, assumed there was no such possibility, that Ballow did not want a settlement, that he wanted a strike or to negotiate to "impasse" a legal stalemate under which the company was entitled to declare further talks useless. Once at impasse the company could unilaterally impose new working conditions, in effect a new contract (though unsigned and open-ended) representing management's most extreme positions. The unions could provisionally accept the new conditions and keep working while talks continued. But in that case the union's impotence would be plain to everyone, including its own members. Or the union could reject the imposed conditions and go on strike. Reaching impasse is, in effect, how companies "strike" against their unions.

Nevertheless, here Kennedy was trying to convince Ballow that the only way to reach a settlement was for the company to back off from its absolutist position on manning. The company's position was completely unrealistic, he told Ballow. I can't ask 400 pressmen to approve a contract when I can't tell them whether 100, or 200, or 300 of them are going to lose their jobs.

Ballow, as he did dozens of times in the course of the talks, just looked at Kennedy and said: "Are you saying you can never agree to our proposal?"

By any reasonable standard the answer was yes. But Kennedy could not say yes because then the negotiations might be at impasse. But he could not really say anything else either. He could not accept Ballow's proposal. Nor could he offer a counterproposal because the union had already offered a small reduction in the number of men on a press. If Kennedy offered more now, he would be on the precarious slippery slope called "negotiating against yourself." He would be one step from free fall, where you start begging your opponent to accept deals he would never have imagined he could get at the outset. It had happened to Mike Alvino over at the drivers' talks. Alvino was so desperate to get Ballow to move off his basic position that he was turning the talks into frantic one-sided bidding wars—"We'll give you one hundred jobs right now." No response from Ballow. "Okay, we'll make it 125."

No, now that Ballow had said the ritual words, there was really nothing of any substance that Kennedy *could* say. Law and custom and Ballow were demanding that he *not* communicate. So he responded in the ritually required fashion: "We are prepared to negotiate anything," which of course was not true.

"It's a ritual dance." That is what they all say. "Negotiations are a ritual dance." It is the labor lawyers' favorite metaphor. It would be trite except that it is deeply true, especially in a negotiation gone bad. It is hard to think of any other aspect of American business life so thoroughly, infuriatingly ritualized, so determined in its substitution of symbol for sign, so rigidly formal in the accepted modes of expression, or where deviation from prescribed form can be so disastrous, or where realistic communication is more thoroughly suppressed.

It is not always this way. Most negotiations are straightforward; two sides with at least a modicum of trust between them get together, give little thought to the law, a mere bow toward ritual, and make a deal. But precisely because American labor law is designed not to achieve any particular substantive outcome, but simply to compel employers and employees to talk, it has accumulated a great many rules about *how* they should talk. When there is no trust across the table these rules for talking can become rules of ritual noncommunication.

So it was in the *News* talks. The philosophical chasm between the two sides, Ballow's relentless aggressiveness and psychological warfare, the unions' increasingly paranoid interpretations of the company's increasingly bizarre behavior, and the law itself, conspired to turn the negotiations into a comedy of terrors in which each side was absolutely convinced it knew just what dastardly thing the other was doing, and both were usually wrong. Each side was convinced the other was deliberately sabotaging the negotiations. And each side, to avoid being ambushed by the stratagems of the other, devoted a great deal of energy to avoiding anything like straightforward communication.

Ballow is the ultimate ritualist, a man who lives to negotiate. He treats negotiations as a world unto themselves, or like an especially dangerous professional sporting event in which winning is the only thing and the rules have nothing to do with the outside world. He seemed obsessed with avoiding ever being caught at a legal disadvantage. At the negotiating table, it seemed as if he could always see himself in court three years later trying to defend his performance of the rite to a federal judge.

It can be argued that Ballow was pursuing a remarkably coherent process that very nearly worked. But the unions, solid realists to whom every ritual thrust and parry could mean a job lost or gained, alternately found him incomprehensible, vicious, or dangerously divorced from reality. Usually a step behind the ritual but convinced that they saw through Ballow, the unions undertook a deep strategy of their own and came much closer than anyone on either side ever realized to handing him the game. What neither side ever did was break through the dance and raise the possibility of walking to the future together.

There were ten separate negotiations for the ten unions. Their styles differed markedly. The drivers, the least unionlike of the unions, negotiated in a mob, their fractious negotiating committee at times numbering more than thirty. They were disinclined to theories, Kheel's or anyone else's, and hated committing anything to writing, which made it almost impossible to get them to offer formal counterproposals. The

drivers were less afraid to strike than the other unions because many or
most of the drivers believed they could beat the company in the streets.
Alone among the unions they negotiated out in Queens, in a hotel near
LaGuardia Airport, so they could make a quick getaway, Alvino said
jokingly, from angry members after eliminating their jobs.

The mailers, under McDonald, usually came without legal counsel
(though Kheel hovered in the background). Their negotiations with
Ballow were among the most bizarrely ritualistic and uncommunicative,
in large part because the tiny, aging McDonald, who must have loathed
Ballow, is also reflexively polite and averse to conflict. He found it
necessary to devote a great deal of time to reassuring Ballow that he
thought he was basically a good man. McDonald could take an amazingly long time and an enormous volume of words to say no.

The talks with the white-collar Guild were like a labor relations
version of *Who's Afraid of Virginia Woolf?* Not only did Ballow and Barry
Lipton hate each other on sight; the rest of the Guild negotiating committee and the rest of the King & Ballow team had almost exactly the
same mutual reaction. The reporters regarded the K&B crowd as redneck "law thugs." The lawyers thought the reporters obscene, self-
obsessed know-it-alls, amateurs who could not control either their
tempers or their language.

The pressmen, on center stage, were the most professional, the best
advised, the most disciplined, and hewed most closely to the Allied
Council strategy as it evolved. Jack Kennedy and his Skadden, Arps
lawyer Michael Connery could be fraternal twins. Both were tall, erect,
exceptionally intelligent, good-looking men. Both can be good talkers.
But they defy, as successful Irish leaders almost always have, every
cliché of the stage-Irish "beer-guzzling, back-slapping"[1] pol. As in Daniel Patrick Moynihan's description of the legendary Tammany leaders
Croker and Murphy, they are "the least affable of men,"[2] masters of
strategic taciturnity.

At a wake for an Irish New York City cop of the last generation, you
can always pick out the homicide detectives, especially the brass. They
are the hardest, most dangerous-looking, self-possessed men in the
room. They are the men in whose faces the Irish iron mask of self-
discipline (of equal use in bearing forty years of celibacy or in plotting
a rebellion) has become a crucible of barely contained violence. Connery and Kennedy are not quite that—Connery too thin, cosmopolitan,
and well dressed, Kennedy a tad too fleshy and forgiving—but in an-

other life they could have been. In the talks with Ballow, Connery took taciturnity to new heights by never attending the sessions: he sent a team of associates in his place, headed by a young lawyer named Larry Marcus, and controlled strategy from behind the scenes.

Style aside, however, all ten unions (even the printers, who declared from the beginning that they would cross any picket line to preserve their lifetime job guarantees) soon reached similar conclusions about the company's intentions. Even those who did not accept the most extreme version of the Kheel theory—that the company would have actually preferred to kill the paper—could not believe Ballow wanted a genuine negotiated settlement.

Nothing Ballow did seemed to the unions to make any sense—if he wanted a deal. His stance at the talks was as uncompromising as the company's proposal was radical. On most major issues he hardly moved an inch off his original position for the first six months of talks. As Don Singleton, a *News* reporter and member of the Guild negotiating committee put it, "He threw these contracts down on the table, and said this is the way it is going to be, and that was that. He had no interest in our positions or the history of the existing contract."

Ballow did not appear to care a great deal about money. Most of the opening proposals included at least modest wage increases. The Guild was offered a large wage increase, and Ballow repeatedly told the unions he was willing to "go out and come back to this table in half an hour with more money" if they would agree in principle to the company's new order.

Kennedy agrees that "wages were never an issue." But he did not find that reassuring. Kennedy wants the company to care about money. If all the company cared about was money the two sides could easily have compromised on manning. Financially, the difference between a manning table Kennedy says the pressmen could have accepted, say nine men on a press (down from thirteen or fourteen, with buyouts for the men who lost their jobs), and the company's "open manning" plan, which effectively would have meant seven to eight men on a press, was not great. Open manning was "not a money issue—it is an ideological issue," says Kennedy. Ballow "is not a pragmatist—he is an ideologue." What the company wanted was control. "In nonunion companies Daddy knows best and nobody argues."

Ballow is not a dour or severe man. He has a big, almost garrulous personality, and is a clever storyteller in the grand, slow Southern manner. James Grottola, the printers' new president, says flat out, "I like Bob Ballow. He is a charming fellow. You can talk with him about everything and anything, and he is never shy in expressing his viewpoints." Grottola's handwritten negotiation minutes have big blank spaces in them covered only by the words "Joke Time."

When Ballow is not being charming, however, he can be viciously blunt. He shows almost no concern for maintaining the convention, so precious to the unions (though of course they rarely follow it themselves), that the company and the unions are on the same side. Even Gold, the devoted Ballow disciple, says, "Bob was unbelievably aggressive at the table. He would say things about these people that would make you squirm. That they were incompetent, they had held a gun to the company's head, they had gotten away without having to work for years."

McDonald or Alvino would talk about how well the company and the unions had always gotten on—in the past twenty years there had been relatively few strikes and the drivers always struck less than anybody— and Ballow would tell them that was nonsense: the unions had not had to strike because they had all "the muscle" and they could "extort" whatever they wanted from the company. Then after virtually calling the union men liars, thugs, and extortionists, usually in a calm, matter-of-fact, even friendly tone, he would say, "That's all right. You had the power, I don't begrudge a union for taking what it can. But we are just going to put an end to that now." Says one union advisor, "There were guys right on the committee who would have lost their jobs," or have been demoted to "associate pressman" at a lower rate in pay under the company proposal, and Ballow would tell them that instead of resenting it they should be grateful for having been paid for doing nothing for twenty years.

Ballow says he does "not believe in holding anything back or hesitating to put the whole truth on the table." Frankness was particularly in order in New York, where "we were not only trying to negotiate a contract, we were trying to change a culture," and "to persuade the unions to get off this thing that they have all the muscle and they can shoot us down, because it is not true anymore." But for the unions it was simply proof he did not care how angry he made them because he did not want to settle, he wanted a strike. As for the alleged need to change the work culture, union leaders were skeptical as well.

Connery, probably the most prestigious, high-powered counsel for any of the unions, says he "never believed in the genuineness of the Tribune Company's need or intention" to change the culture of the plants. "I thought it was just a negotiating device, an excuse for why their demands were so extreme and inflexible, a rationale for their attack on the unions." He concedes that in some industries automation demands a change in the work culture especially "if you are coming with a clean slate and you can create a new culture without having to eradicate an old one." But he never believed this was "was the right strategy" at the *News*. The work force was too deeply "steeped in its own culture," too unwilling to change. Trying to make them change would be an enormous waste of time and resources.

Connery is also a technological skeptic. He simply does not believe Computer Assisted Manufacturing is that big a deal, at least for newspapers. (He believes it has more powerful implications for other industries.) Newspaper presses, he says, "are not so complicated" as to demand a cultural revolution. All that was needed was "consistent, tough management," which the *News* had not had. "You don't need to 'convert' these people," he argues. "You can monitor the performance of a press fairly easily, you check the speed, you check the number of papers coming off, you check the number of web breaks. It is fairly straightforward." Connery and his clients had a narrow vision of what the technology could do. The company, however, had long given up trying to broaden that vision. At the table the unions responded in kind. For months Kennedy's only response to the company's open-manning clause was to suggest a reduction of roughly one man per press, and perhaps two or three on new equipment, though the latter proposal was meaningless, since no one yet knew what the new equipment would be like.

Equally unsettling to the unions was Ballow's devotion to principles that struck the unions as alternately abstract, insincere, or insane. He refused for months to seriously discuss buyouts[3] (traditional lump sum payments to men whose jobs would be lost) on the grounds that it was wrong to pay people to surrender jobs that had never been necessary. "There's no justification," Ballow told Kennedy on May 10, "to pad the pressroom for years and years with extra people and now that we have to eliminate these extra people to pay a bonus." Buyouts are for "when a business does something that eliminates jobs due to new equipment. We don't have that now . . . these people . . . were just employed because the union had more muscle than the company."

It was another Ballow tactic, however, that really convinced the union leaders Ballow wanted a war. In addition to the core, substantive provisions essential to the company's post-industrial vision, the contracts were full of provisions whose only apparent purpose was to destroy the unions. Some of the anti-union clauses were as petty (if disrupting) as denying the unions use of the *News* premises for union business. But the Ballow contracts also would have eliminated the union security clause, which effectively requires every member of the bargaining unit to be a union member (or under recent Supreme Court rulings, to pay "core" union dues). It also would have eliminated the union dues checkoff by which the company holds union dues out of members' paychecks and pays the money directly to the union.

This was going for the jugular. As one senior union advisor put it, "Union security and dues checkoff is absolutely vital, the lifeblood of the union. Nothing means more." Without checkoff unions have a very difficult time getting their members to pay up. "Institutionally unions are far more interested in security and checkoff than getting another fifty cents an hour" in wages for their members. There was no way Ballow could expect to get this stuff, say union leaders. The anti-union clauses were proof positive he was just jerking them around.

Whether or not they accepted the Kheel theory, all the union presidents had come to the table doubting the company's sincerity. A few weeks into the talks, doubt had become certainty. Meeting constantly now under the aegis of the Allied Council, they soon hammered out a joint strategy:

First and foremost there would be no strike. Most of the leaders were convinced the company was too well prepared and if the unions struck they would probably lose. A strike was what Ballow wanted; so they would make sure he did not get it. So powerful was the union commitment not to strike that in early May, McDonald, speaking on the record, told newspaper industry analyst Robert L. Wiley of Furman Selz that even if the company declared impasse and imposed new working conditions that could eliminate 1,000 jobs, "he would nonetheless tell the remaining employed workers to go to work on management's terms."[4]

The second part of the strategy was to keep Ballow from getting to impasse. Avoiding impasse without actually reaching a settlement is tricky. You must create the illusion of progress in the negotiations, because if there is no progress the talks are at impasse. On the other hand you must avoid real progress even on minor points, because as smaller issues are cleared off the table the remaining major and intractable disagreements stand out more boldly. Impasse again. Also, you must not tell anyone you are stalling, or be too obvious about it, because stalling violates your legal obligation to negotiate in good faith. And you cannot tell anyone the unions have all agreed to this strategy together because that is coordinated bargaining, which is also illegal.

The unions adopted what they called the "rope-a-dope strategy": absorb every body blow the company hurls but never hit back by striking. Keep negotiations moving just enough so that you never offer the company a clear shot to the head, a knockout blow by impasse. Slow down the talks, raise diversionary issues the company cannot refuse to discuss, submit numerous information requests the company will be legally obliged to answer at the cost of weeks of work and delay. Make substantively meaningless but legally satisfactory contentions. But most of all wait and wait and wait while the company, which is spending at least $4 to $5 million a month on strike preparedness, security, and lawyers, uses your midsection for a punching bag and finally, like George Foreman against Ali, drops from exhaustion.

Most of the unions had been stalling from day one of the negotiations, and would have done so even if they had believed in the company's good faith. It is standard strategy for unions to negotiate slowly when they expect to have to make concessions. But as the strategy was formalized the unions started avoiding the table altogether, stretching out the time between negotiating sessions to two to three weeks, cutting sessions short, devoting hours to discussing such trivia as safety committees and jury duty. As Barry Lipton, president of the Guild, proudly puts it, "We spent months separating fly shit from pepper."

The strategy was formalized with help from AFL-CIO national headquarters. In May 1990, McDonald organized a meeting between the Allied presidents and Tom Donahue, secretary-treasurer of the AFL-CIO. Months before, McDonald and his colleagues had persuaded the national organization that the situation at the *News* was of national strategic importance. This was a New York strike at a major media property. That guaranteed national attention. More important still, the Tribune Company was a highly visible, ideologically anti-union company, employing one of the nation's leading union-busting law firms and committed to using replacement workers to destroy unions, at a time when the AFL-CIO's top political priority was to get national legislation restricting the use of permanent replacements.

Donahue, says McDonald, had seen the point immediately. He did not need to be told about Ballow, who is high on the AFL-CIO's enemies list of union busters. He put the *News* situation in the hands of Joe Schantz of the AFL-CIO's newspaper-organizing committee. He promised financial help. Now, at the May meeting, he arranged for the unions to meet with Sam McKnight, a Detroit labor attorney who had successfully fought off Ballow's assault on the unions at Channel 2 in Detroit.

Within a few weeks McKnight, at the AFL-CIO's expense, would come aboard as a full-time consulting organizer for the *News* unions. Though McKnight believed a strike was inevitable, he believed striking alone or on the company's terms would be a disaster for the unions. He had used the boycott to fight Ballow in Detroit, with some success, and that was the strategy he urged on the unions in New York. Stay on the job, stretch things out, and prepare a circulation and ad boycott against the *News* that, combined with the millions the company was paying for strike preparedness, would make the Ballow strategy unsustainable. The unions were moving in that direction anyway, but McKnight helped formalize and finalize the union strategy.

The strategy was summarized in a June 16, 1990, memorandum from Joseph Uehlien, of the AFL-CIO's Strategic Approaches Committee, to Joe Schantz, from the AFL-CIO's Department of Organization and Field Services, describing the conclusions of a meeting a few days before between most of the Allied presidents and McKnight. The memo stressed the "importance of downplaying negotiations." Ballow was not there to negotiate and the unions should not fool themselves. Although "it is critical to avoid impasse," the unions "should relax the vigilance with which meetings are scheduled and the seriousness with which negotiating sessions are approached." It was essential to "keep everyone on the job no matter what happens." At the same time, however, the company should be led to believe the unions might strike. "To this end fake strikes, leaking disinformation, and perhaps even selective quickie strikes may be deployed." The active part of the strategy was to be the circulation and advertising boycott, which would be officially launched on Labor Day.

The union strategy was perceptive, inspired, took account of most of the available facts and the apparent balance of power. And it was dead wrong. Ballow believed the company could win a strike especially if it came at the right time. But he did not want a strike and his aggressiveness was not aimed at provoking one. On the contrary, he wanted the unions to do just what they did do: persuade themselves they could not win a strike and rule it out. "What we want to do is scare them out of striking," he said. As for McKnight's boycott strategy, the history of the union movement makes it perfectly clear that boycotts are what unions do when they are too weak to strike—and they usually fail. The *News* unions had only two good options. They could work out a settlement with the company, which at best would allow them to become partners in a new post-industrial enterprise but at least would let them live to fight another day. Or they could call the company's bluff and fight, pick the right moment and strike. Instead, the McDonald, Kheel, McKnight strategy pinned them helplessly in the middle. They had misread the dance.

The unions misinterpreted Ballow's aggressiveness, says Gold, because they took what he calls the "amateur" view of negotiations, though most people might call it the commonsense view. Amateurs, says Gold, assume that negotiations always lie along a simple continuum from conference to confrontation. At one end of the continuum, negotiations "go well" and differences are "worked out" relatively amicably; while at the other end things always come to some dramatic conclusion: strike, lockout, or a sudden conversion after one side or the other sees the light—or blinks.

To Gold this is as silly as imagining that Super Bowls are either "worked out" amicably or settled by mass murder. No one thinks that Super Bowls lie along a continuum at one end of which there is no need to play the game because both sides really like each other, and at the other end of which the game is stopped because the players are behaving too competitively. The game always goes on.

Negotiations, in this view, are a war game, a continuous contest of strength and skill, in which both parties come to the table eager to use every advantage to win. Only amateurs assume that aggressiveness or ingenuity is meant to derail the game rather than win it. The unions, says Gold, ought to know that you bring every weapon to the table to start. They always do. Why is the company obliged to be nice? Why should Ballow's aggressiveness mean he does not want to deal?

Ballow, says Gold, usually starts a negotiation with the maximum *possible* bad news, which in most cases is the destruction of the union. The nuisance issues, the anti-union clauses, raise that possibility, but they are tools meant not to provoke a strike but to procure a settlement.

Ballow says he dislikes strikes because "they are expensive and it takes many years to heal the wounds." They are also one of the few ways he can lose. In a strike all sorts of random things can happen. The unions can turn violent and, as happened to him in the Wilkes-Barre *Times Leader* strike in 1978, the local authorities may decide the better part of valor is to let them get away with it. His client in that one, Capital Cities, owners of ABC, as good as lost that strike, ending up with a rival union-run paper in a town where Cap Cities once had a monopoly. And even if the company wins the strike, it can lose in court. Two, three, five years later the courts can decide that the company had negotiated in bad faith, or that he had forced the unions to strike by declaring impasse too early, or had committed any one of dozens of other "unfair labor practices" that can transform an "economic strike" into an "unfair labor practices strike." In that event, the court could order the company to reinstate any permanently replaced strikers and give all the strikers back pay for every day of work missed, and even go back to the old contract—a complete and potentially bankrupting disaster.

The core of the Ballow "process" is patience. Some of Ballow's contract talks go on for years. Gold says in this case he and Ballow expected the talks to take about a year. To make the process work the company must be willing to wait while Ballow uses the law and its sometimes bizarre rituals to make the wait as painful as possible for the unions.

Contract expiration is the first important milestone in the process. In this case it came on March 31, about six weeks after talks started. American labor law obliges both sides to continue to observe most of the expired contract while talks continue. The exception is that the company is not obliged to observe any provision in the contract treating permissive rather than mandatory subjects of collective bargaining. Anything the company is not obliged to bargain over it can unilaterally change once contracts expire.

Some time after contracts expire, Ballow often stops the union dues checkoff, which is a permissive subject. From then on the union will have to collect dues individually from the members; typically only 50 percent pay up. Eventually he may cut off company contributions to the union health and welfare funds, which means the workers lose their health insurance unless the unions themselves pick up the tab. He announces from the very beginning that there will be pay raises in the final contract, but they won't be retroactive to the date the old contract expired. So every day that goes by in talks is a permanent loss to the membership.

By themselves these are real burdens to the unions, especially relatively small and poor ones. But combined with everything else Ballow is doing, the pressure to settle even on unfavorable terms can be very powerful. The company has given every indication of being ready for a strike. The guards are walking up and down the hallways. Although, contrary to union belief, Ballow, knowing how unpredictable labor law can be, does not set out singlemindedly to get to impasse, eventually he will get there and have the right to impose conditions. The unions have told their own members a strike would be too risky, but without strikes unions are ultimately impotent. Soon the members will see that the unions can neither fight for them nor provide for them. The unions will then face not only bankruptcy but rebellion by their own members, possibly even decertification. On the other hand, the anti-union provisions in Ballow's contract would be just as fatal. The unions are between a rock and a hard place. All of a sudden giving in on a lot of the substantive issues seems like a way out.

That is how Ballow gets a deal.

The *News* unions did not understand. But Ballow is a hard man to follow. Unlike an "amateur" negotiator who imagines that negotiations are a simple matter of the two sides putting their differences on the table and talking out possible agreements, Ballow, during the early stages at least, is delivering a primarily psychological message about power. That message is delivered with brutal frankness; yet crystal clarity on every detail is not necessarily an advantage. Certainly it is no advantage for the unions to realize he wants to avoid a strike.

The combination of Ballow's aggressiveness and the eccentricities of American labor law can make him even harder to follow. In fact his obsession with the law can make him incomprehensible even to other labor lawyers. As one union advisor put it, "So often he just seemed to be playing this deep game all by himself, by these rules he cared about enormously and which nobody else even knew. It was ridiculous sometimes."

Ballow absolutely insisted, for instance, on keeping the anti-union clauses on the table until after the major substantive issues were settled. Gold says there were two relevant legal considerations. The first is that "regressive bargaining," that is, reducing the attractiveness of an offer over the course of negotiations, can be construed as an unfair labor practice: an attempt to disrupt negotiations by throwing monkey wrenches into a deal late in the proceedings. If the company puts a weapon like no dues checkoff on the table, then pulls it away to show "goodwill," then puts it back on the table again because showing "goodwill" did not help procure any concessions from the other side, it can be guilty of regressive bargaining. If the union then strikes, years later the company can be ruled to have forced an unfair labor practices strike and be made to pay tens of millions of dollars in damages.

Keeping the weapon on the table, Gold says, helps *prevent* strikes. Under the law, if the union strikes the company may be able to declare impasse and impose new working conditions. But legally the new conditions cannot be more severe than the offer the company had on the table at the moment of the strike (or the declaration of impasse). If the company has been offering $10 an hour and the union strikes, the company cannot impose a wage of $5 an hour—even if it is paying that wage to replacement workers.

The reason for this is that the imposed conditions still constitute an offer to the union. "Permanently replaced" union members are not fired. They have a right to come back to their jobs under the imposed conditions, providing their jobs are still vacant. If their jobs are not still vacant, the replaced workers have first dibs on a waiting list. Imposing conditions worse than the company's last offer would be regressive bargaining. So Ballow keeps the anti-union clauses on the table as long as there is still a possibility of a strike or a declaration of impasse. To get a settlement, he wants strike or impasse, including the imposed conditions, to be as painful a prospect for the unions as possible.

Gold says the company could have "lived with" a strike on March 31, 1990, the day contracts expired. That early, of course, the company still had its "total victory" offer on the table: open manning, no work rules, virtually no seniority, all the anti-union provisions. With six months to go before the holiday ad season, the company would be in a good position to outlast its employees. If the union refused to settle the strike, it would pay the ultimate price as its members trickled back in to work. The imposed "terms and conditions" of employment would include the anti-union clauses, and the union might well go under.

On the other hand if Ballow gave in to the unions on dues checkoff and union security, and the unions still struck, the replacement workers might be compelled to join and even pay dues to the union. A strike does not put an end to the "bargaining unit," the set of workers that according to the NLRB must decide collectively to join the union or leave it. All the replacement workers would be in the same bargaining unit with the men they replaced, and under a union security contract all might be equally obliged to sign up with the union.

The same reasoning helps explain Ballow's reluctance to offer a buyout until late in the talks. "If we don't propose a buyout and they walk out, they get nothing," says Gold, but if there is a buyout on the table and the unions strike, the buyout remains part of the offer.

If the unions were not going to strike early, Ballow and Gold did not want them to strike ever, certainly not until after Christmas. They wanted to keep the unions pinned to the table, with union funds running low, the membership on edge, the officers afraid of a members' rebellion, until the leaders came around to taking the company's "economic" offer in exchange for eliminating the anti-union provisions. "We wanted," says Gold, "either our [total] proposition with an immediate strike or our economics with no strike."

Ballow wanted the unions not just to face reality, he wanted them transfixed by it. He had the Tribune Company spend millions on strike preparations and then for months played an uncompromising game at the table to freeze the unions into inaction—until they would despair and look to him for a way out.

"He does it on purpose," says Gold. "It's like being in a bar eye-to-eye with this big slugger who keeps teasing you and provoking you, just about daring you to punch him. So you get ready to punch him. But then he turns sort of friendly and says, 'Go ahead swing, and I'll kill ya.' He'll bait you and bait you and make you want to swing, but the idea is not to get you to swing but to make you realize you are afraid to—and then you have to back down. And then he's got you, you've softened once and you will keep softening."

It almost worked.

CHAPTER 11

A Heartbreak Away

Attack—Repeat—Attack.

Admiral Halsey

OF the ten unions and ten negotiations, three mattered: the pressmen, the drivers, and the Guild. The drivers and the Guild mattered because no strike could succeed without them. But if the pressmen settled, then the war would be off.

The pressmen were the pattern-setting production union. They dominated the plants. In the company's view they set the pattern of abuse. If they agreed to a post-industrial contract, then none of the other, smaller production unions could really resist. And despite all the hostility and distrust, all Ballow's psycho-legal war games, and all the union's stalling, the two sides came breathtakingly close to an agreement.

The talks got off to a rough start. At the first session on February 13, 1990, Kennedy started off with a demand that reflected everything that had gone wrong since the MIP. He told Ballow the union would not discuss how many men would work on a press—the central issue in these talks—until it knew what the new plants would be like. Kennedy wanted a link between investments and contract concessions, in effect a new Mutual Investment Program, but this time a legally binding one.

Ballow's answer was dismissive: The company can afford to build what it wants. The purpose of reducing manning is not to come up with the cash to build a plant. For that reason the company's building plans are not a subject of negotiations. "It is management's decision what and where we build." As for negotiating manning on the new equipment: "Don't worry about that since we are negotiating a contract with no manning clause."

This was typical aggressive Ballow legalism. Under American labor law if either side gives a reason for a negotiating position, for example, if the company says, "We need payroll reductions to pay for a new plant," then the other side can ask for documentation for the reason: "Tell us what equipment you are going to buy." In amicable negotiations the rule does not matter—exchanging information helps people reach agreement. But these negotiations were a legal and psychological war for control over the business, and Ballow virtually always refused to let the unions in on any information that would allow them to share a management role.

Skadden, Arps associate Larry Marcus then objected to Ballow's proposal to allow the company to use part-time employees for some pressroom work: "On the face of your proposal you could run the pressroom with part-timers making minimum wage." Marcus was exaggerating. But Ballow merely said you "can't get people at minimum wage to fulfill highly skilled jobs." That apparently innocuous little crack was in many ways archetypal Ballow: it could have been designed to make unions first fume and then squirm and then face the weakness of their position. The unions will talk about the value of skilled workers, and the members cherish their image as craftsmen. But if their skills are so valuable, why are they so afraid the company will replace them with minimum-wage workers? Why are they afraid to strike? Why are they so powerless?

A second session was not held until February 28, fifteen days later. (The union from the very beginning sought to stretch out the time between meetings. Most meetings ended with Gold offering a string of possible dates for the next session and the union turning down most of them.) It was devoted mostly to a discussion of company uniforms and laundering. A third session was not convened until March 9, just three weeks before contract expiration. Uniforms and laundering were again discussed extensively. The union wanted the company to launder the uniforms more often. A reasonable request. But one mustn't forget who is in charge. Ballow took the position that if the company was to provide fresh uniforms, then the men would have to wear them. Any man out of uniform would be fired.

Some real issues were discussed, especially seniority, which under the company's proposal would be modified so that in deciding, for example, the order in which men would be called back from layoffs, the company could consider a man's performance as well as his seniority. The union took the position that there was no need to add an assessment of qualifications to the equation because although not everyone was equally qualified, everyone was qualified enough, "not equally, but competent," as Larry Marcus put it. It was a simple, sincere, but intractable disagreement. The union was devoted to solidarity and protection of a whole class of workmen of varying abilities, to cushioning them from the ruthless assessments of the market. The company imagined a plant of, by Brooklyn standards, ruthless efficiency with work teams hustling and competing to be the best, as they did in Chicago and Orlando. Seniority was designed precisely to relieve workers from that kind of pressure.

At the fourth meeting Larry Marcus presented a union counterproposal on work shoes and uniforms. Ballow accepted it immediately and suggested that as provisions were agreed to, the two sides should initial them with the understanding that "there won't be a complete agreement until all the provisions are put together in a package." It is a fairly standard procedure, but Marcus refused, apparently out of concern that Ballow was trying to rush them toward impasse by closing off future discussion.

Most of the rest of the fourth meeting was taken up with a discussion of a plant safety committee. As the discussion dragged on, Ballow became impatient and sarcastic. He began needling Kennedy about the union's stalling tactics. If this was the union's great plan for avoiding "impasse, they better come up with something better." He ragged Kennedy about the Allied's (possibly illegal) agreement that all the unions would stall together and none would sign before the others.

"There is no coordinated bargaining," Kennedy shot back.

Ballow kept riding him, suggesting that the other unions must not be telling him everything. "They're making a liar out of you," he teased, not pleasantly. "The other unions have admitted it."

Then on March 20, at the fifth meeting, there was a change of tone, a straightforward if inconclusive discussion of manning and buyouts. Both Ballow and Kennedy put their real concerns on the table, and had there been more trust in the room, they might have made some progress. Ballow explained that the union had made great contracts over the years "and I have great respect for that. But it is in your interest now to reevaluate where you stand. We need to know how willing you are on manning. You don't have to respond today. This is not a trick. . . . But a substantial number of people won't be here in the future. . . . We're here to negotiate for that future. . . . Whatever jobs there will be here will be good jobs at high pay that everyone will be proud of."

It was a fairly sincere effort on Ballow's part and Kennedy responded in kind: "The union wants to be flexible," he said, "but the company is not offering any job guarantees or any buyouts or any new presses." The union wants to be a part of the process of building a new paper, he explained, but that means negotiating about working conditions and manning on the new presses.

This last was a point Ballow would not yield on; the company was absolutely unwilling to be bound in any way on the new plants. He could not give Kennedy any satisfaction.

The two men moved on to buyouts, but the discussion broke down on the issue of who would make the first move. Hundreds of pressmen may lose their jobs, Kennedy told Ballow, but "the company is taking the position that there will be no . . . buyouts or guarantees."

Ballow disagreed. He was only saying it was "not the company's place to propose" a buyout. The union knows "who their people are and what they need." But as usual he ended with a sting: "We don't have to guess [what you want]. If the union does not have any ideas then neither does the company."

Marcus objected: "You are speaking too cryptically. We can't understand" what you have in mind.

Ballow replied, "We are not talking about somebody going to Florida on an annuity" at the company's expense, not "something the person retires on," but "we want to do something to make it less traumatic."

The discussion stalled there because Kennedy argued the union could not make a buyout proposal until they knew the number of jobs lost. That tied buyouts back to the question of manning, where there was no ground for agreement, since the company was absolutely unwilling to guarantee a minimum number of men on the press—the supervisors would decide. Still it had been the most substantive discussion so far and might have been the starting point for real progress.

It was not. In session No. 6 on March 26, just five days before contract expiration, the parties took a giant step backward.

Jim Hoge had made an announcement in *Newspix*, the *News*'s in-house newsletter, that the *News* would invest $300 million in a new plant. Ballow and Gold hated that sort of thing. "Negotiating in the press" they called it and were convinced it could cause only trouble. It did.

Kennedy brought a copy of the story to the meeting and used it to take the discussion back to the new equipment, which he wanted linked to the contract. Ballow, who seemed as annoyed at Hoge as at Kennedy for making them retrace old ground, irritably tried to dismiss the issue as dilatory. But Marcus and Kennedy insisted it was vital because the company was looking for "concessions" that could only be justified if the company was going to survive and invest in the future. If there wasn't any proof of that, why should the union members voluntarily give anything back?

Ballow, annoyed, snapped that it wasn't a concession to "eliminate abuses" and stop "paying people for no work."

Kennedy called a union caucus. When his team came back in he gave Ballow a manning proposal that eliminated, on average, about one worker per press per shift. To the union team this was a huge concession, high-risk leadership. Even though the numbers were small, the union was taking the first step to propose concrete manning reductions in their own work force. (They did not consider the company's open-manning plan a concrete proposal.)

Ballow thought otherwise. The union proposal was ridiculous, unresponsive, an insult. Calmly but threateningly he lectured: "This is a long way from where we have to be. . . . The union is playing a game . . . but there are a lot of jobs on the line and if the union continues to play this game many people will end up losing their jobs." He repeated his threats to train replacements right alongside the union pressmen.

The implication was clear: If the union would not respond, it would lose not a third or half its jobs but all of them. The company would bust the union and replace them all. "If you can deal with it, fine; if not, that's fine too. We would prefer to have the union represent our people, but we aren't going to have twice as many people performing the job as necessary. . . . We're trying to be patient [but] . . . we're getting into a very dangerous area where the union is saying we dare you and the company is saying we dare you."

Kennedy tried to interrupt the torrent, weakly protesting that the union was "just trying to get an agreement to protect our people."

Ballow was relentless: "You can't protect all of them. We don't need them and we can't go on carrying twice the number of people."

Pete Gaynor, from the pressmen's negotiating committee, interjected: "Does the company just feel they are out and that's it?"

Ballow shot back, "That's right!" Unless, he added, the unions had another suggestion? But no one made a move.

Okay, Ballow told them, if they wanted to be stubborn about making a buyout proposal for their own men, fine. "After this is over Larry

[Marcus] and I will still have our jobs, but many of these pressmen will not. I hope you have good notes and I hope you can explain to your people why things did not work out" better for them.

Marcus and Gold briefly diverted the meeting to other subjects but Ballow wouldn't let it go: "It is a shame you're playing around with so many lives. We will do whatever is necessary to protect ourselves. We will have a clear conscience that we did what we had to do." A few minutes later the meeting was over.

At the next meeting, just three days later, Ballow took another tack. Appearing to accept that the union needed some rough-and-ready sense of how many jobs would be left under the company's open-manning proposal, he brought in a technical expert, Tom Steck, to talk to the union guys, pressman-to-pressman. Steck had logged almost fifteen years as a pressman and then as a pressroom manager at the *St. Petersburg Times* and the *Chicago Tribune,* and had recently been brought in by Hoge and the contingency group to be senior (which in the newspaper business means "night") operations manager at the *News*'s Kearny, New Jersey, plant.

Steck explained how he would run the Kearny pressroom under an open-manning system. He would use a "stable crew concept": semipermanent teams would assume virtually complete ongoing responsibility for each press, excluding only heavy technical maintenance, but including all prep, cleanup, and light maintenance. They would do other available work around the plant on nights when the team's press was not running.

The union wanted numbers. Steck, trying to be helpful, suggested, as a baseline number, that the minimum he thought strictly necessary to run a typical press would be six men, including the (nonunion) crew chief. He did carefully explain that for a variety of reasons an actual crew would almost always have more men than that.

The pressmen were skeptical of Steck's numbers and a little embarrassed by them. But they could see Steck was for real. He had been able to run presses with six men partly because he was a pretty hot pressman himself. The discussion was surprisingly amicable and professional, suggesting that the company might have spent the previous year more profitably talking to its employees rather than demonizing them.

Ultimately, however, the Steck meeting caused more trouble than it cured. As hard as Ballow had fought against being pinned down to a specific number, henceforth Steck's six-man-per-running-press figure would be enshrined as the company's unofficial manning goal, even though, as Steck said, the Tribune Company assumed not only that typical crews would be a bit larger, but that some teams would work on maintenance and preparation on nights their presses were not running. Steck's six men stuck in everybody's mind—even Ballow used the number occasionally. The six-man estimate made it appear that the company would be eliminating more than half of the pressmen, and that unionized job slots would be reduced by nearly 60 percent. The real goal was on the order of 33 to 40 percent.

At the ninth meeting on April 6 it was as if none of the good exchanges from the Steck meeting ever happened. Kennedy showed up angry because he had gotten a letter from Gold stating that the contract had expired as of March 31. Ballow had promised repeatedly not to make any legal moves against the union without giving fair warning, face-to-face at the table. Now Kennedy thought he had done just that. "So much for eyeball-to-eyeball," he cracked.

Ballow tried to explain that he had not *done* anything. The contract expired automatically. By law, however, the substantive terms of employment continued in force as long as negotiations continued. Nobody would lose jobs or pay. All he had meant by his previous promise was that he would inform the union in advance if the company meant to exercise any of the optional legal rights it gained when contracts expired, such as stopping dues checkoff, or, later, declaring impasse or "imposing conditions," which it was not doing yet.

It didn't help. The meeting degenerated into an exchange of sarcasms and an argument over whether one of the company's "pressroom analysts" had "tapped" a pressman "on the shoulder" or "punched him out."

The next two meetings on April 10 and 12 were almost completely unproductive. On the 10th, Ballow, Kennedy, and Marcus argued interminably over a clause in the union's proposal which said that if a foreman sent a man home early he would still get paid a full shift. The union asked if Ballow had any objection.

He did not. Of course the company would pay for eight hours if a man was called in unnecessarily. The law requires it. But Ballow could not leave it there. Just don't expect it to happen, he added. We expect our supervisors to use the work force to its fullest potential, not send people home early.

Incredibly Kennedy and Marcus heard this as an objection to the union's proposal. They heatedly explained that the way it worked now was that after the night's work was done the foremen gave *all* the men a "good night" and they went home, getting paid for a full shift even if they got off early.

Ballow now took the opportunity to deliver a sermon about how at the new *Daily News* no one was going to get paid for not working and any foreman who sent men home instead of finding productive things for them to do would not be a foreman the next day.

Again the union seemed to think Ballow was saying that the men could be paid by the hour rather than the shift and could be sent home without being paid. The two sides carped at each other until they had gone through this sequence three times and were tired of talking about it.

April 23 saw perhaps the least constructive session to date. At an earlier meeting the union had asked the company to come up with a dollar value for the union's proposed manning reductions, something the company was better equipped to do than the union. The company agreed and sent Kennedy the numbers. Now Kennedy launched into a lengthy analysis of whether the company's figures were right.

Ballow tried to cut him off, telling him he was "missing the point." The numbers don't matter because the union's proposal is irrelevant; there will be no manning tables.

Kennedy and Marcus would not give it up. They wanted the *News* to redo some of the calculations. Marcus explained long-windedly all the reasons this would be useful.

Not only was Marcus stalling but Ballow and Gold thought he was being infuriatingly blatant about it. The union had promised another proposal on manning today. Ballow demanded to know where it was.

Marcus said they didn't have it, but he said if they could get these new calculations from the company (which meant another delay), "maybe there would be another proposal on manning."

By now it had been more than a month since anything like a useful discussion. The union was stalling not only more seriously but more skillfully. Kennedy and especially Marcus had gotten embarrassingly good at sucking Ballow and Gold into discussions of issues that were substantive in themselves—like the dollar value of the union's manning proposal—but led nowhere. And although in theory Ballow was willing to negotiate forever, in practice it was unpleasant and even dangerous to have the other side control the pace. It could give them illusions of power that would allow them to avoid looking Ballow's grim new reality in the face.

At the next session, on April 27, Gold and Marcus got into a furious argument over the company's proposal to eliminate the shape, or hiring hall, and instead hire through the *News*'s human resources department so that all pressroom workers would be permanent *Daily News* employees.

Marcus, having earlier discovered that he could push Gold's buttons on this point, cheerfully explained that the union did not control the hiring, which was flatly untrue.

If the company found a qualified black pressman, Gold shot back, could it give him a job today? (The pressroom then as now was virtually all white.)

No, said Marcus, he would have to go to the end of the shape line. But, he said, the company controls the shape. (Actually the shape was run out of the union chapel chairman's office at the *News*.)

Something about the way Marcus could, on this issue especially, call black white, and say it as if he expected to be believed, really got to Gold.

"Stop giving us that crap," he shouted at Marcus. He was even angrier than he seemed. Gold is a great admirer of Ballow and of the Ballow technique. In theory he buys Ballow's premise that patience is the greatest virtue. But he is not a patient man. He was furious about the pressmen's stalling and furious they were doing it so well, not so much for any tactical reason, but out of sheer frustration at their refusal to play the game he had come for. Gold had joined up for what he hoped would be a "Super Bowl" of labor relations. He loves to negotiate and he loves all the legal complexities implied in Ballow's approach. But then Marcus just sat around smiling and imitating Ballow's Southern accent. What was Marcus doing here anyway? he wondered. He'd most likely never even done this before, Gold was sure. Connery, a partner at Skadden, he thought usually handled the pressmen. It was maddening. These guys wouldn't play. It was like going to a ballpark to watch a great slugger, a childhood hero, and then see him get intentionally walked four times in a row. Gold was beginning to lose what patience he had. Over the next few months he would more and more find himself thinking maybe the best thing would be for the two sides just to slug it out in the streets. (In fact, sending associates to the table and keeping the responsible partner in the background is a cherished tactic at Skadden, whether because it makes opposition lawyers lose their cool or because associates are better at stalling than partners.)

For more than six weeks after that meeting, virtually nothing happened. There were sessions on May 1, 4, 10, 21, and 25, and June 14, but most of them were short. More than half the session on the 4th was spent arguing over who was responsible for the infrequency of meetings. Ballow harangued the union for refusing to meet on nights or weekends or go into the sort of round-the-clock sessions that could really get things moving. Gold, to drive the point home, ended the meeting by offering even more meeting dates than usual. The union refused all Gold's dates this time, but then offered the 14th and the 22nd, which happened to be the only dates in the next two weeks on which the company could not meet: Gold and Ballow were already scheduled to meet the drivers. Gold could have sworn they were doing it on purpose.

Then, at the end of the twenty-fourth session, on June 14, there came what seemed like a possible break in the stalemate. The union proposed bringing a federal mediator into the negotiations and Ballow immediately agreed.

The session convened at 2 P.M. on June 21. Each party first met separately with federal mediator Kenneth Kowalski, so the two parties did not get together until 4:45. Kowalski started by explaining what each side had told him were their concerns and that "the goal is to work to a vision of coming up with a contract." That was about all he ever got to say.

Preening for the mediator, each side spent most of the time either blaming the other for the lack of progress and for not making or responding to serious proposals, or refuting what it figured the other party was telling the commissioner in private.

It was an angry and loud meeting. Yet precisely because both sides tried to make their positions clear in front of the mediator, the argument finally narrowed down to a point, the very point where Ballow wanted it: manning. Open manning not only would save the company tens of millions of dollars, but it would do more than any other single contractual provision to restore the company's power on the floor. Moreover, focusing the talks on manning, especially in front of the mediator, would make it hard for the unions to stall. If Ballow could establish that manning was the dominant issue in these negotiations, then the inability of the two sides to make progress on that issue would demonstrate impasse. To avoid impasse the union would have to give ground on this central issue.

Much of the session was spent arguing over which side was being evasive on manning: the company, which had made its open-manning proposal at the first meeting and never budged; or the union, which had made several manning proposals, none of which included large reductions. Yet in the course of all this tit-for-tat, the mire of the past five months began to clear.

Ballow dominated, pounding home again and again the point that good-faith negotiating does not mean you keep dribbling out insignificant changes in your position as the union had done, but rather making your position clear as the company had. "The only real issue here," he said repeatedly, was whether there was anything the company could give the union that would convince the union to agree to a contract without a manning clause. It was open manning that the company wanted above all else, said Ballow, and open manning was what they had come to the table to get. They had been clear about that from the beginning. If there was any possibility the union could agree to open manning, then everything else—wages, seniority, union security, and the rest—"would all fall into place."

Kennedy objected that it was the company that was not negotiating on manning: "Since the beginning you have not moved one inch, you have not made one proposal after your original proposal."

"That's right," Ballow snapped. "This is the major overriding issue in these negotiations. We want to decide the number of people we need to work in our pressroom. It's like that all over the country in all but a very, very few newspapers. Your union has agreed to this all over the country and it has signed contracts with this type of clause. The question is: 'Is there anything we can do to cause you to agree to this?' "

It didn't work. Kennedy would not name a price, but tried instead to keep the ball in the company's court. "Try to convince me" was all Kennedy would say.

Ballow shot back that the company could convince the union only if the union would tell the company what it wanted.

Marcus cut in: "Make us a proposal."

"You have our proposal," Ballow snapped.

"We reject your manning proposal now," Marcus replied.

That was the end of substantive discussion. The union changed the subject, nothing else was accomplished, and the meeting ended a few minutes later.

In the coming weeks the sessions would continue to be marred by diversions, nitpicking, sarcasm, rope-a-doping, bluffing, and legal game playing. Still, this first session with the mediator had a permanent effect; with an outside witness there it became more difficult to avoid the central issue. From now on, manning would dominate most sessions. Ironically, just as the ten-union strategy of "deemphasizing negotiations" was being engraved in stone—or at least into official AFL-CIO strategy memos—Ballow and Kennedy were beginning to talk for real.

Not that they agreed. On June 27 there was a long discussion of buyouts for men who would lose their jobs. Ballow refused to budge from his position that the company would not be the first to propose buyouts. The company had always proposed first in the past, he explained, because it was weak and the unions were strong, but now the unions would have to accept that they did not have the muscle they once had. They were going to lose the excess manning but they should come up with something to cushion the blow.

Kennedy objected: "You've always said that what happens to the men is my problem."

"Yes, it is your problem," Ballow answered. "But that does not mean the company would not be willing to listen to any [buyout] proposal the union is willing to offer."

A few minutes later, Ballow brought the question back to manning and tried to use the offer of a wage increase to forge a deal: "We're not through with wages. The company has never pleaded poverty. If the union will agree to our manning proposal today, I will take a few minutes right now and I will come back into this room with more money."

Ballow used stick as well as carrot, now waving the threat of impasse almost constantly as the summer wore on: "We've given you our position on manning again and again," he would say, again and again. "We want to know what your bottom line on manning is." Was the union saying "there is nothing the company can do" to get the union to change its position—a legal trigger phrase for impasse? "We are reaching the end of the process," he would say; for the good of your people, you must tell us what your final position is. On July 30 he told the union, "We're getting to the end of the road," not, he says now, because he was ready to declare impasse, but just to prod the union into moving.

Ballow remained as blunt and sarcastic as ever. On July 9 Marcus raised the issue of the proposed cuts in apprentice pay (at the *News* under the hiring-hall system a man could be an "apprentice" for decades) and sarcastically asked if the pressmen were supposed to be grateful to the company for keeping their jobs at "half pay."

Ballow blithely told him they should be very grateful that they would still have jobs after muscling the company out of money for years. If Pete Gaynor (who was an apprentice and whom Ballow liked to pick on) was upset about getting a big pay cut, then as a union member "he should have taken responsibility to straighten out this [the overmanning] years ago."

Despite this sort of thing, and despite the fact that all the participants, including Gold and Ballow, remember the pressmen's negotiations as an exercise in frustration and futility, the truth is Ballow's tactics were working.

Though Ballow told Hoge and some others on the management team that talks would probably drag on through the new year, the talks were probably at impasse by late summer. Gold was now besieging Kennedy with letters arguing that the talks were at impasse and if no progress was made on the central issue the company would be within its rights to declare so. In late June and early July Ballow suddenly accepted the union's wording on a number of the minor issues that had been cluttering up the talks, thus sweeping from the table a number of the union's diversionary tools and clearing the decks for a legal declaration of impasse. The rope-a-dope was stretched thin. The union became convinced that the company was about to declare impasse. Ballow had boxed the union in. They would have to deal or fight.

On August 20 the two parties met and checked off a list of issues on which they had already agreed. Then they made a more systematic list of remaining disagreements on some of the less important but not insignificant issues. The session was businesslike and efficient. Both sides tried to move things along as briskly as possible. It was a stunning change.

Then, about an hour into the meeting, the union made the first move on buyouts. Kennedy handed Ballow a buyout proposal similar to the one it had accepted in 1987, adjusted for inflation. The numbers were high (neither side could give me the exact figure) and probably unrealistic given the new balance of power. And the buyout proposal was accompanied by a manning proposal that was little changed from the one Ballow had found completely inadequate. Nevertheless, someone had decided to move first. It was a powerful breakthrough.

Ballow's first reaction was maddening. The proposal was unacceptable, he said, because it was for a voluntary buyout. We are not interested in voluntary buyouts, he explained, because the company wants to control who is in the work force. When the manning is reduced the company wants to keep the best and get rid of the worst.

This at least was a substantive if somewhat ambitious objection. But then, noticing that the union had simply photocopied the 1987 buyout agreement and filled in some new numbers, Ballow launched into a long harangue about how the union hadn't "really put any thought into this proposal at all; it's not even updated."

Marcus suggested Ballow counterpropose an involuntary buyout.

Ballow snapped back that the company had said all along, "We aren't interested in proposing buyouts." This was obviously disingenuous, since he had never said the company would not counterpropose, it had just insisted the union go first.

Finally, despite months of begging for a buyout proposal, Ballow told the union he was not interested in buyouts at all: "Just so you don't leave under a false impression, we are not interested in buyouts, but we will look at your proposal."

Ballow chopped off discussion with a sarcastic remark, claiming that buyouts might not be necessary because under the company's proposal "some people may quit" anyway because "they will have to work." He then picked a fight over some alleged sabotage at the plant and the session ended.

Ballow kept this up for more than a month, which actually added up to only two more meetings, the first of which, on September 10, was very brief. At a ninety-minute meeting on September 26 he spent much of that time elaborating on his "xeroxes aren't serious" theme: "We've spent more time studying your proposal than you did preparing it," he said, and if "you are not any more serious than that in what you want to do for people who are displaced then I can't help them."

Beneath this apparently bizarre objection, however, there was a serious, classic Ballow point. The whole point of the negotiations process is to get the unions to confront the reality of their situation, to take to heart the overwhelming imperatives for change, to accept deeply and fully the new balance of power. A fill-in-the-blanks proposal might be just as good in terms of facts and figures as a brand-new draft, but it suggests, he says, the moment is not yet ripe for any move by the company. If the union cannot show that it has taken the trouble to really think through the buyouts or even retype them, he told me, then it has not "seriously engaged in the negotiation process." Instead it has "demonstrated a lack of seriousness" and therefore it was still "not time for us to propose."

The union, now all the more convinced that Ballow only wanted a war, caucused, came back saying they could meet no longer that day, and refused to schedule another meeting until mid-October, eventually settling on October 17, three full weeks later.

On the 17th the union returned with a new buyout proposal. The economics were similar to its August 20 proposal but otherwise the union had made a real effort to meet Ballow's objections. The proposal was freshly drafted with all the dates right and it made provision for both involuntary and voluntary buyouts. The company, throughout the negotiations, had rarely requested caucuses. Ballow now asked for one, though the meeting was only eleven minutes old.

The company stayed out for two hours. The union had moved. It had demonstrated seriousness. It was responding to Ballow's reality lessons. The company returned with a three-page handwritten buyout proposal of its own. The numbers were much smaller than the union's, but they were substantial, adding up to roughly $30,000 per job. (Five months later, after an economically ruinous strike, the unions would settle with Robert Maxwell for about $40,000 per job.) There were some burdensome details, the money was to be paid out over a year, and the offer was contingent on having a complete ratified contract by December 1.

Nevertheless, measured against the futility of the previous eight months it was a gigantic event. Both sides had named their price in the central issue, manning reductions. They were far apart but both offers were serious. Only dollars, not principles, separated them. The final price would surely be affected by the manning agreement, but both sides had agreed in principle to a basis for making such an agreement.

Nine days later, before the two sides could meet again, the *News*'s nine[*] unions would be on strike.[1]

---

[*] Excluding the printers, whose lifetime job guarantees effectively took them out of the picture.

CHAPTER 12

La Forza del Destino

Character is destiny.

Heraclitus

DON Singleton, a veteran *News* reporter, had served with some reluctance on the Guild negotiating committee during the 1987 contract talks. In late 1989, however, he volunteered to return to the committee for the 1990 round.

Singleton was not looking for a fight. He knew the *News* needed help to survive; and he had no illusions about the featherbedding in the plants or the corruption in the drivers union. He was convinced Hoge wanted to "break the pattern" of lax management. He was determined not to let the Guild be used in a strike waged to defend the abuses of other unions. He went on the committee, he says, to be "a voice of reason" on behalf of like-minded *News* staffers, men like politically conservative columnist Bill Reel, who were afraid the Guild might get involved in a fight they had no business in.

Six months later, and more than three months before the strike, Singleton made headlines by walking out of the negotiations and demanding that the Guild strike now, immediately and unilaterally. Long after the strike, as he tells the story of how he became a "labor radical"—which is how the Tribune management routinely refers to him—he can barely control his anger. "Ballow never intended to negotiate with us. He would walk into the room full of men who had come there willing to sit down like partners to save a newspaper we had invested our lives in, and just start insulting people. Every move he made was to provoke a strike or to get us to impasse. He knew how to offend people and used it as a tool."

To Singleton, Ballow's tactics were a disaster for both sides. "His idea of negotiations was that he or one of his law thugs would come to a table, present a proposal and say, 'This is the way it is going to be, take it or leave it.' It was as if he thought he didn't need to do anything but show us how tough he was. He had no experience in New York. He never seemed to know who he was talking to. He spent his life down South beating up on weaker unions in anti-union cities. I think he thinks a union is a union, and what you do with unions is show them that you hold more cards than they do, and that you are a hard SOB who is ready to do anything to win.

"The Tribune sent in somebody with more balls than brains and really that's why they lost the strike. People like me they could have talked to, but after Ballow was finished, nobody was talking to anybody and the only way this was going to be settled was in the street, and in the street they lose."

The pressmen were the key to a settlement, but the Guild and the drivers were the key to a strike. The company needed the Guild in part because most of the Guild members—especially the reporters and the ad salesmen—would be extremely difficult to replace in the short term. Both jobs depend on a network of relationships and a feel for the home-town that can be built only over time.

Far more important, however, the Guild would change the political and class status of the strike and its treatment in the press. As Barry Lipton pointed out, if the Guild members at the *News* went out, Guild reporters at the other three papers could be counted on to treat the strike as sympathetically as possible. All of a sudden a fight the press might otherwise have seen as a downmarket story about unsympathetic, middle-class, white-ethnic, socially conservative, backward, and proba-bly corrupt unions threatening to kill off one more New York paper might be transformed into a fight starring a union that the city's poli-ticians especially feared to offend, one with which all the city's powerful elites could sympathize, a union made up of high-profile, literate, new-class, liberal, crusading, white-collar "people like us." This was crucial. Public opinion and the quality of press coverage would matter enor-mously—because of the other union that mattered, the drivers.

There was only one way for the unions to win a strike: stop the papers from getting to the newsstands that accounted for 80 percent of the *News*'s sales. There was no way to do that legally. The drivers them-selves could be easily replaced; it is simpler to train a truck driver than a press operator. The only way to stop the paper from being sold at the newsstands was to terrify the dealers into refusing to carry it. The drivers were the only union that was really up to that job, a union of hard men, many with criminal connections, and a reputation (perhaps even a deliberately exaggerated reputation) for having connections with even harder and more dangerous men. If the drivers struck, the dealers might lie down. But if the drivers stayed in, few men of the other unions would risk the drivers' wrath by themselves going after the dealers. If the drivers did go after the dealers, however, they would need political protection, otherwise the police and the 3,000 FBI agents that call New York home might be all over them. That meant the drivers needed the press on their side, to downplay the violence, to persuade the public that it was rare, random, and of uncertain origin, and to persuade public officials to let the drivers get away with it. So if a strike came the unions needed both the Guild and the drivers—the Guild to provide cover for what the drivers would have to do in the streets. If the company could keep either union from joining a strike it would almost certainly win.

It should have been easy with the Guild, with whom the company had few substantial differences. As one senior advisor to another union put it, "The strategy should be obvious, don't negotiate with the Guild, just anoint 'em. Give them a big raise, renew the current contract, congratulate them on their great victory, show them where to sign." Even Barry Lipton, a notoriously difficult negotiator, "could not have said no."

That was the company's original plan. But management by committee intervened. *News* editors wanted more freedom to make job assignments on the merits rather than seniority. The advertising managers wanted to eliminate a whole raft of work rules that forced their people— many of whom were at best reluctant union members—to behave like factory workers rather than enterprising salesmen. One such rule for instance declared that some ad staffers could only take calls from clients, some could only make calls to clients, and never the twain should meet. And then the Guild did have some especially costly benefits none of the other unions had, including exceptionally generous severance and sick leave policies.

The company believed the core contract proposal that resulted was generous. It included a 30 percent pay raise over three years. But it was not an anointing. The company did insist on some substantive concessions. Even worse, the usual Ballow union-harassment clauses—no union security clause, no dues checkoff, no Guild facilities in the *News* building—were all tossed in for negotiating purposes.

Management claims it was willing to compromise on the givebacks. Hoge assumed they would. Gold says flatly: "If at the right moment [the Guild] had offered to sign immediately, taking the 30 percent, but refusing the concessions, we would have moaned and groaned but then we would have signed and they would have picked up a 30 percent raise for free." Everybody says they recognized the strategic importance of pulling the Guild out of the game.

It didn't happen. Personality, prejudice, and political ideology got in the way.

Ballow and Barry Lipton loathed each other almost on sight. Lipton calls Ballow "an animal, Neanderthal in his approach. He walks one path—toward destroying the work force. He is like a fighter who head-butts a lot and constantly hits below the belt."

Ballow and Gold and the other lawyers returned the compliment: they found Lipton offensive, amateurish, obscene, childish, and worst of all, a union romantic. Even Ballow, reluctant to be quoted criticizing an opponent, calls Lipton, "a clown, a fool, silly, ridiculous . . . inadequate."

Lipton, a short, stocky man with a graying brown afro, is under normal circumstances pleasant, courteous, intelligent, and hospitable. As a negotiator he can be very difficult. Even the leaders and advisors of the other unions think so. One senior union advisor says, "Barry will always be the last one to do a deal and he will have trouble doing it volitionally," i.e., the only way he will come along is under duress and then he'll come kicking and screaming.

Measured by self-interest alone, the Guild had little to gain from the strike. As Ballow occasionally put it, "They don't have a dog in this fight." If the company succeeded in humbling the production unions, Guild members would actually be better off, richer, and their paper more likely to survive. The Guild might even gain members, because the editorial department would grow. Yet Lipton was among the most militant union leaders.

Lipton wholeheartedly endorsed the unions' rope-a-dope strategy. And unlike most other union leaders (who still will not admit on the record to their stalling tactics), Lipton likes to brag about how he wasted time arguing such earthshaking issues as how long a reporter who is up for jury duty should be allowed to get back to the office after he is released for the day. At the very first meeting, and several times thereafter, Ballow asked Lipton to pledge that when the Tribune Company and the Guild reached agreement, the Guild would sign and not wait for the other unions. Lipton refused.

The stalling tactics were against the Guild's interests. Stalling is a tactic for concessionary bargaining: if the new contract will be worse than the old, what's the rush? But the Tribune's opening offer to the Guild was a clear signal that the Guild could negotiate an improved contract, especially if it was willing to sign early and leave the other unions to their fate.

Management suspected Lipton's motives. They thought the reason he so valued solidarity with the blue-collar unions and put their interests ahead of those of his own members was that he wanted to become the president of the Allied Council. A more likely explanation is that Lipton is an archetypal member of a very odd union. It was ideology, white-collar guilt, and union romanticism, not Barry Lipton's alleged ambition, that triumphed over the Guild's own interests.

At the *News*, the Guild is largely made up of white-collar ethnics one or two generations removed from blue-collar backgrounds. Though many or most Guild officers are from the noneditorial departments, at times of crisis the organization is dominated by male reporters simultaneously proud of their status as professionals and even intellectuals, yet also bound and determined to be real, honest-to-goodness, regular union guys like their dads or granddads and uncles and cousins.

Most of the reporters are liberal in their political views. And even the conservatives among them, like former *News* columnist Bill Reel, tend to be populists—conservatives devoted not to the abstract dexterities of the invisible hand but to the solid virtues of neighborhood New York. Their politics, their heritage, and their ambivalence about leaving it behind, the identity of the *News* as a paper written for people who not only are not part of the "new" class but are alienated from it, their need for solidarity with their blue- and pink-collar readers, all combine to make many of them deeply susceptible to union romanticism and to the temptations of playacting the working-class hero.

Lipton himself was enormously susceptible. One of his great concerns seems to have been to prove that the Guild was just as tough as the blue-collar unions, though a lot smarter. Lipton says proudly: "I think [Ballow] thought the Guild would crumble, that the craft unions were a lot tougher, but we were a hell of a lot smarter and more resilient than they expected." When asked about the violence that came with the strike, most of the union leaders downplay it. Lipton by contrast is almost bursting to say that the Guild did its share. "The drivers were not the only people out there. Our own people were involved in that," he claims (not very realistically), as if to say, "We may use word processors but we are tough guys too."

Lipton's efforts to prove that the Guild were tough guys too were often seen by some as more comical than intimidating. One Guild member, a longtime reporter who attended a number of negotiating sessions, says, "I knew we were doomed when I watched him in that room with these suits. The King & Ballow guys were assholes but Lipton couldn't handle them. His way of negotiating was just screaming curse words, 'you f——ing bastard you f——er.' I am no sissy pants but . . . they could care less that he does that. They were playing him like a piano. It was almost like it was a show, like [Lipton] was screaming and cursing to impress the people who had come to observe this."

Yet though Lipton and his colleagues would put their own members' jobs at risk to maintain solidarity with the blue-collar unions, the Guild leaders loathed the idea of being thought to be like the craft unions or the craftsmen. Repeatedly in the negotiations, Lipton, or Guild secretary-treasurer Tom Pennachio furiously denounced Ballow for offering the Guild "craft proposals" or for "treating everyone the same." Lipton, explaining some of the animosity between the negotiators, proudly points out, "Our people are creative and they expect to be respected. . . . By the nature of their work they are intellectual. They enjoy a middle-class lifestyle." But Ballow treated them "like factory workers in a nonunion plant in the Deep South. . . . He offended our committee."

There is another and uglier thread running through the anger of the Guild: class prejudice against Ballow, a self-made Southerner. To put it bluntly, the Guild leaders did not like being in the power of a man they saw as a "Southern redneck." Not grasping Ballow's legal genius, they saw only a country boy who had gotten his law degree from the Nashville YMCA night law school, a man whom many of them instinctively regarded as their moral and intellectual inferior, a presumed racist and bumbler, a little bit like the fat, dumb sheriff from "The Dukes of Hazzard." Ballow may have had his way with those weaker, dumber unions down South, but in the Guild's eyes he sure wasn't ready to take on the boys from the city that never sleeps. That he did take them on, with utter self-confidence, and looked for months like the probable victor, was intolerable.

Ballow, however, was not playing Lipton like a piano. The reverse was more nearly true. Lipton says he wanted to get under Ballow's skin and he did. Ballow was offended by Lipton's antics, particularly the obscenity. And he seemed constitutionally incapable of ignoring the implication that the union was not afraid of the company and had not contemplated the gravity of its position. Ballow denies his personal feelings affected the course of negotiations. But, goaded by Lipton, he did get embroiled in fights over trivia like jury duty and lunch hour policy. He was as stubborn about the anti-union provisions with the Guild as with any of the other unions, though they had no tactical place in these talks. His behavior persuaded rank and filers like Singleton that it was the company that was stalling and that Ballow wanted a fight with the Guild too. By alienating men like Singleton and Bill Reel and even some who opposed striking but did so weakly because they were disgusted by the company's behavior, Ballow worsened the odds in what would turn out to be a close battle to keep the Guild on the job. But much of the credit for Ballow's misplay must go to Lipton.

The acrimonious atmosphere of the sessions was only made worse by the chaos in which most of them were conducted. Under arrangements established by the Guild, the principal negotiators, Ballow, Gold, King & Ballow lawyer Michael Oesterle, et al., sat at the head of a very long table or series of tables, while their counterparts, Lipton, Tom Pennachio, and union business agent Robert Vann, sat at the foot, more than fifty feet away. In between sat as many as twenty Guild members, in theory members of the negotiating committee, but in practice almost any member interested enough to stop by. While the principals tried to talk, the "committee members" pretty much pitched in whenever they wanted to, on whatever subjects caught their fancy, often screaming at or denouncing their own principals as well as Ballow and company. As Lipton said, they were "creative" and "intellectuals" and they were a "committee," and the result was very often as maddening as those three words used together would suggest.

Practically speaking the talks ended after only six sessions. At that sixth session an especially heated, and in this case racially charged, argument broke out. The scene was typical mayhem as the principals tried to make themselves understood over the crosstalk of the creative intellectuals. Michael Oesterle from King & Ballow had been asking for an explanation of some point in the Guild's proposals. Gold was speaking when Guild business representative Robert Vann, who is black and not talkative, gestured as if to interject and make a point. Dave Hardy, another black Guild member, was also there.

Gold (points at Vann and says [sarcastically according to Guild members]): Oh look, I see Bob Vann finally wants to say something.

Lipton (to Gold, speaking): Put your finger down.

Gold: That's how I talk. When I have the floor I speak and when you have it you can.

Lipton (shakes his finger at Gold)

Gold: Don't shake your finger at me.

Mike Oesterle: The idea here is to try to negotiate a contract in clearer language. When I read something and it is not clear to me that is when I have to get it cleared up—

Tom Pennachio (to Gold, but Gold thinks to Oesterle): Now wait a minute, when are you guys going to quit making wisecracks and start negotiating?

Gold: What do you mean about us making wisecracks? We have answered all your questions and now we want to get answers on our questions.

Pennachio: What do you mean interrupting a business rep? How dare you treat a business rep that way! You'll be taken care of later.

Gold: Are you threatening me?

Hardy: He's not threatening you, it's a promise. Listen chump—

Gold: Don't call me chump, call me Ed or Mr. Gold.

Hardy: I am sick and tired of listening to a bunch of Southern rednecks.

Pennachio (to Hardy): Now let's cool off. (To Gold) I'll get you my own way.[*]

Gold: I am not going to listen to people threaten me.

Hardy: That may be the way it works down South but not in New York. I'm tired of listening to whites, on whites, in white, motherfuckers.

Oesterle: We need to have a caucus and let everyone cool off.

Lipton: We're cool.

Oesterle: We're going to leave. (Points at Hardy) He needs to cool down.

In the end Ballow not only did not "anoint" the Guild, he ignored them. After that sixth meeting Ballow and Gold turned the Guild ne-

---

[*] Pennachio denies threatening Gold.

gotiations over to a B team of negotiators and never met with the Guild again until the waning days of the strike. Ballow says that he always intended to turn the Guild negotiations over to Oesterle after a few meetings, and that Lipton's demeanor had no effect on his decision to leave. Be that as it may, Lipton, who wanted the Guild to stick with the craft unions, and to be in on the fight, had by that measure beaten Ballow hands down.

Mike Alvino came into the negotiations a frightened man. By late spring 1990, the NMDU, the drivers union, for the first time in decades, was on the defensive at the *News*. Bill Deering, the former UPS executive brought in by Hoge to straighten out the *News*'s distribution operation and prepare for a possible strike, had made far more progress than anyone expected in getting the drivers under control, cutting back on theft, no-show jobs, and bogus or unnecessary overtime.

When Deering arrived the *News* had a grand total of three nonunion line supervisors for the drivers, one at each plant, supervising hundreds of men. Instead of waiting to get union supervisors to drop their cards, Deering, who had spent years riding herd on Teamsters for UPS, addressed the problem directly, by adding more than thirty nonunion supervisors to his staff. With this force on the job he cracked down hard on theft and waste. In less than a year he uncovered more than two dozen malefactors and fired them. He harassed the bootlegging operation further by reconfiguring routes and transferring drivers. In part because the company suspected the trucks were being used in other illegal activities, he made and then enforced a new rule requiring the drivers to return their trucks at the end of a shift, rather than bringing them home. When Deering arrived the *News* believed it had been losing as many as 80,000 papers a night to theft. Less than a year later that number was below 20,000.

Similarly Deering was able to cut back very sharply on no-show and cush jobs, and unnecessary or wrongful overtime. When Deering arrived, the *News* had well over 700 full-time-equivalent job slots for drivers. Deering established that the *News* needed about 410 full-time positions. Roughly 250 could do the work of a typical day, the others would be for weekends, sick and vacation leave, and special operations. Many of the jobs and much of the overtime were not clearly written into the contract. Some had been established by written but informal agreements, some were by verbal agreement, and some were based on pos-sibly obsolete or otherwise disputable language in a contract that had not been cleaned up for years.

This meant he could go after a lot of the most blatant abuses (legal or not) without renegotiating. All it would take was a diligent supervi-sory team of sufficient size, which he now had, the guts to fire people, and the patience to pursue disputes into arbitration. He did it. The jobs established by verbal agreement were the easiest to eliminate; arbitra-tors would overturn even long-standing practices if they had little de-fensible purpose and there was nothing in writing to back them up. Even practices specified in writing could be attacked if conditions had changed so much as to render the practices meaningless.

Diligence paid off. Deering investigated and investigated, trimmed and trimmed, arbitrated and arbitrated. He won in arbitration about half the time, though as he and his team got better at it their record im-proved. In the summer before the strike he was winning routinely. In less than a year he eliminated more than one hundred of the least defensible job slots and cut overtime substantially. In one year, without a new contract, he had saved the *News* more than $7 million in payroll costs, about half its 1989 deficit, and more than 10 percent of its total goal of eliminating $50 to $70 million in labor costs. He believes he would ultimately have been able to cut the drivers down to about 500 jobs and minimal unjustified overtime—without changing the contract.

NMDU leaders, especially those involved in corrupt activities, were appalled. Surrendering a few jobs was one thing—some union leaders had made quite a bit of money over the years selling out the jobs of rank and file members. But Deering was attacking the NMDU as a business. The bootlegging operation, the overtime abuses, and the no-shows, which produced millions of dollars a year for union leaders and their cadre of followers who made up the Newspaper Delivery Mob, were gravely threatened. And Alvino was letting him get away with it. Lots of people were very mad at Mike.

It is not entirely clear how Alvino became president of the NMDU in the first place. Many consider him a man of limited intelligence, out of his depth even among many of his fellow drivers, a weak man with little real leadership ability. Moreover, he is rumored to be allied with men from the weaker of the two mob factions in the union, the one including associates of the Bonanno family rather than the Luccheses. (The NMDU is deeply factionalized, two of the two major conflicts being the

Italians vs. the Jews, and allies of the Lucchese crime family vs. those of the Bonannos, though there are innumerable subfactions and temporary alliances cutting across crime family and ethnic lines. The Bonannos are dominant at the *Post*, but union-wide—and city-wide—they are much weaker than the Luccheses. New York's famous "five families" are really four and a half. The Bonannos are the runt of the litter, smaller and weaker than all the others and not always treated with respect. It is not unknown for the four other families to hold an all-families summit meeting without so much as telling the Bonannos.) But not only has Alvino never been publicly identified as a Bonanno associate, but long-time observers of the union, including law enforcement officials, warn that the internal politics of the drivers union are supremely enigmatic. Cosa Nostra "associates" are not necessarily controlled by their families. "Constitutionally" only "made" members are under rigid family discipline and there are few such "made" men in the union. Most NMDU leaders and their cadres are very tough men in their own right, not easily pushed around even by the mob. Neither the Lucchese nor the Bonanno family can simply order the election of a particular president. And the NMDU, however corrupt, is also a functioning union whose elections can turn on legitimate union issues with rank-and-file members uninvolved in corruption deciding the outcome.

One theory is that Alvino was elected because, despite any possible Bonanno connections, he was accepted by the Lucchese faction in preference to tougher, smarter rivals who would be more difficult to deal with. And Alvino seems always to have had the ability to go along and get along with the other guys. Though his testimony helped send former union president Douglas LaChance (alleged to have ties to the Luccheses) to jail, neither LaChance nor the Luccheses ever exacted serious retribution.

Former NMDU president Jerry Cronin, who downplays the Mafia's influence in the union, has a more mundane explanation. Alvino is a weak man, he says, but he can give a good speech and is an effective demagogue. With these tools, he put a lot of work into making a comeback in the union. "You could always get a following in the NMDU," says Cronin, by telling men they are not getting everything the contract guarantees them. So, he says, Alvino would walk into one of the plants "and start finding [management] violations everywhere, and get himself a big audience by constantly referring to the details of the contract," which he convinced the men he knew like the back of his hand.

Cronin calls most NMDU members "naive." They not only have no sense of how close the *News* was (and is) to bankruptcy, but think the company is rolling in dough, he says. Some members quite literally believe "the contract is law." When *USA Today* came to the New York area, though it did not have an NMDU contract "members thought there was no question, that it was a law that the NMDU delivers all papers within a fifty-mile radius of the city, and therefore it could dictate terms." Because of this naiveté the members will follow anyone who says they can always have more. In short, they believed in Alvino because he was absurd.

Alvino had wanted badly to be president. But he certainly had never wanted to find himself president in the middle of a war, especially one that seemed likely to destroy his chances of winning a second term. He was already being blamed by union leaders such as business agent Seymour Goldstein for the devastation wrought by Deering. LaChance was about to be paroled and would want his job back, especially if Alvino screwed up. Alvino was eager for a deal, and he made that clear to Ballow.

A typical small union negotiating committee consists of half a dozen to a dozen members. The drivers negotiated in a mob, bringing as many as three dozen men to many meetings, representatives of various factions who wanted to ensure that their own perks and goodies would not be dealt away. The result was a bit like a bad comic opera in which the chorus gets far too much to do.

The drivers' private caucuses away from the company were long, noisy, inconclusive, and out of Alvino's control. Ballow and Gold could hear loud fights through the walls. They fought among themselves even during sessions with management. One session broke up because the drivers got into an argument over whether it was right to distinguish (for seniority purposes) between a man who missed two weeks of work without permission because he went fishing and a man who missed two weeks of work because he was kidnapped. The fight ended with a union executive committee member shouting to anyone who would listen, "What the fuck is the difference between a kidnapping and going fishing?"

It actually took weeks for many on the drivers' committee, including Alvino, to catch on to what the company was asking for.

Early in negotiations Alvino had told Ballow the company would get "relief," that he knew the union would lose positions, but he was prepared to do what was "necessary." But at the sixth session, more than two months into the process, only nine days before the contract would expire, it became clear Alvino had no idea what the company thought was necessary. He cheerfully remarked that it did not sound like the company really wanted much from the drivers and they should have a deal soon.

Ballow was dumbfounded. He had just finished explaining, not for the first time, that the company's core demands might cost the drivers nearly 200 regular jobs (not even counting thousands of hours of lost overtime and gratuitous no-shows). He pulled the meeting up short and for a few minutes virtually changed sides, carefully explaining to Alvino just how rough the company's proposal would be on the drivers. "There is going to be tremendous impact on your union and loss of jobs . . . people may be hurt, we need to talk about the effects . . . people will be losing jobs and therefore we want to know what ideas the union has on how to make the transition and how to make that easier . . . the union has to give some ideas. There's 144 people who are going to lose their jobs from the retie operation [alone]. . . ."

Ideally management wanted a drivers' contract that would give the company the same freedom to build the sort of quality-oriented, customer-conscious work force they hoped to build in the plants. The company's original proposal to the drivers, for instance, also included open manning and eliminated decades of work rules that strictly governed how hard the men could be worked, how full the trucks could be loaded, what size the bundles could be, and of course when overtime would be paid. But the situations in the plant and on the road were quite different. No technological revolution loomed for truck drivers. The number of drivers on a truck was either one or two, and even the company admitted two were sometimes necessary. As for those work rules, well, the men worked alone. Most of the rules represented gravy for individual drivers rather than systemic obstacles to efficiency.

Realistically management wanted three things from the drivers. The first was an end to theft. As Deering had shown, this was primarily a management rather than a contractual issue. The one way the contract could help would be by moving the drivers entirely out of the packaging area of the plant, shifting all packaging jobs to the mailers union and closing down the "odds room" where drivers retied standard-sized bundles into packages that exactly suited customer orders. The odds room facilitated theft, and getting the drivers out of the building altogether would make life very hard for the Delivery Mob.

The next objective was to eliminate featherbedding and bogus overtime. Again Deering had shown that a lot of this could be eliminated by aggressive management, but to finish the job the company needed a "zipper clause" eliminating all previous side agreements to the contract.

Finally, the *News* wanted to eliminate, at one stroke, about 150 jobs devoted to distributing "the colors." Most of the color inserts distributed in the *Sunday News*, including the Sunday magazine, were printed by an outside contractor who delivered them to the *News*'s Kearny, New Jersey, plant. There *News* drivers "retied" the bundles, adding a superfluous additional plastic tie. Then the bundles were distributed to newsstands and other outlets by a separate group of *News* drivers, in effect a parallel delivery system. Management wanted to eliminate the retie, and have the regular *News* drivers deliver the colors during the regular workday.

These were substantial changes. But they were easier to quantify and simpler to pin down in a negotiation than what the *News* wanted from the production unions. On the plant floor the company was in an all-or-nothing struggle for control of the production process. With the drivers, compromise should have been possible, because even a partial victory would have been valuable. But instead of taking Alvino's weakness and the company's limited needs as an invitation to end these negotiations quickly and pull the drivers out of the strategic picture, Ballow went the other way—he pushed harder.

At the seventh negotiating session in late March, Ballow brought in Deering to do what Tom Steck had done for the pressmen: explain in detail how the new system would work. Deering did a good sales job, showing that his new system, though it would eliminate 25 to 40 percent of current jobs and millions of dollars in overtime, in most ways would be better for rank and file drivers who remained. Though the Kearny retie and the colors operation would be eliminated, some jobs would be added back, because the regular delivery routes would be made smaller and more numerous. Drivers would work shorter hours in a far better-organized system with more time to do customer service. Most would report not in the dead of night but at four in the morning to already loaded trucks. They would save—and make—the company enough money to make their jobs really secure for the first time in more than a decade. And as better service boosted circulation more jobs would be added back.

The drivers' committee sounded more receptive than the pressmen had. Though Deering had been making them crazy, they did not hate him the way the production unions hated Dick Malone. Not that they were ready to agree. The Deering plan, though appealing enough for the rank and file drivers who would remain, not only would have eliminated about 200 jobs, it also would have played hell with the Delivery Mob—especially that bit about the trucks being preloaded. But it was possible to imagine a compromise.

At the very next session, however, Ballow made an early compromise almost impossible. He announced that the *News* was considering a radical new plan: selling the drivers' routes and turning the routemen into independent businessmen whose income would depend on how many papers they sold and how efficiently. Current union drivers would be given preference in the bidding to buy their routes, though not an absolute right of first refusal. And the company would help with financing.

In some ways it was a great idea, ironically inspired by management's grudging respect for the bootleg operation, which did a better job than the company at distributing the paper in some neighborhoods, particularly black and Hispanic ones. Giving all the drivers, including the "criminal entrepreneurs" among them, a legitimate incentive to improve customer service and increase circulation might be just what the *News* needed to win the circulation wars against *Newsday* in Queens and Brooklyn, or open up new territory across the river in New Jersey.

The plan had been floated by Hoge in the press some weeks earlier, but it was not part of the original company proposal. Ballow had never mentioned it, and the union ignored it. Announcing it now almost as an afterthought, however, two months into negotiations, right after Deering had spent hours selling the virtues of another system, was either foolhardy or deliberately provocative and possibly both.

Everything Deering had said at the previous meeting was now irrelevant—under the new plan there might not even be a company-run route system. The new independent routemen would not be union members, the men would work for themselves. Instead of losing 25 to 40 percent of its membership at the *News*, the union might lose 60 or 70 percent. The independent routemen would destroy the bootleg operation.

Under the best of circumstances the company would have had a slim chance of selling such a plan and it would have taken months of preparation and some very powerful sweeteners. But management had not even seriously discussed the idea with Deering (the idea had come from circulation sales and Deering was still in distribution). When Alvino asked, "Why didn't Bill tell us about this?" Ballow simply told him, "He probably doesn't know, this is something we have been talking to the marketing people about and Bill hasn't been in on it."

Alvino was dumbstruck by this new move, but Deering, when he heard, was furious. He never had any faith in Ballow's negotiating style and like the union leaders eventually became convinced Ballow was trying to force a strike. Selling the routes, he says, was not a serious business proposition but "a farce, a Ballow ploy" to impress the drivers with how tough he was, to scare them or provoke them. "It was just a hammer. . . . They dangled it as a threat but it had never been seriously prepared. It was never presented to us for our analysis." (Hoge says it was a serious plan. It was the way he wanted to run distribution.)

UPS, where Deering had made his career, is a Teamster-organized company and Deering is no union fan. But his years at UPS also taught him that tough and resourceful management can wring good performance out of even the toughest unionized work force. Deering's success in curbing theft, no-shows, and phony overtime persuaded him that management did not need total victory. He had eliminated more than 100 job slots without changing the contract. "Four hundred twelve [jobs] was the final number we wanted," he says. If all the company got from the contract was the zipper clause and the elimination of the colors system, "We would have been 90 percent there." They did not get there in Deering's view because "Ballow felt that by being strong he could negotiate complete control," and instead he provoked a fight. "The union had always taken the position that they would give us manning concessions." But instead "we gave them a . . . contract that basically said you eat, shit, and sleep where and how and when we say. . . . [Ballow] used every tactic to humiliate and degrade them, and we would never listen to them."

Ballow's hammer worked, but it worked too well. When Alvino realized that cutting some legitimate jobs or surrendering a few overtime or no-show deals wasn't going to satisfy Ballow he began to panic. Negotiation sessions began to swing back and forth between emotional extremes, with Alvino alternately all but begging Ballow to offer him a deal he could sell to his members, and angrily warning that the drivers were tougher than Ballow realized.

Alvino wanted three things from Ballow: to replace his open-manning proposal with a number, to give buyouts to men who lost jobs, and above all to back off on selling the routes.

In return, Alvino, unlike Kennedy over at the pressmen's talks, made clear he was willing to cut nearly as many jobs as the company would have cut itself under open manning. He would agree to eliminate the fifty or so men on the retie line in Kearny. He might be willing to eliminate the whole colors delivery system: "If you think we are going to boo-hoo over 150 jobs we're not. We have the balls to do what we have to do," he told Ballow. "All I need is for you to tell me the number so I can see what the hardship is." He had "to be able to go to the membership and say we have X amount of steady jobs." But the company had to make a solid proposal, he said again and again. "The men won't cut their own positions."

As spring and summer wore on, Alvino appeared to become more and more frantic; a desperate and almost pathetic figure, embarrassing to some members of his own committee. Soon he was "negotiating against himself," promising lavish cuts if only the company would agree to a number and drop the idea of selling the routes; when Ballow said no, he would promise more lavish cuts. He'd heard from Hoge and Sloan that the company wanted to cut costs by 25 to 30 percent; he wanted Ballow to know the drivers could do that, no problem. Not enough? Well maybe, he told Ballow in June, the company should "add to its proposal and cut the routes down from 135 to seventy"; that would be "fine," but they have to forget about selling the routes. A few weeks later he walked into a meeting and said, "There are now 704 regular situation holders at the *News*. I am willing to cut that right now to 604," if Ballow would agree to set a number and not sell the routes. (Alvino's counts don't match the company's.) Ballow simply replied, "We are not going to guarantee a number." Alvino could only lamely reply, "Okay we'll cut that to 575."

Alvino, the federal mediators, and Tom Gleason, the drivers' lawyer, told Ballow repeatedly that there was no possibility that the union would agree to selling the routes. "Even if we were friends and sitting down at a barbecue in Tennessee," Alvino told Ballow, "I could never agree" to sell the routes. "There is no plane and no car fast enough to get us out of town" if we tell the membership we have agreed to this.

Ballow would only reply that he thought he and Mike were friends but they were still going to sell the routes and the union had to face that.

Alvino offered an alternative, an elaborate but possibly workable incentive system whereby the drivers would earn bonuses for increasing the circulation on their routes. For the drivers, who with their horror of writing things down hardly ever made formal counterproposals, and who lived for the side deal, the gentlemen's agreement, and allegedly the greased palm, it was a remarkably sophisticated and progressive proposal, especially considering that unions traditionally loathe incentive proposals. Ballow dismissed it summarily: "This . . . offer, if you want to call it that, only demonstrates that the union agrees that our concept of selling the routes is the way to increase circulation."

Alvino even had a clever buyout idea: If the company absolutely would not budge on selling the routes, the *News* should put the profits from the route sales into a buyout fund. With the routes selling for six-figure fees, the company could offer record buyouts and that might do the trick. Ballow flatly refused, saying the company wanted the windfall the sales would bring.

Gold says he and Ballow did not expect the union to agree to selling the routes. They hoped their "hammer" would make Alvino eager to agree to almost anything else, and by late summer they thought they were succeeding, and told Hoge there might soon be a deal. They were deceiving themselves. They had not understood their adversaries.

The drivers are not self-righteous men. Like many predominantly Italian-American unions, the NMDU shows little interest in union ideology, union romanticism, or traditional union values. Ballow was an adversary, even an enemy, who wanted to take away money and jobs the union wanted to keep. But unlike the Irish-led production unions, most of the drivers' leaders seemed to regard this not as a crime that cried out to heaven for vengeance but as a perfectly natural desire, albeit one that should be thwarted. During NMDU negotiations there were no grand speeches about the company's iniquities. In discussing the strike afterward, the drivers, unlike other union leaders, did not denounce the company for its impious anti-unionism, as if somehow companies had a moral obligation to be pro-union. Neither at the table nor in post-strike interviews did they talk much about the anti-union clauses in Ballow's contract.

In part because of this lack of self-righteousness Ballow and Gold were both far more comfortable with the drivers than with any other union. Despite many angry and silly moments, the drivers' negotiations were more relaxed, businesslike, and even friendlier than any others. As Ballow says, "The drivers were not choir boys, but they were much more straightforward," freely admitting (though not on the record), for instance, that the unions had agreed to stall and that no union would sign until all were ready. Ballow still talks to Alvino several times a year. And when Ballow had a hip replacement more than a year after the strike, he says, a number of the drivers called him in the hospital to wish him well.

Ballow and Gold had numerous off-the-record sessions with Alvino, Gleason, Diana, and other members of the negotiating committee, something they rarely did with other unions. During these sessions Gleason made it clear they were not going to get the routes sold. But, says Gold, he also told them that if they gave in on route sales and also cooled down their rhetoric a bit, Alvino, Gleason, Diana, and company would try to get a deal through the executive committee.

Gold calls Gleason the most professional negotiator from any of the *News*'s ten unions, someone who never "shadowboxed" and who understood the ritual dance. But precisely because they found the drivers and their lawyer more congenial than the other union leaders, and because Gold also believed the company was getting good intelligence ("G-2" Gold inevitably calls it), including reports from a *Daily News* employee who was dating a well-informed driver, they badly overestimated how well they were doing. Gold thought the final deal would be "pay only for work done, elimination of unnecessary [drivers' helpers], and elimination of the retie line but not the whole color operation," and that it would come in the fall.

His "G-2" was not good enough. Neither Gold nor Ballow realized how much they had weakened Alvino by their own tactics or how disgusted much of the executive committee was by Alvino's weakness.

One of the most discontented was Seymour Goldstein, a union business agent who was responsible for day shifts at the Brooklyn, Garden City, and New Jersey plants. Goldstein, a much smarter and tougher man than Alvino, had announced months before that he was going to run for union president against Alvino in the 1991 election. Goldstein is by his own description a "hothead," who as a business agent believed it was his job to fight the company at every turn and bitterly criticized Alvino and his ally Mike Diana for letting the company have its way.

Diana, the "nightside" business agent for the *News* drivers, tried to cooperate with some of Deering's changes, in effect following at the plants the same conciliatory strategy that Alvino was trying at the table.

Goldstein fought for a hardline policy on both fronts. He led the opposition to Deering's reforms. He effectively assumed some of Diana's responsibilities on the night shift, where he had some supporters at all the plants. As Deering remembers it, if there was a dispute during the Brooklyn night shift involving a Goldstein supporter, and Diana intervened with a supervisor to resolve the issue, the Goldstein man often refused to have the matter settled until Goldstein came down. And if Diana did settle a case involving one of Seymour's supporters, Seymour might show up in the Brooklyn plant the next day in a rage, upset the deal, and demand to renegotiate it.

Alvino was ready, even eager, to let go of the retie operation at Kearny, about fifty jobs. In fact as Ballow banged away at him it seemed he might even do it without getting a good buyout package for the men who would lose jobs.

Goldstein was furiously opposed; during the regular negotiating sessions it was almost the only substantive issue he ever spoke to. The company suspected the retie line was Goldstein's electoral power base and this was why he was so vocal. (Business agent is an elected position.) Goldstein denies that. But the retie line, claims Gold, was a rich source for the rackets. According to Gold, because the work really was unnecessary, it was a good place to plant no-shows. The Sunday color sections were a lucrative target for the bootleg operation; and controls were lax in the retie operation.

As the talks progressed Goldstein became more obviously discontented. He and Alvino snapped at each other in front of the company and there was real animosity between Goldstein and Gold. At the last meeting before the strike Goldstein threw a contract book at Gold and called him a "motherfucker."

Goldstein was convinced the negotiations could do no good, especially in Alvino's hands. He saw clearly that time was on Ballow's side. Behind the scenes he "was telling Mike we are never going to get a contract. There was a window of opportunity and it was closing." Unlike leaders from most of the other unions, he wanted a strike.

The window of opportunity was the Christmas advertising season, which starts just before Thanksgiving. Goldstein says he believed that if the company got through Christmas, its best money-making season of the year, without a strike the unions would be helpless to resist if the company declared an impasse. "After Christmas when advertising was slow they would have made their move." A strike, he believed, "was the only thing to do. If we did not have the strike there would be no *Daily News* today." He was not alone; the other unions might pride themselves on the cleverness of their no-strike policy, but by late summer a significant portion of the drivers' leadership shared Goldstein's views. LaChance, out on parole and getting ready to run for president again, may have been among them.[1] (In any event, LaChance seems to have profited from the strike. He was arrested afterward for illegally participating in the management of a wholesale distribution company that sold the *News* during the strike. The case has not yet come to trial.)

Despite all Ballow's efforts at intimidation, the members were ready to fight too. Ballow was in the business of scaring unions straight. But he had never faced a union like the drivers. Unlike Alvino, most of them were not scared. They were just mad: at Deering's crackdown, at the firings, at Ballow's demands, his bullying of Alvino, and at Alvino's weakness.

The other *News* unions, for all their own excesses, and their pride in controlling the plant, almost always thought and spoke of themselves as victims, united victims, victims strong in their solidarity, victims righteous in the pursuit of justice, but victims nonetheless.

The drivers did not think of themselves as victims. By the fall many of them were looking forward to a fight, not only because they had never lost a fight but because for all their devotion to business they were basic and violent men absolutely unwilling to be pushed around no matter how much it cost them to push back. Don Corleone, a man so admired by most Cosa Nostra members and associates that one might think he had actually lived, would have said they had balls, a compliment he reserved for men who would fight regardless of cost or gain, for principle alone, not the lofty principles of union romantics, but the principle that men who let themselves be pushed beyond a certain point were no longer men. They were about to earn the compliment.

CHAPTER 13

The Battle of Wounded Knee

That job can be done sitting down, standing on your head, standing on one foot, playing with yourself, or whatever you want.

NMDU leader

GARY Kalinich was a member of the drivers union, though he did not drive a truck. His job was to watch a tying machine bind bundles of newspapers and feed them onto a conveyor belt leading down to the waiting fleet of *News* delivery trucks. While watching the tying machine do its job, Kalinich was also supposed to place a protective top sheet on each bundle. This was a mindless and unnecessary job that could have been easily done by reliable and relatively inexpensive automated equipment. Gary Kalinich's top sheets could have been a metaphor for everything that was wrong with the *News*. But Gary Kalinich and his top sheets were destined to be transformed not into metaphor but history.

Jobs in packaging had long been a matter of contention between the drivers and the mailers. From the company's view anything having to do with bundling, counting, or moving newspapers into the trucks should be mailers' work; letting the drivers pack and count is an invitation to theft, especially if the drivers union happens to have ties to the Mafia. But the drivers, always far more powerful than the mailers, had fought for a share of these jobs and often had gotten their way, including control of the odds room, where drivers customized standard bundles into the precise sizes needed by particular customers.

Thus the mailing or packaging area is one of the few true mixed union sites in the plant. The result is not harmonious even at the best of times. The mailers resent the drivers as interlopers and their resentment is multiplied by fear. Go to the Brooklyn plant and try to talk to a mailer; as likely as not his first concern will be to make sure he is out of earshot of the drivers; his second concern will be to tell you not to "go out there," that is, to the loading dock, the drivers' turf: "You don't want to get close to those people and they never talk anyway." Now, of course, the tension was far higher than usual. Deering's crackdown, including the firings, made the packaging floor more orderly and efficient, but it did not improve tempers, any more than did a life of daily readiness for a bloody war that apparently would come only when the other side said so. And then, there was Seymour Goldstein.

With Diana, as some of the men saw it, falling down on his job by making things too easy for the company, the "dayside" union business agent, Seymour Goldstein, began spending more time on the nightside, especially at Garden City but also in Brooklyn.

"Officially that was Diana's job," Goldstein explains, but "Diana had a different kind of relationship with the company. His was not hostile. Mine was hostile. When the *News* wanted changes I stopped them. I stopped them every which way I could."

Despite or because of a quick temper and an abusive manner, Goldstein became something of a hero to some of the men, a real leader who would fight the company, not beg for a break, as Alvino had been doing at the table.

On the night of Wednesday, October 24, Gary Kalinich showed up for work in front of the conveyor belt. But instead of standing up and facing the belt, Kalinich sat down on some nearby metal shelves.

At approximately 11:30 P.M., a mailroom supervisor named Bob Gable told Kalinich he would have to stand up while attending the conveyor belt. The company says Kalinich had his back to the belt, that he was reading a newspaper, and that he was putting on the top sheets by reaching over his back without watching what he was doing, with the result that the sheets were going on crooked and fouling the tying machine. If the machine jams, the conveyor stops; that in turn can shut down the presses.

Kalinich refused to get up. He had torn cartilage in his left knee, and the doctor's note recommending he stay off his feet. He was doing this job because he had tripped over some plastic baling wire in his truck in June and had been on temporary light duty ever since. Besides, as one union leader commented, "That job can be done sitting down, standing on your head, standing on one foot, playing with yourself, or whatever you want."

The Battle of Wounded Knee, as it would be dubbed, had begun. Gable and Kalinich were arguing angrily when Seymour Goldstein walked up and, according to Goldstein, told Kalinich, "Sit down if you are in pain."

Company sources claim Goldstein told Kalinich, "You stay right where you are [sitting down] and put the top sheets on! You work for me." By then the tying machine had jammed again, Gable was trying to show Kalinich how to fix it, and then make him fix it himself. Kalinich, says the company, refused to cooperate. Some other drivers joined in the argument supporting Goldstein and challenging Gable's right to direct Kalinich, because, in the union way of looking at things, Gable was a mailers' supervisor and could not instruct a driver. But Gable was one of the new nonunion supervisors brought in by Deering, and the company believed that the old restrictions did not apply to nonunion supervisors. Whoever was right, the machine had now jammed again and a crowd was beginning to gather. This was beginning to get serious.

Dick Malone, the production manager for the Brooklyn plant, was called down to the floor. Malone told Gable to give Kalinich "one more chance to be accountable to you or face disciplinary action." He also says he said Kalinich could get a chair and sit, as long as he was facing the machine. That was not unusual, says Malone: lots of men sat in the packaging area. Then he called Steve Guida, Deering's protégé and successor as director of distribution, down to the floor and told him to deal with Goldstein.

Guida is a young, exceptionally bright, personable but tough, UPS-trained manager who, like Deering, who brought him to the *News*, cut his teeth in the business dealing with Teamsters. Like Deering, he understands that successfully managing a force of unionized drivers means prevailing in a constant power struggle without being a martinet—grasping the difference between never giving in on a principle and never giving an inch. Like Deering he was good at it; the drivers had made bigger gains in efficiency than any other department, but neither Guida nor Deering was hated by the drivers the way Malone was by the printing unions.

Guida, thirty-one years old, now became the point man in the dispute. But he had little room to maneuver. Unfortunately, the Goldstein incident had already become an issue of principle and Guida and everyone else began to act by the book, responding in a preprogrammed fashion to threats from which the company had decided long ago it could not back down, like a NORAD computer in a Hollywood nuclear nightmare relentlessly marching toward a war of mutual assured destruction.

Even before the June 17 AFL-CIO memo outlining the proposed union strategy, the Tribune Company was sure about one thing: the unions would stage a series of slowdowns and stoppages, some overt, some covert, like deliberate web breaks or conveyor jams. The unions had been doing it for years. It was their tactical bread and butter, their most effective weapon in winning the side deals and verbal reinterpretations of the contract that had given them rather than the company control of the plant floor. For a commodity more perishable than the fish it is used to wrap, a one-hour slowdown is devastating. Time and again managers had decided it just wasn't worth paying that price to win on what taken alone might be a small issue; by giving in on hundreds of small issues over decades management had emasculated itself.

The only way to fight back, Hoge's team had decided, was on principle: zero tolerance for slowdowns, shutdowns, or any illicit interference during the run. Men who broke the rules would be disciplined, up to and including suspensions or firing. A plantwide work slowdown or stoppage would be dealt with just as aggressively, if necessary by declaring any stopped workers to be on strike, removing them from the premises, and bringing in "permanent replacements."

Ballow made the point very clearly at the pressmen's negotiations when he told Kennedy if the presses ever again shut down to protest the appearance of a suit on the floor, "We will send people in to run those presses." Part of the purpose was psychological, to show the unions that the balance of power had changed, to make them feel helpless and prompt them to make concessions at the table. Part of the motive was legal: by establishing that the company would not tolerate such behavior the company would be in a stronger position legally if an incident such as that about to happen at the Brooklyn plant ever did happen. Mostly, however, management simply wanted to take away the unions' most destructive weapon—not only now during these negotiations but permanently.

To put an end to deliberate sabotage once and for all required a principle. You could not stand tall sometimes and back down on other occasions, because that would still leave the unions an incentive to use the tactic. Like governments that announce they will never negotiate for hostages, the company had to be willing to risk a few potentially explosive incidents in order to deprive their opponents of a fearsome weapon.

As Guida saw it, Goldstein had forced the principle into play. As a union rep, he had a contractual right to be at the work site, but he was contractually forbidden to direct the work force, which he had done by telling Kalinich to sit down. That was management's prerogative. If management had overstepped its bounds, Kalinich and Goldstein could file a grievance to be settled later by the prescribed arbitration procedure. There had to be some consequences; simply stopping Goldstein from interfering this time was not enough: it gave him no reason not to try it again. Goldstein would have to go.

Depending on whom you talk to, Seymour Goldstein had either been testing the company's limits, trying to provoke a strike, or just being "hostile" (Goldstein's own interpretation) for some time. Just a few weeks before, Goldstein had been refused entry to the Garden City plant because he would not sign an entry ledger (a new requirement for union officers not on shift). About thirty drivers walked off the job for two hours in support of Goldstein. A strike had been averted only because Bill Deering and Mike Alvino had been able to talk Goldstein and his men back inside before a busload of replacement workers arrived on the scene. But the bus had been on the way.

Guida was determined that Goldstein would get no slack this time. Guida considered Goldstein a troublemaker, and believed he had either deliberately provoked the Garden City incident or at least used it to find out if the company really did have replacements ready to roll. Nevertheless Guida started by trying to do himself a favor. Mike Diana had asked to be alerted if Goldstein got involved in an incident at the plant. So Guida rang up Diana and said, "You got Seymour here; there's going to be a problem. He's probably going to be thrown out of the building."

Diana, extremely upset, urged Guida not to do anything irrevocable before he could get there, which was fine with Guida. If Diana could get Goldstein to leave voluntarily, the whole thing might blow over.

It didn't. Guida and union Vice President Robert Polletta met with Goldstein to discuss the situation. Diana joined them. Goldstein told his side of the story: he had not been directing the work force but only helping a fellow human being in pain.

In Guida's mind there was no question Seymour had countermanded a supervisor's orders. He told Goldstein he would have to leave.

As Guida remembers it, Goldstein then said, "Fine. Just let security escort me out."

Guida, who hoped to do this as undramatically as possible, said, "You have your choice, do you want to go out alone or do you want security?"

Goldstein said, "I want security."

As Goldstein was escorted from the building, Polletta and Diana practically begged Guida not to eject Goldstein.

"This is it," they kept telling him. "If you do this, they're gone and not coming back . . ."

Nevertheless Guida was surprised a few minutes later when some supervisors came into the office where he was still negotiating with Polletta and Diana and told him that work had stopped, a number of drivers had left the building and were milling around on the street, and about fifty mailers and drivers were standing idle at their work stations.

Guida turned to Diana and told him, "Get the guys back in here; find out what's going on." The two union officers went outside to try to calm things down but were back within minutes telling Guida they couldn't do anything. The drivers had walked out in sympathy with Goldstein and would not return until he did.

"It doesn't look too good," they told Guida. "You've got to get Seymour back. . . . If this happens we're all dead. This is the beginning of the end. . . . Don't you see, this is not what we wanted?"

Guida would not budge. He not only accepted the policy of zero tolerance for slowdowns and walkouts, he truly believed in it. As a distribution manager he lived for the minute saved and suffered through every delay. His brief tenure at the *News* had convinced him the company could never build a decent distribution system if the unions could shut down the company every time they wanted to prove a point. The very essence of Guida's job, first under Deering and now with himself in charge of distribution, had been to establish what he regarded as a normal labor-management relationship, to maintain management's rights to direct the work force. If the unions had a problem they would just have to play by the rules, stay on the job, and file a grievance later. Even the Teamsters did that. No negotiating with terrorists.

Now the NORAD computer really began to roll. After the brief Garden City walkout a few weeks before, the company team had worked out in some detail a contingency plan that would bring Gold, Ballow,

Gene Bell, Human Resources head John Sloan, and to a lesser extent Hoge directly into the loop if another incident occurred. By refusing to allow Goldstein back into the plant, even at the price of a walkout, and informing Malone that the situation could not be resolved, and that the work force had walked off the job, halting production, Guida triggered the plan.

Shortly after 2:20 A.M., according to company records, Malone informed Gold the drivers had walked, Gold called John Sloan to tell him what was going on, and Sloan, as per plan, called Hoge. But Hoge did not assume direct control of the situation or make any of the crucial decisions in the next few hours. The plan did not call for him to do that, and it was the plan to which everyone now responded.

Brumback ally Gene Bell, the Tribune VP for newspaper operations who was informally serving as the *News*'s general manager for the duration, took responsibility for such local operational decisions as getting the replacement drivers, on call at a hotel on Long Island, under way. Ballow was on the West Coast, but at 2:30 A.M. (a rare Gold lapse into round numbers) Gold set up a conference call that lasted 174 minutes (his old self again) among himself, Ballow, and at different times Sloan, Bell, Malone, and Guida.

Ballow, Gold, Bell, and the others were not, strictly speaking, making decisions. The script had been written long before. The company would replace workers who had walked, and do it so quickly that the walkout would not delay even that day's paper. But the company still had a legal obligation to respond appropriately to any decisions the union or individual workers might make. A worker, for instance, is not "replaced" until a new man is on the job; the men outside had a legal right to come back in until then, and any company action to prevent their return would be an extremely serious unfair labor practice. Ballow and Gold's primary objective now was to keep the situation clean legally.

Alvino called Gold while the conference call was going on. As Gold remembers it, Alvino was "panicked not angry,"[1] and tried to convince him to put a stop to the incident at least for tonight by letting Goldstein come back. Gold refused.

The first busload of a dozen replacements arrived within less than an hour of the walkout. "If I could have had a topless dancer in the neighborhood, I couldn't get twenty guys together that fast," Augie Spiers, a drivers union official, later cracked.

The violence started immediately. The driver of the bus, which bore Pennsylvania plates and carried a few guards as well as the dozen drivers, tried to pull up to the main entrance on Pacific Street. He found the way blocked by an angry crowd. Next he headed around the block to a back entrance, but instead slammed into a trash can barricade improvised by protesting drivers. A mob pelted the stopped bus with a barrage of rocks, bricks, and trash cans, smashing the windshield and mirrors, and a side door. Some press accounts put the number of attackers as high as 200. The bus driver pulled out, radioed for help, and retreated to the parking lot of McDonald's on Tillary Street.

A new bus with more replacements met the first, and both buses proceeded back to the plant. The handful of police officers who had arrived told the bus drivers they could not yet guarantee their safety, and the buses retreated again.

Sometime in the next few hours, a crowd of strikers broke into the nearby fenced and walled parking lot full of *News* delivery trucks, fire-bombing three and slashing the tires and puncturing the radiators of forty more.

Meanwhile some of the police officers on the scene tried to mediate, urging Guida to let the workers back in before things got out of hand. Guida says he told them they were welcome back. Legally they had not yet been replaced and had every right to come back. But now there was a new wrinkle: Not only could Goldstein not return but, Guida said, no driver who had broken the law would be allowed back in.

Substantively the point was moot; the officers had not yet made any arrests (though they would shortly) and there was too much confusion to sort out who had thrown things at the buses. But it was another company condition and the drivers were in no mood to play according to the company's rules. They stayed put.

By the time the first bus of replacement workers arrived about 200 drivers were out on the street, including nearly all that should have been inside and many of those who would normally be outside by the loading docks. Thus in the company's version perhaps as many as 200 men had struck—most of the Brooklyn shift except for the men who had already left to do their routes before Goldstein was escorted from the plant. The union saw things very differently. The next day, Alvino and many drivers claimed that although about thirty drivers had originally walked out in sympathy with Goldstein, the rest were forced out of the building by management and refused reentry. A driver named Vincent Pelligrino told *New York Newsday* columnist Jim Dwyer, "They sent us outside to back in the trucks while they were throwing out our business agent. And we turned to come back in, and they told us, 'You're out and stay out.' Now they say we walked out."[2] According to other reports *News* managers told some drivers either outside or near the door that if they wanted to work they would have to walk around the block to the east entrance. This caused a considerable argument and the managers eventually told the men to go where they were told or leave.[3] The drivers would eventually make a formal charge to the NLRB that they had been forced out of the building against their will, an offense that might have been enough to turn every day of the strike that followed into an unfair labor practice strike, rather than an economic strike, costing the company tens of millions in back pay for striking workers and forcing it to reinstate any replaced striker.

Outside, the protesting drivers controlled the streets. It was not until about 5 A.M. that the police felt strong enough to try to clear the area around the plant. They made the first two arrests of the strike, both of drivers, one for disorderly conduct and one for letting the air out of the tires of a delivery truck. Ten Sanitation Department tow trucks arrived to clear away the forty disabled *News* delivery trucks. By then the immediate area around the plant had been sealed off by more than one hundred police equipped with riot gear. But it was not until 7:20 A.M., just about five hours after the replacement workers had been called, and long after the last truck carrying an A.M. edition normally would have left the Brooklyn plant, that the replacement drivers were escorted into the building by police. Members of the other unions were cleared from the building by security and some replacement workers for other departments began arriving, though only the drivers, and only sixty of them, had been officially replaced. The first delivery trucks, each carrying two replacement workers—one driver, and one security guard handling a radio connecting the truck to *News* security forces—did not roll until 8:25 A.M., six hours behind schedule. When they did roll they moved in convoys of three with police escorts front and rear.

The next day a *Times* reporter asked Gary Kalinich if he believed the incident had been deliberately provoked by the company. "Oh, most definitely," he replied.[4]

The belief that the Kalinich-Goldstein incident was a setup is commonly and passionately held on both sides, though of course people disagree about which side did the setting up. Many company people believe it was set up by Goldstein, perhaps at Doug LaChance's instigation. Most of the union people believe it was set up by the company, on orders from Ballow and perhaps Brumback.

There are exceptions. At least some senior union sources believe Goldstein deliberately set out to start a strike; and some former *Daily News* managers are convinced that the incident was the company's doing. Either might be true, but the available evidence for either is slim.

The company case for saying Goldstein did it on purpose relies on only two or three pieces of what could be called evidence, thin and circumstantial at best. Goldstein thought the drivers should strike and made no secret of it. And Goldstein had been the cause of the Garden City incident only three weeks before that nearly produced the same result, which leads Hoge, Gold, and others to conclude he was provoking incidents on purpose until he got lucky and started a strike. Goldstein is believed to be a LaChance ally. Cronin says he wanted to be a LaChance "clone." Some *News* executives believe LaChance wanted a strike because Alvino would not survive a strike politically. Finally, even in the first few hours, the union violence, the three truck firebombings for example, had an organized feel to it. As Gold remarks, "I know the drivers are tough guys, but I don't think they carry Molotov cocktails around wherever they go. And slashing tires and puncturing radiators on forty trucks is a lot of work. Someone was ready."

Goldstein vigorously denies he provoked the incident on purpose: "If I had the opportunity and the authority, I would have struck them a long time ago. But it was not up to me. I just got lucky."

Goldstein in turn believes the company planned everything. "It was a setup. They knew I was going to be there. . . . They knew how short my fuse was." What really convinces him however was that he almost was not there. He says he was in nearby Freddy's bar, the hangout for guys from the Brooklyn plant, talking to Daniel McPhee, a pressmen's business rep, when he got a call from a company supervisor, not a union guy but one of the new management supervisors, who told him there was a problem at the plant and could he please come right over. He does not remember the supervisor's name but says that if he hadn't gotten that call he never would have been around when Kalinich had his run-in with Gable. "If I wanted to precipitate a strike that night I would have

been there" in the first place. McPhee does not remember seeing Goldstein that night.

Bill Deering also believes the company either deliberately provoked
the incident or else jumped on it as a way to precipitate a strike. Deering says that if he had been at the plant he could have gotten Goldstein
to cool off and back down again, as Deering got him to do during the
Garden City incident. The reason Deering was not around on the 25th,
he says, is that Ballow was annoyed that Deering had resolved the
situation in Garden City instead of allowing it to escalate into a strike
(although he says he never heard Ballow say this). One week later
Deering was given a raise and a promotion to director of circulation
sales, a department staffed mostly by Guild members, from which Deering would have no direct contact with the delivery system. Guida, Deering's protégé, was put in Deering's old place.

Deering believes the move was made so that if there was a future
incident, Ballow and Gold, and Malone, the loyal Tribune Company
executive so hated by the pressmen, would control the situation without
the interference of somebody of Deering's stature. "They . . . put Steve
Guida in my place. . . . Steve is a good kid but I was in a totally different
financial and professional situation. They really were not in a position to
push me around."

Hoge says the reason Deering was moved to circulation sales was that
he had quickly proven himself one of the best managers in the company, and the man who had been in that slot was making no progress.
Ballow says he had no part in reassigning Deering and credits Alvino,
not Deering, with resolving the Garden City incident. Guida, who is
close to Deering, says he knows of no reason to believe Deering was
kicked upstairs because of the Garden City incident. He does say he
believed in taking a harder line than Deering did. Deering, he says, has
great skill in talking out a tense situation, but Guida believes that if you
have to "talk out" a potential strike whenever the union gets mad, the
company will not be able to make any progress in building the business.

Deering's testimony is far more damning than anything that can be
said for the "Goldstein did it" theory. On balance, however, the notion
that the company conspired to provoke the incident makes little sense.
It would have been an enormous legal risk for little gain. A strike proved
to be so provoked would almost certainly be ruled an unfair labor practices strike rather than an economic strike, bringing enormous financial
penalties on the company. Tens of millions of dollars would depend on

keeping secret a conspiracy known to three people at a minimum (Ballow, Gold, and at least one manager at the plant) and suspected by many others, including Deering, who would be likely to be in a position to offer damning circumstantial testimony.

And for what? The company believed it was making progress with the drivers. At the last meeting with the pressmen the two sides had for the first time exchanged significant and mutually responsive buyout proposals, suggesting that they could agree at least on the context of a settlement.[5] Even if the company had wanted a strike, October 25 was, give or take a few days, the worst day of the year to provoke one. The next sixty days were Goldstein's "window of opportunity," the holiday ad season when the company would have the most to lose and the unions would have more economic leverage than any other time in the year. January would be the time for the company to provoke a strike. Moreover, as Longson points out, in late summer the company cut down on costly strike readiness, in part because the lawyers had made it clear there probably would be no impasse declaration and therefore probably no strike until after the new year.

Nor is any conspiracy theory necessary. The combination of Goldstein's hostility, the frustration of the drivers, the company's policy of zero tolerance for slowdowns, the general air of brinkmanship inspired by Ballow's approach, the eagerness of everyone charged with executing the contingency plans to do their jobs well, the decision to go on automatic and remove human judgment, particularly Hoge's, from the equation in the event of a work stoppage, all together provide a quite adequate explanation for what happened.

Guida's decision to stand firm had put into motion forces that would eventually drive the Tribune Company from New York. And yet even today Guida, Gold, Hoge, and nearly everyone else who was involved on the company's side that night say it was the right decision. After all, they say, it was never certain that they could save the *News*. The one thing that was clear was that unless management regained control of the workplace, the paper would die. There was no point to deceiving themselves; if they couldn't stop the walkouts they couldn't win the larger battle.

As Guida put it, the company had to finally say to the unions, " 'You can walk, but this time we're going to put the paper out. We're not going to cave. The game has changed.' And they said, 'We're out. You can bring your replacement workers in and we'll see what happens.' And the gloves came off, and that's what happened that night."

And that night anyway, that was all that happened. Even as the replacement-driven trucks rolled on the morning of the 25th, the brink still had not been passed. There was still time for both sides to step back, to shout "do-over," to announce offsetting penalties and agree to repeat the play. The real mystery is not why the two sides went to the brink the night before, but why in the clear light of day, in full view of the abyss, they did not step back.

CHAPTER 14

No Do-Overs

We saw an opportunity to take the paper into the modern age.
Edward Gold

ALVINO was beside himself.

As much as any union leader he had wanted to avoid a strike. Repeatedly during negotiating sessions he had lamented to Ballow that his term as president, which he had wanted so badly, had come at a time like this. Now he seemed overwhelmed, betrayed, angry all at once.

All morning long he told anyone who would listen that the drivers had not struck and had no intention of striking. They had been locked out. Even allowing for the honorable romantic tradition of union hyperbole, his interviews with the press verged on the hysterical:

"I feel like Berlin is better off than we are," he told some reporters. What had happened was like a "war movie, where the Nazis come to town and pick out who is going to be hostages."

All morning long, as Alvino raged, the company's contingency plan raced along. The complicated machinery set up by Longson's contingency team, and more than a year of planning and training and tens of millions of dollars' worth of preparations swung into action.

The *News*'s spruced-up human resources staff began arriving at the 42nd Street headquarters at first light. The building was already ringed with police in full riot gear, including helmets and face shields, adding a sci-fi touch to the always surreal sight of Manhattan's concrete canyons at dawn. Human resources manager Robyn Hill and her staff immediately began preparations to hire hundreds of people in the next few days, some of whom would be put to work that very night, and transport them into the plants via guarded, bulletproof buses.

That morning the *News* began flying in employees of Tribune Company papers from across the country to serve as the backbone of the replacement force. The earliest set of replacements would be working round-the-clock shifts, like medical interns on perpetual call, not leaving the building for up to two weeks. In part this was for security reasons, and in part it was because experienced workers were at a premium. In any event, the first men bused into the plant were not just going to work; they were setting up camp. Hill had to play quartermaster as well, supplying cots, blankets, underwear, socks, and perhaps most important given the prospect of the next two weeks, deodorant.

And then, suddenly, there came a pause in the action, one last chance for both sides to step back from the brink.

Alvino, McDonald, and Kheel resolved to go see Hoge. They wanted to make an end run around the lunatics, as they thought of them, who were controlling events, and make a last plea to work things out. Alvino and company decided to appeal to Hoge's decency, which they still believed in, partly because he had been so invisible while Ballow pursued his battle plan.

At 3 P.M. they strode into the lobby of the *News* building and asked for Hoge. But even in this dire hour, the man who had been a phantom for months refused to see them. Instead they were met by Gold and two King & Ballow lawyers, Mike Oesterle and Bud Johansen.

Alvino's proposal was simple: Let's call the whole thing off. There had been no strike. Nobody had meant to strike. It was a misunderstanding. Everyone, even the thirty or so guys who had originally walked out in solidarity with Goldstein, wanted to forget the whole thing and come back.

The lawyers replied in full-bore legalese. The drivers, or at least some of the drivers, had struck, giving the company the right to "permanently" replace them. It had permanently replaced roughly sixty, the number of replacements who were brought in last night. Even the men who had been replaced were not fired, they had conditional legal rights to return to their jobs should those jobs become available. But those jobs were not available at this moment; they had been filled by the replacements.

Moreover, he continued, once a strike had commenced, none of the men who walked out could come back except by making an "unconditional offer to return," that is, an offer to return under whatever working conditions the company established in lieu of a contract. Alvino had established a condition: all the men who had walked out, even those who had been replaced, must be allowed back in. That made his offer conditional rather than unconditional and gave the company the right to reject it. The company did reject it.[1]

Alvino and company tried another tack. Okay, they explained, we disagree about what happened last night. The contract provides a way of settling such disagreements. We should submit any dispute about what happened to arbitration. The arbitrator might well find the company within its rights to suspend or even fire Kalinich, and maybe every single man who walked off the job. Wouldn't that be good enough? After all, if these guys did do something wrong it was more like insubordination, the kind of thing one guy, or even a crowd of guys are fired for, not a strike for which you go after the whole union.

No, said the lawyers. The company was through being threatened with walkouts. On this issue we will not submit our fate to arbitrators. Besides, Gold pointed out, these guys burned three trucks and vandalized forty. That's not just insubordination. There is no way the company can pretend that something very serious had not happened. However, the company certainly does not wish to force the drivers into a strike or to punish all for the actions of a few. So all the unreplaced drivers were perfectly welcome to come to work tonight under normal conditions (the legally continued terms of the lapsed contract). The replaced workers, however, would not be allowed in. If the union thought the company was wrong it should go to the NLRB or to court. If the union won, the men would have their jobs back with back pay.

But who exactly had been replaced?

Oddly enough, the crucial legal issue was not how many people had walked out, but how many people had been brought in to replace them. It is not by walking out that a man loses his spot, but by the act of being replaced. The drivers legally could have come back in at any point until the replacement workers actually arrived on the job.

In the company's view sixty men had been replaced because at least that many had walked and that was how many replacements the company brought in. But, also in the company's view, it was not necessarily the men who walked who were replaced. Given the nature of employment at the *News*, wherein the company guaranteed a certain number of positions or job slots, but it was the union that maintained the "priority" lists that decided who worked when, it made more sense to speak of replacing not men but job slots. Besides, things had been pretty confused last night. So the company's position was that the sixty lowest-priority full-time drivers would be designated as the men who had lost their job slots to the replacements. If any of those men showed up they would be turned away.

The lawyers were confident their position, which to common sense seems grotesquely unjust, was legally unassailable. But legal or not, there was no way the union leaders could accept it. Alvino could never sell it. By now the rank and file were ready, even eager to fight. The war had actually begun. Goldstein, furious that the drivers had not yet made serious contingency plans of their own, was already helping to organize men to fight the company in the streets "with a vengeance," as he would later say. It would take some doing to keep the membership from striking even if the company accepted the arbitration proposal. Alvino told the lawyers the company would have to back down or there would be a strike.

Gold replied that it was their decision. The company was not forcing them into a strike. It was outrageous to blame the company for what the union was about to do, simply because the company refused to be intimidated by wildcat strikes and slowdowns. If there was a strike it would be on the union's head.

Alvino, Kheel, and McDonald left.

The company would stick with the program. Even now at the brink of a strike at the worst possible time of the year, with Ballow apparently winning at the table, the company would, in classic Ballow style, fully enforce its legal rights, admit no weakness or fear, act as if it regarded the unions as powerless and a strike as an inconvenience at worst and an opportunity at best. Even now at the brink of a shooting war it was the psychological war that kept the company's attention. Above all the company seemed to want to hold on to the advantages of its own growing will to power, nurtured by eighteen months of finally being on the offensive, of doing the intimidating after decades of being intimidated. Even now the Tribune Company would continue to try to force the union to respond to its agenda. Never again would it willingly put itself in the position of responding to a union threat, or playing by the union's rules.

Hoge's continued unavailability was a symbol of the company's determination to stick with the program. Months before, Hoge had agreed to disappear. But, says Gold, some of the lawyers still worried that Hoge would pick some critical moment to try to decide events with a single dramatic gesture, as befits an "amateur" who believes in "strategy" rather than "process." That afternoon was just the sort of moment an amateur might choose to throw away months of inexorable psychological, legal, and economic warfare, say by offering to call last night off if the union would sit down right now and make, say, three key concessions. That would change the whole atmosphere of the negotiations, setting up a crisis-inspired mini-negotiation separable both psychologically and in principle from all that had gone before, a unique episode with its own parameters, imperatives, and, most important, its own deadlines applicable to the company as well as the union. The likely result of that sort of thing was that the company, having admitted into negotiations the sense of urgency it had worked for months to banish, would end up settling for one and a half of its three demands—a good showing in ordinary times but a disaster when one had spent more than a year and many millions of dollars on a plan to get it all.

Gold need not have worried. Hoge had no intention of blinking. Although Hoge "knew there was room for play" that afternoon, he saw there was not as much room as might be hoped. The company, like the unions, had to react not only to what the union had done but what it might do. Because Hoge believed that Goldstein had been deliberately trying to provoke a strike on behalf of once and future president Douglas LaChance and that "Alvino was not a strong leader . . . and not really in control of that union," he feared a strike might be coming anyway, no matter what Alvino said or the company did. If that were the case, the contingency plan must not be derailed. Only a handful of American newspapers had ever successfully published through a strike, none had ever done so in a pro-union city in which 80 percent of a paper's circulation was through newsstands, which is to say, in New York. The *News* could not sacrifice the slightest advantage.

The company, Hoge and most of the team believed (Gold is an exception), could win a strike only by having its way from the very beginning: never miss an edition, keep up the momentum, keep advertisers and readers on board, and crush the strikers psychologically. Even though the company had moved to a lower level of alert in the past few months, with fewer guards actually on duty and fewer emergency replacement workers on immediate call, "never miss an edition" was still the goal.

One of Hoge's fears was that backing down now would create a logistical nightmare for next time: "You've got replacement workers you have trained and they are sitting there month after month. You bring them in. Then you fire them the next day." You lose not only "credibility" but the replacement workers. If they "were not going to be used they would have no more incentive to stay."

Long after it was all over, Hoge maintained he still would not have changed the decision: the *News* had run out of time, it could not afford the drawn-out half victory it might end up with if it blinked now. "Remember, we are losing a lot of money at this time . . . we are looking at big losses this year, bigger the next year, negotiations with no end in sight, we could be doing the same thing and losing twenty, thirty, forty million next spring. So you can't give away your sword."

With Deering and Guida riding herd on the drivers, and Malone doing the same with the production unions, the *News* was a dramatically different company than it had been a year before. The paper had operated in the black in September and in the first three weeks of October, and probably would have made a profit for the quarter. Bill Deering and Barbara Kalish, a holdover from the pre-Ballow labor relations staff, both of whom took the "Brumback mantra" to "take control of the business" to mean literally and simply reasserting a normal labor-management relationship, would say that the mission had been largely accomplished. So one might ask, why go to war? But Hoge would argue that the company had been able to make such progress only because it had its "cannon on the ridge." It could not spike them now.

Longson, who like Ballow was out of town at the time, agrees: "If we had said 'do over,' that's probably what would have happened; they would have discovered a way to strike us without striking us. And if they could engage in intermittent walkouts three or four times a month, they could substantially disrupt the paper and have a lot of the effect of a strike without calling a strike." As Ballow adds, "How many times do you let them disrupt your business and then say 'all is forgiven'? They had been doing it and doing it and sometime it had to come to a head. Yes, we had to consider that this might bring on a strike, but they had things to consider too. They had choices to make and we had choices to make. But it had to be understood that we would not take it anymore. We had had a bellyful."

For Gold, the devoted Ballow disciple, as always the crucial considerations were not logistical but psychological.

"You can't just 'blow things over,' " Gold says, because you are then saying you are not willing to take a strike. "If we said we don't want a strike, we would lose control. And all along we had been gaining more control" over the business and at the bargaining table. So at the meeting with Alvino and company "we were playing hardball" but "we did leave them options."

Gold still feels it would have been easier for the unions to back down than for the company. The unions could send everyone but the replaced men back to work, drag the company before the NLRB, and probably win (though the company, he says, would probably win on appeal in federal court). The practical damage to the workers, meanwhile, would be minimal. "If you have a union [hiring] hall, a few dozen guys" being replaced "does not mean anything" because the replaced men "could be shuffled into the *Times* or the *Post*."

Gold makes one last psychological point, perhaps the most important, because it illuminates the effect of Ballow's strategy on the company itself: you cannot *appear* to be ready for a strike, he explains, without *really* being ready for a strike, psychologically as well as logistically. "The whole time we had a split personality. If they are not going to strike we are not going to force it, but we were always ready." By the night of the incident the atmosphere was like "a prize fight. It was two heavyweights going toe to toe."

And now the union, in the company's view, had swung first.

"They had damaged the equipment. They had firebombs the first night." This was not the way the company had planned for things to go, but now "we saw an opportunity to take the paper into the modern age" and "we believed we were ready and we could handle it."

The company answered the bell.

For the drivers, the earliest shift would start at 9 P.M., when the "countrymen," the guys who hauled early editions of the paper up to Connecticut, or upstate New York, or out to Pennsylvania, normally checked in. But by dusk dozens and soon hundreds of drivers began gathering near the Brooklyn plant, at the corner of Dean Street and Sixth Avenue.

Not far away is one of Brooklyn's most visible[2] monuments, the Williamsburg Bank tower, topped by a large clock, a good old-fashioned clock with illuminated red hands, visible for several miles.

When the bank clock showed a few minutes before nine, Mike Alvino stepped out from the crowd and began walking toward the plant door where the drivers normally entered.

The men from the corner followed.

As he reached the corner of Carlton and Dean, Alvino stopped, turned, and shouted back to the men behind him that all the nine o'clock starters should come up to the head of the line with him. When the clock showed 9:05 the procession was stopped by a police barrier on Pacific Street.

Alvino squeezed past the barrier, and stood alone for a moment on the other side.

He was a weak man who for months had been frightened and out of his depth. But now, relieved of the burdens of strategy and politics, no longer bedeviled by inscrutable labor lawyers or impetuous union rivals, now just a good captain on the street, Alvino played his part well.

Alone on the other side of the barricade, he shouted, "All countrymen here."

Twenty-four men filtered out of the procession and joined the union boss.

Alvino led them to the plant door, where they were met by Alan Waters, a supervisor. Waters asked Alvino who was coming to work.

Alvino's list included one Willie Gladdick. Waters consulted his own list, which showed Gladdick as one of the low-priority drivers that had been designated as "replaced." He told Alvino that Gladdick would not be allowed in.

The two men talked for nearly fifteen minutes but to no good. Finally Alvino and all twenty-four drivers turned and walked away. But before he got out of earshot of Waters, Alvino turned around and shouted back:

"We want all these people [the replacement workers] in our unit, at $600 initiation fee and $30 a month dues."

As he approached the barricade and the crowd of waiting drivers, somebody handed Alvino a bullhorn. At 9:45 by the Williamsburg clock, Mike Alvino shouted through the bullhorn, his voice coming out loud but slightly distorted by the cheap electronics, in the way emergency announcements in New York always seem to sound:

"We are at the point of no return. We are officially on strike for unfair labor practices." Then as if to emphasize that this was not about money: "There ain't five cents on the table."

Within minutes an emergency meeting of the pressmen's union, called at nearby Freddy's bar, voted to join the strike.

"They have driven another brother union to an unfair labor practice strike," Jack Kennedy told his men. "We are not going to work for the *Daily News* tonight. We are going to work for the union."

Within a few hours seven more unions announced that they were either joining the strike or, pending such a decision, would honor their brother unions' picket lines. The printers refused to put their lifetime contracts at risk and said they would cross the lines and come to work. That was all expected.

The one worrisome note for the union leaders was that the Guild had not yet joined the strike. Tonight anyway, Lipton would not go beyond a commitment to observe the picket lines until further notice.

Kennedy's letter to Gold making the strike official stressed that this was not an economic strike. The union had struck against unfair labor practices, including the company's "poisoning" of the atmosphere of negotiations, harassing workers at the plants, and refusing to negotiate in good faith.

The next day the drivers union filed an unfair labor practice complaint against the *News* with the regional NLRB, charging that the events of the night of the 24th and the early morning of the 25th were the result of a conspiracy to perpetrate an illegal lockout of the work force. Several months later the regional general counsel of the NLRB agreed to prosecute the complaint against the *News*. Such an agreement is equivalent to a preliminary finding that there may be some merit to the complainant's case. But the strike ended and the paper was sold to Robert Maxwell before the general counsel could bring his case. The matter became moot, and history was deprived of any official, neutral inquiry into what had happened that night.

Now the drivers and some of their brothers from the other unions went out, as Seymour Goldstein would say, "with a vengeance."

On this, the first official night of the strike, vengeance mostly took the form of larger, better-organized versions of the previous night's activities. At all three plants buses carrying replacement workers were attacked by hundreds of rock-, bottle-, and brick-throwing picketers. In Garden City several busloads of replacement workers were repeatedly turned back from the plant by volleys of rocks and bottles hurled from a crowd of as many as 300 strikers. At the Brooklyn and Kearny plants workers chanting "scabs, scabs" smashed windows and windshields of several buses that had already delivered their workers and were trying to leave the plants. At both the Brooklyn and Kearny plants delivery trucks were set on fire. In Manhattan at around 5 A.M. Friday morning a delivery truck burst into flames at Seventh Avenue and 42nd Street, the replacement driver escaping just in time to avoid serious injury. In Brooklyn the replacement driver of a *News* truck stopped on Eastern

Parkway was pushed out of his truck and punched. He was hospitalized with injuries, and the truck was towed away. Outside the Brooklyn plant, two police officers were hurt and one picketer, Joseph Kenniff of Westbury, was arrested for second-degree assault and criminal possession of a weapon, which turned out to be a rock. In the course of the night there were three arrests in Brooklyn, two in Kearny, and six in Garden City.

Every plant was behind schedule. The first *News* trucks to roll that night did not leave Kearny until nearly 2:20 A.M. Friday morning. Two trucks pulled out of the complex and were pelted with rocks but were able to get away because a cordon of eighteen police officers in riot gear kept strikers from blocking their way. Garden City and Brooklyn were even further behind schedule.

Not all the strikers were so effective. In Brooklyn, shortly after midnight, about one hundred strikers began an informal demonstration, marching from Pacific Street and Sixth Avenue toward Flatbush and Atlantic and chanting, "Don't buy the *News*." Perhaps the futility of a small group of protesters marching around the lightly peopled streets of Brooklyn after midnight had just begun to dawn on them when they noticed a replacement bus parked on the corner of Atlantic and Flatbush with only the driver inside.

This made more sense.

As the crowd swarmed toward the unprotected target one woman striker shouted, "Tip it over."

The crowd responded and began rhythmically rocking the bus side to side, each time a little bit closer to flipping it, as the terrified driver scrambled to find a safe place from which to take the fall.

The bus was just about to go when a single riot-equipped police officer showed up and succeeded in chasing the strikers away. The strikers consoled themselves for this slightly shaming setback by marching back toward the plant, near which they captured some wooden warehouse pallets, perfect for making a bonfire in the street, which they did.

Two days after the strike began, reporter Alex Jones wrote in the *New York Times*, "The strike by unions at The Daily News is just what the paper's management had been hoping for, and from the union perspective even trying to provoke, but it is a disaster for the paper's labor leaders, who had sought desperately to avoid a strike if at all possible."[3]

That was the almost universal opinion in the city, and not only among reporters. Before the week was out even some top union advisors had convinced themselves that the strike was lost because the *News* had managed to print and distribute close to 600,000 papers for Friday, raising the total to 700,000 for Saturday, which normally ran only 900,000 anyway.

But a paperhandler named Willy gave another *Times* reporter a more informed view:

"They may try to get the paper out, but they'll never get it out to the streets. And if they do we'll drag it off the newsstands."[4]

CHAPTER 15

The High Ground

Passing moral judgments is a great business, and I am delighted to be in it because of the pay.

Jimmy Breslin

THAT first night, when the drivers, pressmen, and the other blue-collar unions took the fight to the streets, they were not alone. John Roca, a *News* photographer, was one of many Guild members who joined the melee. The only difference was that Roca and his fellow Guild members didn't show up to hurl bricks or set bonfires but to photograph and report on their union brothers who were doing so.

Roca came close to becoming one of the strike's first casualties. Running up to a crowd of strikers, one of whom was busy smashing the windows of a replacement bus with a trash can while others tossed rocks, bottles, and eggs, and another smashed up the taillights with a brick, Roca began doing what he does: taking pictures.

The crowd, apparently thinking Roca was a *News* security officer trying to document union violence, turned on him.

"No pictures!" they shouted, and chased him back up Dean Street, which, fortunately, for Roca, was back toward his car. Along the way, he saw Joanna Molloy, a writer who had joined the *News* just three weeks earlier.

"Get in," he shouted.

Molloy jumped into the car. At the *News* Molloy worked as a gossip columnist, one of two reporters who anonymously wrote "Applesauce," a widely read, full-page, irreverent "around the city" column. Watching Roca work was an altogether different kind of experience.

Burning rubber, Roca gunned the car out after the bus, which had started moving again, fleeing the attacking strikers, and was now just half a block away from the police barricades guarding the entrance to the plant. Following the bus through the crowd of pursuing strikers would have been a neat trick for someone using the conventional procedure of driving with both hands and looking where he was going, but Roca was steering with one hand and shooting with the other.

As he circled the plant his police radio was on with the volume way up and Molloy could hear "ominous messages about medics being called in."[1]

Molloy asked Roca to let her out near the barricades on the corner of Pacific Street. The streets here were clear, the strikers having been herded onto the corners of the intersection, and the replacement buses were getting through, dropping off load after load of strikebreakers.

The strikers seemed to be at least as angry at the cops as they were at the scabs. To Molloy, who later told the story in a vivid diary of the first days of the strike published in *The Village Voice*, the scene was "ugly." For one thing the unions were very politically incorrect. One striker yelled at the cops, "You're all a bunch of women," which made the cops break out laughing because two of them *were* women.[2]

Inspired by this discovery another striker yelled, "Come over here so I can fuck you up the ass!"[3]

Another wit complained, "The cops will probably arrest us tonight. It's Equal Opportunity. There aren't enough white people in prison."[4]

Molloy, young, white, liberal, instinctively pro-union, had to ask herself: "Am I really on the same side as these people?"[5]

Actually, she was not, anyway not officially and not yet. The Guild had not yet struck; nor was it a foregone conclusion that it would do so.

The Guild claimed vaguely to be "honoring the picket lines." But the first night of the strike this did not mean much: reporters in the field had no picket lines to cross, many Guild members had finished their shifts by the time Alvino had called the drivers out on strike, and most of those who were in the *News* building at the time stayed there.

Even the next morning the Guild's Rubicon was still several hours away. Editors and reporters with evening or late-night deadlines did not necessarily report for work at the crack of 9 A.M. For Molloy and other Guild members, that left several hours in the morning free for rumor-mongering and bouts of anxiety over the prospect of striking because Gary Kalinich would not stand up; several hours of irritation at the prospect of giving up their jobs to support blue-collar unions whose excesses, many Guild members believed, were bankrupting their paper.

When Molloy woke, the first person she heard from was Betty Liu

Ebron, her "Applesauce" co-writer, who relayed a rumor that the Guild was allowing members to cross the picket line, at least today. Molloy called Guild headquarters and someone there said that was not right, the Guild was honoring the line.

But that wasn't entirely right either.

The word from Lipton seemed to be that the Guild was honoring the picket line "for now," a dangerously indecisive position. Many, perhaps even a majority, of Guild members were either on the fence or opposed to a strike. If the Guild struck, many or most of these, despite personal scruples and personal interests, would follow. But to hold these people, the Guild would have to issue a firm call to arms. A tentative "for now," would not be enough.

Lipton himself was out in front of the *News*'s 42nd Street headquarters dividing his time between explaining the Guild's position to the media and to a crowd of Guild members who had come down to find out where the Guild stood. Lipton did not have a real answer: the Guild, he explained, was indeed honoring the picket line "for now," but a final decision would have to wait until a Guild meeting, which Lipton said he would call for Monday.

Just about everyone, militants and waverers alike, hated that idea. The company could replace all the Guild members by then and the Guild could end up striking without ever deciding to. Pressed by several members of the negotiating committee, Lipton agreed to hold a meeting right away at Guild headquarters on West 44th Street. The Guild workers on the sidewalk trooped into the *News* building just long enough to pick up what for many would be their last paycheck for months.

Lipton may have been eager to strike. But he couldn't be sure the members would back him. In the spring, the Guild leadership had called the members together to ask them to authorize a strike, generally a routine vote. As *News* reporter Sal Arina, himself deeply skeptical about going on strike, put it, "[Y]ou have to give your negotiating committee some leverage." But the April strike authorization vote turned out to be anything but routine. The last Guild strike had been more than a decade before; many of the people in the room had no strike experience and did not regard giving the leadership the right to strike as anything like a mere formality. Many of them had no desire to get involved in a fight between the company and the blue-collar unions.

At one point in the meeting it looked like the strike authorization would be denied—a devastating vote of no confidence in the leadership and a clear signal to the company that the Guild was ready to roll over at the table.

To get the strike authorization, several Guild leaders took the floor and made a number of vague and probably unenforceable promises.

Accounts of exactly what transpired vary. Arina remembers one union leader promising that the vote that day would have only symbolic meaning: if it actually came to a strike the Guild leaders would come back to the membership for another consultation.

But no union leader had authority to make such a promise. In a more common version, Lipton refused to promise a second vote, but said he would not strike unless the negotiating committee, which included a number of rank and file members, voted to do so.

This swung the vote. As one member commented, "They wanted us to give them a confidence vote . . . but [our reaction was] what, are you crazy? We're going to give these guys, in whom we have no confidence, a vote of confidence? It makes no sense. So the promise . . . was extracted—and I helped to convince people to vote for it. Biggest mistake I made and I will regret it forever."

When the Guild finally gathered in an auditorium at Guild headquarters on West 44th, it was already 1 P.M. At the beginning, the meeting was about one thing only: what the Guild would do that day, or at most through the weekend, honor the picket line or go back to work. From the outset the gathering was noisy and chaotic and angry.

Veteran reporter Marcia Kramer, who had been expected by many to be a leader in opposing the strike, said little at the meeting, which she said was dominated by a "mob psychology."

Arina stood up to say that while he understood "the frustration the members of the negotiating committee feel in not being able to make any progress at the bargaining table," he did not believe the union should abandon its original no-strike strategy.

Political reporter Adam Nagourney, who had voted against the strike authorization, gave what strike supporter Tom Robbins would later call an "eloquent" argument for the same position: "I believe that the drivers have fallen into management's trap. I believe we will fall into the same trap if we follow them."[6]

Lipton and his fellow officers pushed hard for Lipton's original position: no strike but honor the lines. They argued that if the Guild did not formally strike they could deny the *News* the legal right to shed its pension obligations to the Guild. The desire to do this, they believed, was one of the Tribune Company's prime motives in provoking a strike to kill the paper.

Rank and file members of the negotiating committee recounted stories of the company's arrogance and intransigence at the table and urged the Guild to strike immediately. After more than an hour it was clear there was nothing like a consensus in the room.

Many of the members had grave doubts about whether a strike was in the Guild's own interest. The Guild did not benefit from the arcane work rules and static overtime for which the blue-collar unions were fighting: no Guild members were paid for stories they did not write, or for a whole story when they reported only half. Some suspected Lipton's motives. As Arina put it: "It seemed to me he was not thinking first and foremost about his members but about himself, primarily as a member of the Allied leadership—and what kind of shit he would take if he were to act for his own union."

On the other hand even the doves in the Guild were disgusted with the company's behavior at the negotiating table. For months before the negotiations, Hoge had been meeting with small groups of Guild members, telling them the company had no beef with the Guild. In fact once the company settled with the trade unions, Hoge intended to expand the editorial, advertising, and promotion staffs. But the company's less than splendid opening offer and Ballow's hard-nosed style made Arina, like many of the doves, extremely skeptical of Hoge's reassurances. Even with the big wage increase, any proposal that would cut so deeply into the Guild's sick leave and severance pay, and compromise seniority, must have been, Arina reasoned, "designed to be rejected." Even a self-described "registered Republican" like *News* columnist Bill Reel ended up powerfully pro-strike, because the company's behavior convinced him it wanted only to "crush" the unions.

The Guild's self-interest ought to have been the company's greatest ally. But that advantage had been neutralized by the members' anger at the company's intransigent negotiating style. Besides, for the Guild members, self-interest could never be the only issue.

A few days after the strike began, David Hinckley, the *Daily News* critic-at-large and a member of the Newspaper Guild, crossed the picket line. Joanna Molloy, still on probation and therefore still working at her desk, asked him about it.

"Well, ultimately I could find no moral high ground," he told her. "The Chicago people are objectionable. And I do have problems with some of the unions. But it came down to who was going to save the paper, and I think management stands a better chance of that."[7]

The moral high ground. Newspapermen and -women, especially the hard-news folks, have to have it. It is the premise of the profession. Much of the work of a newspaper comes down to, if not explicit crusading for what's right, then certainly reporting on the failures and foibles of others. Reporters are by occupation, if not by temperament, judgmental. Spending a lifetime judging others puts reporters, like clergymen, on the front lines of moralism, playing a role that constantly exposes them to charges—if only from their own consciences—of hypocrisy and moral grandstanding. To make it worse, as might be expected of talented people who join a low-paying profession in part because they prefer fame to wealth, many newspaper folk care enormously about what others think of them. Now they faced a choice roughly between supporting the company and thereby gaining the opprobrium of their colleagues in an overwhelmingly, romantically, pro-union profession; or supporting the other unions, thereby perhaps losing not only their livelihoods, but killing a paper to boot. Was it hypocritical for reporters who crusaded for social justice to vote against the strike? Was it grandstanding to go out in a cause they did not believe in? How would it look?

People who work with words all day have a tendency to believe that being good is mostly a matter of taking the right side—which one does by saying the right thing. Now the reporters were confronted by a choice that needed to be made in action. It had been so easy to judge when only words were at stake, when the judgments were only newsprint proclamations, expired in twenty-four hours. So accustomed were many of them to the primacy of word over deed that several who, in the course of the meeting, declaimed most passionately for solidarity and the strike changed their minds almost immediately thereafter and went back to work. Some reporters later said that the next few days, starting with the meeting and ending with their own personal decisions to go in or stay out, were the worst days of their entire lives. In the weeks that followed an inordinate amount of the press coverage of the strike would focus the moral and emotional traumas of individual Guild members, almost always reporters, wrestling with the decision to walk out or stay on the job. Most of these stories could hardly have interested the general public; but the reporters who wrote the stories seemed to find the intellectual gymnastics and moral agonies of their colleagues endlessly fascinating.

Certainty and conviction were what the Guild members craved. In the next few minutes they got it, in two events that seemed briefly to unite the Good with what was good for the Guild.

At forty-three, *News* columnist Juan Gonzalez was trim, handsome, dynamic: a born leader, an experienced organizer, with a knack for creating consensus. He had not previously been active in the Guild at the *News* but he was no stranger to conflict.

A native of East Harlem and East New York, Gonzalez began his career as a militant during his senior year at Columbia, as part of the SDS-led steering committee that orchestrated the 1968 Columbia strike. Gonzalez was arrested twice that year for taking over university buildings. Soon after, Gonzalez broke with SDS, and helped form the Young Lords party, the Puerto Rican answer to the Black Panthers. As "defense minister" of the Lords, he helped carry out an armed takeover of a Harlem church in October 1970. As an outstandingly effective community organizer, he forced Mayor John Lindsay to increase funding for hospitals and other neighborhood social services.

Gonzalez never graduated from Columbia, and when he left the Lords in the early 1970s he moved to Philadelphia, got married (later divorced), had two daughters, and took up a series of blue-collar jobs, working in a garment factory and a printing plant. He helped organize workers in his garment factory during a strike of the Amalgamated Clothing and Textile Workers Union and in 1978 became the coordinator of the STOP Rizzo movement, a coalition of left and minority activists who successfully opposed a referendum that would have allowed conservative Philadelphia Mayor Frank Rizzo to run for a third term.

Gonzalez got into journalism by taking a course at Temple University and getting a job as a copyboy at the *Philadelphia Daily News*, where he eventually convinced editor Gil Spencer to give him a job as a reporter. He spent ten years at the Philadelphia paper. But he apparently saw no conflict between reporting and political activism, becoming president of the radical National Congress for Puerto Rican Rights. In 1983 he published *The Puerto Rican Fight for Equality and the Revolutionary Movement in the United States: A Marxist Leninist View*. The *Philadelphia News* disapproved of reporters doubling as political activists, and at one point

Spencer reportedly threatened to fire Gonzalez if he did not step down as president of the congress. When the Philadelphia paper went on strike for six weeks in 1985, Gonzalez ran the Guild's strike steering committee. Nevertheless after Hoge brought Spencer to New York to edit the *News*, Spencer brought Gonzalez to New York to become a *News* columnist.

Now in a room full of confusion, Gonzalez had no doubts at all. About an hour into the meeting he stood up to speak.

In a soft but insistent voice he told the men and women in the room a story: by an odd coincidence he had had coffee just the morning before with two union printers, employees not of the *News* but of a downtown financial press.

Those men, Gonzalez said, like the *Daily News* employees, had been working without a contract for months. Then one day management announced it was cutting their salaries by 60 percent, from $21 an hour to $9.50 an hour. These men, he told the Guild members, are a lot like us. They have mortgages too. They have kids in college too. Their lives have been ruined, he said, because their union lost its power.

As he looked into the eyes of those printers, he said, he could see the defeated look of other workers around the country, the air traffic controllers, the Eastern Air Lines mechanics, the men from the *Chicago Tribune*, their unions crushed by Brumback too. Choking back tears now, he told his audience that the Guild had more in common with the craft unions than some people in the room were admitting. The same thing will happen, not only to our printers and our drivers but to everyone in this room, he said, if we let the Tribune destroy the unions.[8]

As James Ledbetter of *The Village Voice* reported, "You could almost hear the minds turning around; as many as thirty members were said to have instantly decided not to cross."

"That," as one striking journalist put it later, "was when Juan Gonzalez became our leader."[9]

Not everyone felt that way. Some reporters thought Gonzalez's speech amounted to little more than cynical manipulation by a professional ideologue, who up to that time had shown almost no interest in the Guild's activities.

One *News* reporter says that the night before, Gonzalez, after a few drinks, gave her the same speech in Extra! Extra!, a Newsie bar. When he did it again at the meeting, she says, "It was like he had been rehearsing the speech" with "the same rhetorical flourishes . . . in this very carefully scripted story." She found the whole performance "self-indulgent." It "made my stomach turn. . . . None of this rhetoric that he takes from his Young Lord days has any relevance to our situation, what about our clerks who could never get jobs with benefits like these?"

Others had had a similar reaction: "When Juan Gonzalez and Jerry Capeci said to follow us," comments Sal Arina, "my first reaction was to run in the other direction." Gonzalez's ideology, his abstract devotion to unionism and fighting the bosses, terrified Arina:

"Most people who came to this meeting feeling either strongly for or against the strike had reasons having to do with their own lives." Some Guild members had family in one of the other unions, and so had a real interest, Arina says, in supporting the strike. Arina had "very concrete interests in not striking": a new home, with a stiff mortgage, and three kids. But he saw Gonzalez as a "political activist." Politics is Gonzalez's "reason for being," he "sees this situation in terms of his lifelong struggle. . . . I don't see it that way." Maybe he would if he were "a single guy and came to the table with a different sense of what was important in life and had . . . different responsibilities." But as it was he was "not here for a political cause."

Another *News* reporter comments: "People like Gonzalez who became big eleventh-hour people were nowhere during the negotiations. . . . A lot of these people stepped in and it gave meaning to their lives at the last minute." As *News* reporter and Gonzalez admirer Tom Robbins later put it, "Juan is having his second Spring '68—and it's exactly what we needed."[10]

The detractors, and all the opponents of the strike, suddenly seemed to be a distinct minority. By the time Gonzalez finished speaking he had seized the moral high ground; transforming, at least for a moment and at least for some, ambivalence into militance.

Gonzalez had also done something else: he had changed the subject. The meeting from this point on, almost without anyone noticing, became a debate not about whether to honor the picket lines that day, but about whether to strike.

The speeches grew more militant—or more "crotch-grabbing," as one dissenter put it. Men older than Gonzalez, men who had families, spoke for the strike. One veteran told the group he was willing "to put my three decades here on the line to win this. These bastards must be stopped."[11] The dissenters or doubters spoke less and less, and some drifted out of the room.

Then came the second galvanizing event. At about 2:30 P.M. the *News*'s company spokeswoman, Lisa Robinson, had announced that the company would "permanently replace all striking employees who do not show up for work today." The company announcement was impossible logistically and therefore legally: a worker cannot be "permanently replaced" until a permanent replacement shows up to take his job, and the *News* was nowhere near being able to replace its entire unionized work force. Moreover, the company was deliberately going slow with the Guild and would not permanently replace any Guild workers for another four days. The company soon corrected their announcement with a plea for Guild members in particular to return to their waiting jobs. It was not soon enough.

Radio news reports immediately picked up Robinson's company announcement. Guild members following the news reported it to the meeting. Lipton wanted confirmation. But then within a few minutes, one or several members—no one seems to be sure how many or to remember their names—burst into the room and started saying, some say shouting, "We're being replaced" or "They are sitting at our desks." This was untrue, but it had an explosive effect. One member recalls that it was like "the way a lynching is started." People began telling each other "we have been replaced, we have been replaced," though they themselves had only heard the news a minute ago second- or third-hand.

Organized discussion more or less ceased. Lipton turned away from the crowd and huddled with the other union officers up on the dais. And then all of a sudden Lipton turned back to his members and said that, in view of confirmed reports that the company was replacing members of the Guild, he was now declaring the Guild on strike.

About one hundred of the members who had attended the meeting immediately joined the picket line. A few others, some because they felt the strike had not been democratically called, immediately crossed. But many simply wandered out of the meeting as anxious and confused, or more so, than they had gone in.

Sal Arina walked over to the *News* building more or less in a daze, not sure whether he would go in or join the line. When he got there he was still not sure, so he walked around the block, eventually going to sit in his car parked on 41st Street. After sitting for about half an hour he drove toward his Long Island home, actually crossing the 59th Street Bridge. But then he stopped, and turned back toward the city. He stopped at a subway station in Queens—the last stop for the number 7 train before it crosses the river into Manhattan. For a while he just stood on the subway platform, debating what to do. He is not sure how many trains he let pass, but finally he wandered out of the station, and headed home for the weekend. He decided not to decide, at least for today. Since he was not scheduled to work again until Monday he would have the weekend to think.

Guild members started calling each other, arranging mini-meetings to discuss what to do; the meetings went on all weekend and through the next week at least. Those hesitating mostly wanted to go back in but preferred to cross the line with a group. A few days after the meeting some eighty Guild members, almost all reporters who had not yet reported for work, met in a playground near *News* headquarters to see if they could reach a consensus. Many of them said they thought the "Guild made a mistake" or that the paper really could go under this time. But few could face crossing the line, certainly not alone. Some like Joel Benenson, the Albany bureau chief, reminded his fellows that sometimes one had to defend principles without hope of a reward. "You have to measure victory differently. . . . I don't want to be a party to union busting." Elizabeth Jensen, another reporter, told a *Times* reporter of a "classic" dilemma: "two options, neither of which really seems right." The group decided to stay out for a little longer, but at almost the same moment more than a dozen *News* photographers crossed the line.[12]

Eventually just about half the Guild would cross (by Lipton's count, though he repeatedly denied it as long as the strike lasted). Lipton had struck without anything like a consensus.

Most Guild members who crossed were from the advertising and circulation departments, or were clerks and secretaries. Among the editorial staff, almost all the photographers, much of the sports department, and a sizable portion of the feature writers came back in. With a few important exceptions, the political reporters and most of the hard-news people stayed out.

The *News*'s most important columnist, Mike McAlary, walked the picket lines for a few days declaring he would never bow down to management. A few days later he signed a six-figure contract with the *New York Post* and henceforth maintained solidarity from within the comfortable confines of his column. Two years after the strike, with the *Post* in financial trouble, he rejoined the *News* under new owner Mort Zuckerman, who, given broad latitude under the bankruptcy reorganization laws of Chapter 11, had fired more than 160 *News* reporters and other Guild members regardless of seniority.

Tactically, the defections by Guild members made it much easier for management to get out a newspaper every day. Strategically, Lipton had carried the day. By officially joining the strike (and with most press reports concealing how many Guild members had crossed) the Guild had done the most important thing it could do: it altered the class status of the conflict. New York is no longer really a blue-collar town, but a new class city. The city's establishments might not have rallied to protect the privileges and possibly corrupt practices of a group of nearly all-white, and all-male, ethnic, politically incorrect, self-destructive blue-collar unions, especially when the most visible union, as the drivers union would soon become, was widely believed to be a Mafia-dominated enclave. But, though the company did not realize it yet, when the Guild joined in, the politically crucial question of how the strike would be portrayed in the press was all but settled.

The Guild had done its part. Now, it was time for others to act.

CHAPTER 16

With a Vengeance

War is cruelty; and you cannot refine it.
General William Tecumseh Sherman

THREE days after the strike began, Sam McKnight, who had helped design the union's no-strike strategy, sounded ready to consider throwing in the towel. He had always believed that a strike on the company's terms would be a disaster, and now it had come.

The first few days of the strike seemed to confirm his worst fears. The *Daily News* had not missed a single edition, exactly the standard the company had set from the beginning. The most skeletal of replacement crews were able to print 600,000 papers that first Thursday night, 710,000 the next, and 1.24 million on Saturday night for Sunday, and 906,000 on Sunday for Monday.

Delivery had been spotty at best, but that looked like a problem the company would soon solve. Most of the first few days' delivery snafus were the result of having too few drivers with too little experience of their routes. From the company's view the situation could only get better. The advertisers showed no disposition to abandon the *News* for moral or political reasons; the prestrike boycott had been ineffective. Advertisers indicated they would drop the *News* only if there was a large and sustained drop in circulation. In the early days of the strike, advertisers eager to guarantee coverage fattened the *Post* and New York *Newsday*, but few of note abandoned the *News*.

The protesters outside the plants had succeeded in slowing the trucks' progress and complicating every task. But these limited victories could not last: the unions could not stage a virtual riot outside of every plant every night; with each passing hour the police were more the masters of the situation immediately around the plants. Police were even escorting delivery trucks to their routes under "Operation Safe

Corridor," a plan the police brass had worked out with the formidable *News* security staff months before. The Guild had been frighteningly irresolute, casting doubt on Lipton's ability to keep his people out. The Guild, particularly the people who worked in circulation, sales, and advertising, was crucial to the advertising and circulation boycotts.

All in all it looked like a loser. And at an Allied meeting on Sunday McKnight "suggested the possibility" that the unions make an "unconditional offer to return" to work, build up the boycott, and revert to the rope-a-dope strategy. But they would have to to do it now. Their legal right to return to their jobs would expire as soon as permanent replacements came on the job.

McKnight got no support whatever at the meeting. One union advisor calls his plan crazy. The members' blood was up; the leadership probably could not cancel the strike now if they tried, and trying might rip the unions apart. This was no time for precise, cold-blooded calculations of the odds. Losing in the street would be far better than surrender; at the least the unions should show the managements of New York's two other papers what they could do. As McDonald had told Donahue at the Allied meeting with the AFL-CIO months before, "If the union was going to be killed we had to fight back . . . even if it meant we had to kill the paper, wreck it, put it out of business. . . . We would have to build the hatred up to win one way or the other."

Within a few days of the strike, the unions' long months of cold-war passivity were subsumed in a frenzy of activity. With the help of Dennis Rivera, president of the hospital workers union, Local 1099, and one of the most able and militant union leaders in the city, a strike fund of more than $300,000 was raised from dozens of New York locals. (Local 1099 gave $50,000 by itself.) The boycotts got serious, rallies were organized, and picket lines were fattened.

These efforts were great morale builders. Morale and money are important in a long war. But strategically, as a plan for winning the strike, all this was nonsense, busywork. Money and morale would help the unions to stay out longer. But that did not mean much unless simply "staying out" could produce a victory. That it could not do.

The unions could no longer win simply by withholding their labor. Their old craft union strategy had declined with the crafts. The pressmen, the most skilled union remaining, aside from the Guild, were replaced with heartbreaking ease: from the first night of the strike the presses ran with crews of a half dozen men or fewer, just as the company had said they could. Malone says in the first days he ran some presses with two-man crews. And though the first few weeks were hectic, soon regular, permanent six-man crews made up primarily of novice pressmen were putting out the paper every night with little difficulty. True the paper was a bit thinner, but soon it actually looked noticeably better than it had before the strike. The replacement crews, working without regard to the old union work rules, maintained the presses far more aggressively, cleaning inkwells that had been choked with debris for years, rebalancing and repairing or replacing worn rollers more frequently, breathing new life into the ancient equipment. The cleaning, sprucing, nudging, and adjusting made it possible to get a dark, clear impression with less ink, so the print was sharper and the paper smudged less in the reader's hand. By January there would be spot color in every edition, a splash of red or blue to make the paper easier to see on the newsstands, something the old *News* had rarely done. The plant itself soon got the most thorough cleaning it had received in years. It was still noisy as Bedlam, but it no longer quite looked the part.

There was no way the unions could win a strike legally. There members were now, in effect, semi-skilled workers and their only recourse was to adopt the classic tactics of industrial unionism.

When industrial unionism was reborn in this country in a three-year blitzkrieg under the leadership of John L. Lewis, president of the United Mine Workers and founder of the CIO, it was delivered in violence. The chief weapon of the new industrial unions was the sit-down strike: the paramilitary occupation by tens of thousands of workers of the nation's coal mines, steel mills, and automobile plants. Lewis reminded labor that its power came not from boycotts, or from the niceties of labor law, but from the strike, from anger and outraged pride and superior force—especially political force.

The great industrial strikes of the 1930s were revolutionary, as strikes must be for men without real economic bargaining power. The strikers in effect proclaimed themselves exempt from the civil authority, assuming the status of combatants in a civil conflict, and under that status seized their employers' property. They won because society, by refusing to use the police or the army to clear the plants, forced the employers to make the strikers a decent accommodation. Revolution, of course, was only a temporary tactic, and most strikers were destined for a permanent place in that peculiarly American social class, the wage-earning bourgeoisie. (Lewis was a registered Republican.) The classic industrial strike is thus, paradoxically, violent, illegal, and yet political. The unions' goal is always to persuade the political authorities to hold their fire, to recognize implicitly the union's right of revolution, to allow them to step outside the law and force from their employers what they could not win in the market or at the negotiating table. Afterward, once the union has established its power, violence, or even the threat of violence, may not be necessary. Future strikes may be relatively peaceful if the company, having been beaten once, shies from using its own ultimate weapons, such as permanent replacements. Then industrial strikes may look very much like craft strikes—the peaceful withdrawal of labor from the market.

At the *News*, however, this evolution was about to be reversed. It was as if the new technology and the company's new zeal, by the very act of taking away the unions' market power, had given them a new power forged from weakness and desperation. The *News* unions were about to be born again.

For the first few days the violence was directed almost exclusively at the *News* itself and especially replacement workers at the plants and along the delivery routes. At 3:15 A.M. on Friday, October 26, the first morning of the official strike, *Daily News* Truck 228 was attacked at Eastern Parkway and Utica Avenue in Brooklyn. The front windshield was smashed and the driver cut by flying glass. He was not seriously hurt. Ten minutes later at Harrison and Fourth Avenue in Jersey City, Truck 369 was firebombed and severely damaged, though the driver escaped unharmed. Another *News* truck was attacked on Flatbush Avenue in Brooklyn by four men who hurled bricks through the windshield. At 4:45 on Queens Boulevard and 47th Street in Queens, a *News* truck came under attack by a group of men hurling rocks and bottles. All the windows were smashed but the driver and his helper continued on their route. Forty minutes later the same truck, now about half a mile farther out on Queens Boulevard, was attacked by two carloads of men with baseball bats who smashed the driver and his helper in the legs. Again the drivers managed to escape without being seriously injured.

Later that morning a large group of strikers formed a human blockade around *News* Truck 303 as it delivered papers along First Avenue in Manhattan, but before the incident could go any further a police car responded to a radioed call for help and the crowd dispersed. At 6:50 A.M. Truck 328 attempted to make its delivery to the newsstands at

Penn Station. It was a key delivery not only because of the thousands of *News*es sold there every day but because of the station's visibility to New Yorkers who were by now intrigued by the question of who was winning. The truck was driven off by a crowd of bottle-throwing picketers.

From all over the *News* delivery area there came reports of thousands of copies of the *News* lying in roadways. A police captain in Secaucus, New Jersey, reported two truckloads dumped in one street. Far out on eastern Long Island at a large home delivery drop-off point near exit 61 of the Long Island Expressway, more than two dozen men waited in ambush for *News* delivery trucks to drop off their loads. Replacement drivers, seeing the ambush, drove off without delivering the papers.

Another *News* truck was set afire in the Sheepshead Bay section of Brooklyn. Several other drivers reported attempted firebombings or attempts to drive them off the road. One striking *News* driver, driving around the streets of Brooklyn on the morning of the 26th, was stopped by police. He was allegedly carrying a container of gasoline, bottles stuffed with rags, Molotov cocktail–style, and a supply of rocks, and was arrested for illegal possession of a destructive device.

The next day was similar except that the number of serious attacks on delivery trucks or other *Daily News* property rose substantially. Another truck was waylaid near an exit off the Brooklyn-Queens Expressway, and the driver was beaten by a man with a baseball bat. Later, a striking driver was arrested and charged with the assault. At 2:30 a bus taking seven replacement workers from the Brooklyn plant was stopped at a traffic light near the Manhattan Bridge when two vehicles, a gray van and a burgundy-colored Jeep (both of which would show up repeatedly in reports of violence over the next few weeks), pulled up beside it. One man jumped from the Jeep and fired shots in the air; seven more men, their faces concealed by ski masks, jumped out of the van and started beating on the bus with baseball bats, then hopped back into the van. Both van and Jeep raced away across the bridge into Manhattan before police could arrive. Again there were numerous reports of trucks being run off the road, their papers being stolen while drivers were making a delivery, or tires slashed, radiators punctured, windows smashed, and unoccupied trucks burned. Replacement workers, drivers in particular, began to receive death threats. By Saturday morning New York City police had made more than two dozen arrests for violence around the plants or attacks on trucks. Eight *News* trucks worth about $35,000 each had been completely destroyed by fire, and sixty more had sustained significant damage.

Yet the attacks on drivers and trucks and violence on the picket line did not and could not stop the paper getting out. Many of the *News* replacement drivers were experienced strikebreakers, and the trucker's helpers were actually security guards trained for labor disputes, as were the men in the tail cars that followed most trucks. Many were veterans of more violent strikes than this; some actually seemed faintly disappointed that the New York unions didn't pack more punch. Four days into the strike, in the wake of numerous firebombings, several beatings, and the occasional gunshot, one guard told the *Times* he considered the *News* strike "mild" by comparison to the coal miners' strikes he normally worked, largely because there was "less gunfire."[1]

The delivery trucks, like the plants, were a hardened target. Moreover, many of the guards in and following the trucks carried video cameras for the specific purpose of recording union violence; truck attacks produced a relatively large number of arrests. Had the trucks been the only available target, every union foot soldier might have ended up in jail before the Tribune Company could be seriously hurt.

A few days after the strike began, the pattern of violence shifted decisively against the *News*'s soft underbelly, the newsdealers and their newsstands. In 1990 the overwhelming majority of the *News*'s 12,000 dealers were immigrants, mostly from the Third World, many from Pakistan, India, or the Middle East, whose life experience had taught them to be skeptical of the law's power to protect them. These were the men whose fortitude and undying loyalty to the *Daily News* the circulation department had taken for granted and of which it had repeatedly assured Hoge and Longson.

Nasir Naveed ran a subway newsstand in Brooklyn. On Friday, October 26, a man who identified himself as an NMDU member told one of Naveed's employees to stop selling the *News* or he would bring other union members to protest in front of his stand. Half an hour later, a man who identified himself as being "from the *Daily News*" ordered the same worker to come out from the newsstand and take the copies of the *News* off the front shelf. One hour later another man grabbed piles of newspapers from the stand and tossed them all over the subway platform. Fifteen minutes later another man took a bundle of *News*es hidden under the shelf and threw it onto the platform. At approximately 4 P.M.

yet another man came to the newsstand, carrying some sort of container concealed within a brown paper bag. He held up the container and told the same employee that if he sold the *Daily News* again he would "pour gasoline on the newsstand, set the newsstand on fire, and burn him alive." The man left and Naveed's employee canceled delivery. Throughout the strike, the man who had visited the stand first periodically returned to make sure the *News* was not delivered.[2]

On Sunday morning, October 28, Abdul Mohammed was at work at the A & S Stationery store on Seventh Avenue in Park Slope, Brooklyn. Suddenly eight men appeared outside his shop. Four stayed outside; four men entered the store, grabbed bundles of the *Daily News*, and heaved them into the street. Don't sell the paper again, they warned Abdul, or something bad will happen. "I can't take the paper or they will kill me," Ali Najeli, one of the store owners, said angrily. "At least in Beirut, I could have a gun. Here if I had a gun the police would come and take me to jail like this," he added crossing his wrists to signify handcuffs.[3]

The same morning, says a dealer named Hada at 290 Avenue U in Brooklyn, "some people came and took all the *Daily News* and they made a fire outside." According to Hada "they were six people, tough, and the police came three times, but what can they do? I don't sell the *Daily News* because I have four kids and I have to watch myself."[4]

That same Sunday at 4 A.M. three men, their faces concealed under ski masks, walked into the Corner 1 Stop, a twenty-four-hour convenience store at 6122 Avenue U in the Mill Basin section of Brooklyn, and warned store clerks not to sell the *News*. Corner 1 usually sold about 800 copies of the *Sunday News* every week, so the store owner was reluctant to comply. But later that morning a group of unidentified men smashed several store windows. Corner 1 dropped the *News*. To this day the windows of the store are boarded up, though the glass has been replaced.

The incidents mounted into dozens and then into the hundreds within days. Young Kim, a dealer in Queens, said striking union members wearing hoods came in two days in a row, threw all his papers into the street, and told him, "If you sell the newspapers something is going to happen to you."[5] Several men armed with baseball bats entered a store at 1510 Avenue J in Brooklyn. According to Shahid, an employee, the men stole all the copies of the *News* in the store and threatened to hurt the dealer if he sold the *News* again. Eddie Lane, who had owned a stand at 49th Street and Sixth Avenue in Manhattan for five years, told the *Times* he had decided "It makes no sense to sell papers" after a man who had been watching his stand told him it "could burn down."[6]

Often the gangs seemed to be following directly in the wake of the delivery trucks. The story told by Mohammed Aiemudden, who worked at a newsstand at 61-50 Metropolitan Avenue in Ridgewood, Queens, was a common one. According to Aiemudden, as a deliveryman dropped bundles outside the stand, "Four men followed him and took the bundles. . . . One man had a baseball bat and said that people who work in the stores should not go out."[7] Sometimes the crews moved so fast no threat was needed. At a newsstand at 42nd Street and Third Avenue a clerk named Arroyo was just a few doors away from the newsstand, getting a cup of coffee, when his three bundles of the *News* were delivered. In less time than it took Arroyo to walk back to his stand, a man pulled up in a car and made off with the papers.

In just five days, from October 27 to 31, nearly 100 newsdealers told either the *News* or the police that they had been threatened or attacked by strikers, most of them apparently NMDU members. The strikers had found the tactic that would win them the strike. In the next three months there were hundreds of acts of violence or vandalism directed against dealers selling the *News*, and thousands of threats or instances of harassment. Union leaders would repeatedly claim that the violence was rare, scattered, and spontaneous, the work of a few men suddenly losing their tempers after being driven to the edge by the company. But the sworn testimony of newsdealers, press reports, company records, and interviews with NMDU leaders suggest a much more systematic campaign. In many cases the same dealers were threatened repeatedly until they stopped carrying the *News*. Even after doing so they were visited repeatedly, in some cases daily, by men checking to make sure the *News* was still unavailable or reminding the dealers their windows still could be smashed, their stores burned or bombed, or they and their employees attacked if they resumed selling the paper. A number of dealers also charged that NMDU drivers for the *Post* or the *Times* told the dealers that if they carried the *News* they would not get the other papers.

By company count there were more than 2,000 "security incidents" of all sorts and in all jurisdictions during the months of the strike. This is almost certainly an undercount, since in many cases company records count multiple intimidating visits to the same dealer as a single incident. The company classified about half of those as serious, e.g., intimidation, harassment, threats of violence, or actual violence. The tallies kept by the New York City Police Department, which count only incidents within the five boroughs, are even more conservative than the company's, but still significant. The NYPD recorded more than 560 strike-related incidents, including numerous instances of harassment or intimidation or threats of arson or bombings, dozens of assaults, several actual or attempted bombings, and dozens of cases of arson and other destruction of property. City police arrested more than 150 strikers. They also arrested about forty *News* workers, mostly for scuffles with strikers.

In many cases frightened dealers who told the company they were harassed or threatened refused to report incidents to the police. Long after the strike, some dealers interviewed for this book refused to discuss what had been done to them. One drivers' union official intimate with the details of the campaign against the dealers—and proud of it—told me the threats and violence "had a great effect on the dealers. To this day they still try as hard as possible to show they are on our side. Like if a dealer gets something stolen from his shop he will tell the driver, 'I know it wasn't you guys: you guys are my friends.' The dealers will never forget this one."

Among the records of violence I was able to obtain are several dozen sworn affidavits from newsstand dealers and employees. The affidavits were taken by *News* lawyers in support of a RICO suit (later dropped as part of the strike settlement) against the NMDU and various union leaders and drivers. The dealers were informed that false statements would be punishable under federal perjury laws. Their testimony suggests that they will indeed "never forget this one."

Newstand dealer 20:
On Saturday October 27 around 2:00 or 3:00 A.M., eight or nine guys drove up in three cars. Two of the men came into the store. . . . They picked up the bundle of *Daily News* and started leaving the store. I tried to stop them and . . . two of the men holding bats came into the store and said "Don't move. Give them the load." . . . One said, "If you sell the *Daily News* here, I'll burn your store and beat you up."

[The next morning] a car drove up with three men inside. One came into the store . . . pulled back his jacket and showed me his union card and from his other pocket he took out a knife, pointed the knife at me, and said "Don't take any delivery." . . . Every day since men have come around to check if I have the *Daily News.*

Newsstand Dealer 26:

On Sunday, October 28, around 6:30 A.M. . . . three or four men came to my window. I had the *Daily News* on my shelf outside. They said, "Don't sell the *Daily News,* I'm union. You know in the Bronx stores got burned, same thing will happen to your store." . . . They took my bundles and threw them in a white sanitation truck.

Newsstand dealer 23:

I came to open the store and found there was glue placed in the locks [a common form of vandalism during the strike]. The locks were replaced by me at a cost of $100. . . . Four men come by, daily sometimes. . . . The regular driver comes inside and says "If you sell the *Daily News* we will break glass." . . . Sometimes they come by three times a day.

Newsstand Dealer 19:

Monday, October 29, around 7:00 A.M. a Hispanic man in his late twenties, medium height and build, entered the store. He said "If you sell the *Daily News* today, I will call ten guys to come here today and make something with you. . . . I'm going to make a fire."

Newsstand Dealer 31:

On November 15 at 8:45 A.M., I came to work at my store. There were two men, one white and one black sitting in a car across the street. . . . The white man took the *Daily News* bundles and scattered them on the street. . . . While I was bending over a bundle of papers, the black man took my wallet out of my pants pocket and ran to the car. Both men drove away, saying that if I did not stop selling the *News* the next time they would be burning the store. My wallet contained $225 in cash and my green card.

Newsstand Dealer 15:

The store has been visited early in the morning on a daily basis. Usually two men enter the store and tell us not to sell the *News* or we will be out of business. Threats are also made . . . broken windows, fire, and so on. . . . Our regular *Post* driver and Metropolitan [wholesale distributors of the *Times*] drivers have also said that if we sell the *News* we will not receive the *Post* or the *Times* and other newspapers.

Newsstand dealer 24:

On 11/1/90 I arrived at my store and someone had put a handwritten letter under my door that threatened to blow-up my store if I sold the *Daily News.*

Newsstand dealer 22:

On Tuesday, October 30, at about 9:20 A.M. two men entered the store. The first man said "I'm a union man. I'm coming to tell you that you cannot sell the *News.*" . . . He said "Now we are friends. If you sell the *News* we will become animals."[8]

From the very beginning the campaign sorted itself into certain patterns. Though NYPD Chief of Detectives Joseph Borelli took the official position that the police could find no evidence that the violence was directed or organized by union leaders, he did concede that the NYPD knew some of the attacks were mounted by the same people or the same cars. A small red car and a brown Caddy manned by strikers who made particularly violent threats were two of about a dozen vehicles that surfaced repeatedly, including the maroon or brown Jeep that attacked the replacement bus at the Manhattan Bridge, a white Toyota, a red-and-black Chevy Blazer, and a green or gray van that often went about with its plates covered, among several others. Much of the violence or serious intimidation seemed to be committed by several gangs that more or less kept together during the strike. There was a gang of three or four men who favored baseball bats and metal pipes as weapons and made especially violent threats. There seems to have been another gang of about five or six men who often showed up in a "white car," perhaps a Toyota, and a group of about eight or nine who moved in two or three cars, one of which was the brown Caddy. On a number of occasions a group or groups of twenty or more men worked together, though usually such large crowds were used in attacks on trucks or major distribution points rather than individual newsstands. Dealers and *News* security were able to give police several license plate numbers of repeat offenders and NYPD was able to make several arrests and convictions.

A *New York Post* van and several *Wall Street Journal* trucks were used for stealing papers. The men in the *Wall Street Journal* trucks allegedly would follow *News* delivery trucks en route from the plant, stealing papers as the *News* trucks dropped them off.

Drivers union sources identify at least two staging areas for the campaign where the men would muster and lay plans before setting out for the day's targets. One base, says a drivers union official, was a cluster of mobile homes parked near the Garden City plant. This location apparently was used as the base from which to launch one of the more serious incidents of the strike, in which several dozen strikers attacked buses of replacement workers on their way from the Island Inn, where the *News* had lodged them.

The main center of operations, say union and company sources, was the roofers union hall in Brooklyn, just a few blocks from the *News* plant. "We used the roofers hall as the place where we met and sent guys to do whatever they had to do," says the drivers union official cited above. There "teams were formed and guys had certain tasks to do. . . . They would do all kinds of things to the rag heads, you know the Muslims that sell the papers. They would harass them something fierce. . . . Locks were glued so they could not open up in the morning. If a guy would not stop selling the *News*, guys would visit him and they would say what could happen to him . . . and of course some buildings and stores got burned down completely. A lot of stuff happened. There were a lot of guys that were very good in the field." For his part this union official laments that the effort was not better organized, which he blames on Alvino's supine attitude toward the company. "We just had to do, he says, whatever we could think of to hurt the circulation of the *News*."

Another source, a former drivers union official who was not present at the meetings at the roofers hall, but who has intimate knowledge of the inner workings of the NMDU, says he was told "at least some of the planning took place at the roofers hall. People with well-known names were involved in the planning." Organizing the campaign was simple and the tactics were familiar from earlier, smaller strikes aimed not at any of the papers but various wholesale delivery companies. "Strike captains would organize field troops of guys to go and attack trucks and newsstands. The NMDU knew every stop and every route where trucks would be. It was real easy to plan."

It was also fairly easy to observe. For months the use to which the roofers hall was being put was little better than an open secret. *News* security personnel, though legally forbidden from putting any union gathering place under surveillance, noted that the cars gathered at the hall every night were the same ones that were hitting the drivers and the dealers. Outside, NMDU members could be seen with walkie-talkies. Mike McAlary, the former *News* columnist who quit to join the *Post* during the strike, even wrote a sympathetic column about a raid staged from the hall on which the union guys allowed him to come. According to McAlary, several dozen strikers, predominantly drivers and pressmen, were gathered in the hall around midnight when "a scout had walked into the room and whispered, 'We're doing a thing in the Bronx tonight.' " The men filed out to their waiting cars and drove up to the Bronx, gathering again, according to McAlary, at the Alexander's Plaza parking lot on White Plains Road. Some of the men carried baseball bats or rapped bicycle chains around their fists. By 2 A.M. there were twenty-one cars in the lot when a "man in a tam-o-shanter" came to give them instructions. The night's target was a *Daily News* drop-off point in the Hunt's Point market, where hundreds of bundles of papers would be delivered for pickup by franchised or wholesale distributors. " 'The *Daily News* truck comes in and feeds the vans,' the tam explained. 'The company will have about twenty ninjas [as the union guys called the contract security force] there. Our job is to stop the truck. I don't care what you do but stop the truck. If you want to burn it go ahead. But if you are going to burn it, remember what the firemen over in Brooklyn told us. Keep the truck doors open. That makes it burn faster.' " He also told the men there should be no shooting: "People won't accept that sort of thing."[9]

As the men waited for the *News* truck to show, some gathered rocks, juggling them "like oranges," McAlary wrote, "in the boredom of waiting for war." But that night, according to McAlary, neither guns nor rocks nor bats were needed. The *News* truck approached the lot at 3 A.M. But it was preceded by a company scout car manned by two security guards, who, seeing the strikers, stopped and "screeched back up the block in reverse," warning the truck driver. The truck swung around and pulled out fast, the ten thousand or so papers it carried never to be delivered.[10]

Fear was the strikers' most powerful weapon. They could no more hit every dealer with a firebomb or even a threat than they could stop every truck. They did not have to.

Liz Willis, who operated a newsstand at Seventh Avenue and 50th Street in Manhattan, was not threatened or even visited by any strikers. But she did not want the *News*. "I love my stand, sweetheart,"[11] she explained to a reporter, and she feared that if she sold the *News* she might show up one morning to find only ashes. Vipul Patel agreed: "We don't want to take the risk for five or six dollars a day"[12] in profit. A *Times* reporter surveyed some forty newsstand dealers. Even most of those who had not been threatened said there was no incentive to sell the paper for a few pennies' profit, only to risk harassment or real violence—or alienate pro-union customers. Similarly, during the second week of November, *New York Newsday* surveyed thirty-three newsstands in Brooklyn, Queens, and Manhattan. Eighteen of the dealers said they had not been visited by anyone from the union. And of the fifteen that did get visits, only eight reported being threatened. Nevertheless, only ten of the thirty-three stands were selling the *News* and every single one of those was inside either Penn Station or Grand Central Station, "two of the most heavily policed areas of the city."[13] Not a single one of the twenty-three street stands would risk carrying the *News*.

Even when the *News* took steps to stiffen the dealers' backbones the plans often backfired. Noorodin Kurji, new owner of the Rego Park News candy store, was repeatedly threatened with dire consequences if he sold the *News*, so he refused to for more than a week. But then a *News* security agent visited him and asked him to start the paper again, assuring Kurji the *News* would protect him from violence. The next day a fire was set at his store, destroying his awning, shattering his front window from the heat, and causing smoke and water damage. Kurji said he was angry not at the unions but at *News* management, which he felt had misled him. He said if the *News* would not pay for the damage he would ask friends of his who owned newsstands not to carry the paper.

In the first few days after the strike, the conventional wisdom, as summed up by Alex Jones in a *New York Times* piece, had been that the unions by striking had fallen into a management trap and it was difficult to see how they would escape from it. Three weeks later, Jones summed up the new consensus, reversing himself 180 degrees: For management, he wrote, the "strike has been like a complex military campaign in which surprising initial success could not be turned into quick and complete victory" because of a "stunning" and "fundamental miscalculation. . . . It came as a surprise to most News executives that most news dealers have been frightened into refusing to sell the paper."[14]

On November 1, only eight days into the strike, Hoge announced that the harassment of *News* vendors had cut so deeply into circulation that the paper had begun giving away 200,000 copies a day. A *News* executive speaking anonymously said that only 50 to 65 percent of the print run, over 875,000 on weekdays, was reaching readers. Executives at the other New York papers were telling the press and advertisers that the *News* was reaching only 200,000 people a day.

Circulation quickly became a game of perceptions. In the absence of hard audits, almost impossible to conduct during a violent strike, advertisers would stay or jump ship depending on whose circulation figures they believed. The widespread reports of violence made low estimates seem credible. Yet the company, in order to get stronger action from law enforcement officials, felt it had to publicize the violence as much as possible.

Just six days later, the *News* cut its print run substantially (Hoge would say only that it was still more than 600,000). Hoge admitted publicly that the paper was available at only about 2,000 of its more than 12,000 retail outlets.

The actual number of newsstands carrying the *News* was about 1,800, according to company records. This was an *increase* from the first week of the strike because in those first few days the company had relatively few driver teams on call and could not even attempt delivery to most dealers. As the *News* was able to offer the paper to more dealers, the absolute number carrying the paper rose nearly every week despite the violence. The problem was that the absolute increase was achingly slow, far slower than the company had expected. The number of drivers and trucks operating was fewer than expected because as long as the violence continued the *News* was mostly restricted to manning the trucks with expensive professional strikebreaking crews. And even as the number of dealers to whom the *News* could offer the paper increased, the result of the violence only became more clear as more dealers refused the paper, or, if they officially accepted it, hid it under the counter, slipping it only to known customers who asked for it. By the week of November 12, according to *News* figures, necessarily the most optimistic, the *Daily News* was being carried by 1,859 dealers; the next week the figure was 1,962 dealers, and by December 4 it was still only 3,183 outlets.

The company's one planned response to a breakdown of the dealer system had been to bring in more street hawkers to sell the paper. The *News* normally used several hundred such hawkers to sell the paper at toll booths, sports stadia, and so forth. For a strike the company had planned to put a thousand additional hawkers on the street, men whose entire livelihood would depend on sales of the paper, with no front windows to be broken or newsstands to be burned down.

Despite repeated assurances from the circulation department in the months before the strike, however, almost nothing had been done about hiring hawkers. Howard Greenberg, made VP for circulation just weeks before the strike, was given responsibility for executing the company's latest desperate plan: recruiting hawkers from the city's homeless. The results were a disaster for the company. Homeless advocates criticized the program as exploitation, and at one point a Dinkins administration official forbade the *News* from recruiting in city-run shelters. *News* spokeswoman Lisa Robinson told the media the *News* had started using hawkers "because there are so many newsstand owners who have been threatened and violated by the union workers." This made the program seem desperate, and dangerous for the homeless workers, which it was, and tended to reinforce the most pessimistic estimates of the paper's circulation. Many of the men looked like the alcoholics and drug addicts they were; few New Yorkers wanted to get near enough to them to buy a newspaper. To make matters worse a large number were posted in the subway (the *News* had to sue the MTA to make this possible), where beggars had been harassing commuters for years.

Most of the hawkers were given the papers free, or nearly so. In order to maximize sales, the *News* was already not collecting from many dealers, in part because papers were so frequently stolen that it was impossible to argue with any dealer who claimed his had been, and in part out of gratitude to dealers who were still on board. At one point the *News* offered the dealers represented by the South Asian News Dealers association $500 per week for any newsstand that sold 250 or more papers a day, but there were few takers. Soon the *Daily News*'s circulation revenues approached zero.

On November 18, the paper claimed a circulation of 600,000, which persuaded no one and only damaged the company's credibility. From then on, more carefully prepared and conservative numbers were released. Hoge, who had come out of isolation, appeared on Channel 7's "Eyewitness News" on December 2 and claimed the *News* reached 4,000 outlets (which contradicted lower figures in a later *News* press release) and got 525,000 papers to readers. A week later, the *News* sent out a release breaking down circulation into home delivery, newsstand, hawker, and wholesale, claiming a total of 552,000.

On December 18 a new company breakdown claimed the *News* had finally reached the 600,000 circulation Sloan had claimed a month before. The figures were accurate in suggesting a slight upward trend from an abysmal but unknown low in early November. But the 600,000 figure was reached only by ascribing 200,000 papers to the hawkers alone, which probably was not true and certainly was not credible. Even worse, the company's figures conceded that the dealers, ordinarily responsible for almost 80 percent of *News* circulation, were selling only 125,000 papers a day, devastating evidence of how effective union violence and intimidation had been.

Though the advertisers had been unmoved by the prestrike boycott, they fell away quickly as soon as it became clear that the *News* was losing the battle in the streets. Some smaller advertisers cut back or dropped out almost immediately: the *News* lost the amusingly named Top Tomato grocery stores five days into the strike. Yet the next day Robert Holzkamp, the senior VP for advertising, could still say that not one major account had been lost, though some of the following Sunday's insert business had been. Just a few days later, however, some midsized accounts, including Liberty Travel and NBO Menswear, told the *News* they would not buy any additional space for the time being; others warned they would not pay their bills until it became clear how many readers the *News* was hitting. Still, the bedrock department store accounts, Macy's, alone worth more than $10 million a year, Abraham and Straus, Alexander's, and others held firm.

As the strike entered its third week the slippage became serious. Fleisher Furniture said it would stop advertising because it had received threats after a TV commercial advised customers to "see our ads in Sunday's *Daily News*." Hillside Bedding, an important midsized account, announced it would get out of the *News*. On November 10, Alexander's ran thirteen pages in the *Post*, an unheard-of event before the strike. Five days later, on November 15, News America Publishing, a major coupon distributor, said it would no longer use the Sunday *News* to carry its color coupon inserts, a decision that cost the *News* $100,000 a week.

The next day Pergament Home Centers, the second-largest account after Macy's, abandoned ship and also announced its intention to seek compensation for previous shortfalls in promised circulation. Finally on Thursday, November 22, the day of the Macy's Thanksgiving Day Parade, in which the *News* had previously announced it would not participate for fear that union violence might disrupt the festivities, Macy's decided to pull out. A&S and Alexander's soon officially followed suit. With their withdrawal, the *News* ceased to function as an advertising vehicle.

Practically speaking, the paper's revenues, minimal since the second week of the strike, were now nil. The *News* was losing between $750,000 and $1 million per day.

Officially the unions credited the collapse in company revenues not to the illegal war on the dealers but to the unions' legal circulation and advertising boycotts. The circulation boycott consisted largely of striking union members visiting newsstand operations and asking them not to carry the *News*, or better, sign a form letter stating they wished to cancel the paper to show support for the unions. The unions collected the signed forms and sent them on to the company, thereby allowing the unions to keep track of who was still taking the paper. Dealers were also asked to post signs or stickers proclaiming "*Daily News* Not Sold Here" or similar slogans. The success of such canvassing, however, depended largely on fear already instilled. As some of the dealers make clear, the men carrying the form letters themselves sometimes used threats or worse. And even strikers who, as Mike Alvino put it, "politely asked" dealers not to carry the paper were, in effect, cashing in on earlier threats or violence against the same or other dealers.

The advertising boycott reaped the rewards of violence primarily in the sense that most advertisers jumped ship only when circulation collapsed. But the terror played a more direct role as well. Targeted advertisers were warned that the unions would picket their stores en masse unless they suspended advertising in the *News*. Such demonstrations are legally ambiguous: union members have a first-amendment right to take their case to the public through informational picketing, for example, carrying signs or handing out leaflets telling the public about the *News*'s unfairness to its workers and even informing the customers that Alexander's department store still advertises in the *News*. On the other hand, federal law forbids secondary boycotts, defined as union activities meant to punish a neutral company for continuing to do business with a company undergoing a strike. It is a judgment call whether fifty strikers standing outside of Alexander's shouting slogans and hurling epithets at customers are simply informing the public of their grievances or trying to intimidate Alexander's by frightening away its customers. But it seems likely that what was happening to the dealers made such protests more frightening.

Later in the strike the focus of the violence somewhat shifted to the remaining advertisers, some of whom had their windows broken repeatedly. Bernadette Castro, president of the Castro Convertible furniture chain and a *News* loyalist, was one of the last advertisers to drop out. She reported receiving death threats for continuing to advertise, as did several other executives. Union leaders representing store workers reportedly warned some of the major stores that they risked labor troubles of their own, including minor sabotage, if they continued to advertise.

The Tribune Company's strategy had always depended on one bedrock assumption: that time was on the company's side. A few weeks into the strike it became clear the drivers were making time the company's enemy. Rich as the Tribune Company was, $5 to $7 million in losses a week was too much for it to stand for long. If the company could not get the dealers back on board the strike would be lost.

For weeks the company clung to the hope the violence would tail off. The drivers' resources were finite, as were the drivers. The police were making a certain number of arrests. The *News* investigation team was arming its lawyers with evidence, and the first lawsuits against violent strikers were filed in late November. As one *News* executive put it at the time, "We're about to start taking people's houses away: blow up a newsstand, lose your house, that ought to settle things down."

The sheer volume of incidents did decline over time. But their ferocity did not; in fact as the weeks passed the proportion of seriously violent incidents rose as the strikers began to pound their message home to dealers unimpressed by mere threats. Suzie Cosimo, the owners of Eddie's Lunch on Eighth Avenue in Brooklyn, had refused to cancel the *News* despite being threatened repeatedly and having all five locks on her security gates Krazy-Glued shut. But when three men in ski masks armed with bats and rocks smashed her windows while she and a storeful of diners looked on she gave up the paper.

An even more terrifying incident took place on November 20 at Tony's Grocery Store, a Bronx bodega that had been warned the day before to stop selling the *News*. At 3:30 A.M. store clerk Ramon Nieves heard and then saw a white male banging on the front window and gesturing for Nieves to come nearer. As he approached he saw to his horror that the man had thrust a Molotov cocktail into the security window. It exploded just as Nieves turned away, escaping with only some facial cuts from the flying glass and singed hair. The store was seriously damaged.

The same week a Westbury 7-Eleven that had refused to stop carrying the *News* after being warned to do so was bombed. The drivers' union men who had delivered the warning, Luke Fox and Russell Kengott from the Brooklyn Plant and Charles Esposito of Garden City, set off two primitive, small, but potentially dangerous anti-personnel bombs—M-80 firecrackers dipped in wax and coated with BB pellets. The little bombs blew out a front window and injured one clerk and one customer. All three men were later convicted of arson and related offenses. One of the worst incidents of the entire strike happened on January 10, 1991, when the Club House News and Smoke Shop on Forest Avenue in Staten Island was destroyed by a firebomb.

A few incidents of this sort were more than enough to keep the dealers terrorized. "Taking people's houses away" was only a solution if it could be done in a timely fashion. The odds were that the lawsuits against the violent strikers would not be heard for months or years.

With circulation and ad revenues gone, Ballow's waiting game suddenly turned into a losing proposition. The company's goal became frankly political: to force the mayor, the governor, and the police to track the violence to its source and put a stop to it.

CHAPTER 17

Getting Over

The industrial union goes on strike for economic aims, but gets and holds them by means that can only be called . . . political, in the sense of power politics.
Edwin Beal and James Begin, *The Practice of Collective Bargaining*

SHORTLY before the *News* lost Macy's, Jim Hoge, after months of avoiding the press, began to reemerge to fight for the hearts and minds of New York. It was an uphill battle from the start.

New York is probably the most pro-union big city in America. Some 40 percent of the work force is unionized. About half of those union members belong to one of the city's powerful municipal unions, the organizational backbone of the Democratic Party.

New York's mayor, David Dinkins, was indebted to organized labor for his victory over Ed Koch in the Democratic primary. New York's governor, Mario Cuomo, had also relied on union support, but lately his relations with the state's unions had been rocky and he was looking for ways to conciliate labor. Neither Dinkins nor Cuomo would overtly support organized union violence. But the unions did not need their outright support, only their passive acquiescence, their tolerance for a relaxation in the diligence with which law enforcement agencies would normally pursue organized crimes. To get even this, however, the unions would have to supply men like Cuomo and Dinkins with an acceptable cover story, not just for public consumption, but for their own consciences. As it happened, rationales were not in short supply.

To begin with, the early-twentieth-century legacy of police violence against unions has made most law enforcement agencies in this country extremely eager to appear neutral in labor disputes. This is more than an inclination; the law itself has trended in this direction. One of the great successes of the labor movement in the 1920s, for instance, was to drastically curtail the use of "labor injunctions," by which courts had declared a vast array of legitimate strike activities illegal, effectively making police into company shock troops. It is a measure of how careful the law has become that even after weeks of violence the Tribune Company never even tried to seek an injunction against union activities easily linkable to violent acts, such as gatherings of more than two drivers union members within fifty feet of a newsstand. Such injunctions are rarely issued today, except when the police department informs the court it is unable to maintain order.

In practice, the principle of neutrality often means law enforcement officials will take only defensive action against strike violence. At picket sites, for instance, the police will keep the strikers and the company men apart and arrest protesters who commit acts of violence in their presence. But many law enforcement agencies are reluctant to go over onto the offensive, to vigorously investigate other acts of violence and trace them to their source. They know that if they discover that union leaders helped organize, or even abetted, condoned, or failed to take reasonable steps to prevent violence, both the leaders and the union will be exposed to massive civil damages. The police could be responsible for smashing not only the strike but the union.

This, of course, is exactly what companies want; it is exactly what the *News* wanted in New York. They wanted the police to officially prove what the company thought was obvious—that the violence was being organized either by the drivers union or some faction thereof, not only so the responsible parties could be locked up but so the union and its leaders could be threatened with bankruptcy or prison if the violence continued.

Official neutrality can easily become acquiescence to violence. In New York, however, acquiescence had another stimulus. New Yorkers are difficult to scandalize and almost impossible to shock. By local standards the violence in the *News* strike was not all that impressive. In a city accustomed to more than 2,000 murders a year, no one was killed. Even more important than sheer habituation to violence, however, is that New Yorkers live in a political, religious, and ethnic culture that has long accepted that skirting the law is an ordinary and necessary part of the life of ordinary citizens.

One reason New Yorkers are so blasé about breaking the law is that New York has so much law to break: many laws mean much corruption. A recent official report on New York City's remarkably corrupt construction industry, for example, concluded that there were two main reasons for the corruption: New York has an excess of available professional criminal talent; and nobody who obeyed all the city's rules would ever get around to building anything. Even respectable developers must bribe, cheat, and lie: if they refused, there would be no buildings.

Large and indispensable parts of New York City's transportation system are frankly illegal, including a huge fleet of gypsy cabs and illegal van services that work neighborhoods into which the city's licensed cabs and buses will not travel. To cope with New York's Byzantine rent regulations an astounding portion of the city's tenants and landlords must break the law every day.

The city's ethnic mythologies celebrate lawbreaking. Don Corleone, the mythical Mafia aristocrat, and John Gotti, the cheap hood in expensive suits, are both folk heroes to Italian-American boys, who confuse the two in their minds. The Irish and the Jews share a history of oppression at the hands of legally constituted authorities that has made them more comfortable than most Americans with civil resistance—one reason they have been so prominent in both the union and civil rights movements. In this city, "Goo-Goos," Al Smith's term for good-government reformers, is still one of abuse. This bizarre confluence of cynicism, ethnic myth, and revolutionary principle yields the New York wink, an exceptional local ability not to see lawlessness, especially if it is, by local standards, muted and in a good cause.

Thus for many New Yorkers a modest amount of union violence can seem simply a way of evening up the odds. The fact that in the *Daily News* strike the violence was committed by a criminal organization on behalf of men who sought to protect no-show jobs, unworked overtime, and profitable street rackets would not necessarily affect public opinion. The men who were getting paid for not driving trucks or not running presses were just *getting over*, like the rest of us New Yorkers who live in illegal sublets, or hop in with gypsy cab drivers. But longshot or no, rousing public indignation and forcing the police and the politicians to act were the only hope Hoge had left.

In the first days of the strike the *News*'s political position had looked strong. Two of the three rival New York newspapers, the *Times* and *Newsday*, covered the first week's violence thoroughly, and the police, through Operation Safe Corridor, did keep the strikers from shutting down the plant and saw the trucks off to their routes.

Union leaders, however, immediately started pressuring Dinkins to cut back police protection for the *News*. Barry Lipton called Operation Safe Corridor "unfair interference," saying it amounted to "[the] city spending money on efforts to produce a newspaper with scab workers."[1] McDonald, meeting with Mayor Dinkins, claimed the police were being used as "strikebreakers."[2]

The response of the city's establishments to this demand was curious. Not a single editorial page took note of the obvious implication—that the union leadership wanted the police to permit replacement workers to be open targets for violence. Within days the mayor would allow Police Commissioner Lee Brown to stop the escorts for the trucks.

McDonald's meeting with the mayor took place on Monday the 29th. Over the next week and a half the company's political and public relations situation deteriorated with amazing speed. In those few days, union violence became a thing to be winked at, or rationalized, or fashionably doubted.

Kheel and McDonald and a few of the other leaders met with John Cardinal O'Connor on Tuesday to ask for the cardinal's moral support for the strikers. After the meeting the cardinal told the press he was convinced the unions "want to operate fairly, to do the right thing." He deprecated the notion that the violence added up to anything more than the sporadic outbursts of frustrated individuals.

The next day a gang of some thirty men attacked *News* delivery trucks and crews at a Staten Island parking lot used as a distribution point for home delivery. When the police arrived they found the rioters in possession of cans of gasoline with M-80 firecrackers taped to the sides. Eleven of the gang were arrested. It was one of the most obviously coordinated acts of violence so far. Nevertheless, the cardinal followed with a letter to Kheel defending the unions even more forcefully. He was "convinced the union representatives have not only denounced violence, but sincerely abhor the use of violence under any circumstances."[3] Kheel read the letter at a public rally in front of *News* headquarters on Thursday, November 1. At the same rally, Sonny Hall, president of the transportation workers union, declared, according to some press accounts, "If we see anybody selling the *News* in the subways, their ass belongs to us." Hall denies the remark. Barry Feinstein, president of Teamsters Local 237, and Stanley Hill, executive director of District Council 37 of the municipal workers union, proclaimed "there will be no peace in this town until we win."[4] Striking columnist

Mike McAlary told the crowd, "We're winning, there's no question. You've almost got to be a scuba diver to read the *Daily News* because all the papers are under water." City Council President Andrew Stein and Manhattan Borough President Ruth Messinger also spoke for the unions.

The cardinal's letter and the rally were a perfect example of a public relations paradox that would endure throughout the strike. One set of highly respectable union supporters such as the cardinal and later the mayor, the governor, and leading police officials could suggest the violence was grossly exaggerated, and certainly not the fault of the unions; while almost simultaneously more roguish supporters could virtually admit the unions were winning because of the violence and then threaten more violence if the company did not surrender. It was the New York wink perfected.

That night the police canceled Operation Safe Corridor, depriving the *News* trucks of police protection. Hoge, arguing that the result could be a riot at the plants, asked Brown to at least guarantee the trucks safe passage beyond the police barriers at the plants. Brown agreed, but one step beyond the barrier the trucks were now on their own.

The press coverage began to turn decisively against the company as well. In the strike's first week the *Times* had run a number of thoroughly reported stories vividly detailing the violence against *News* dealers and its effects on the paper's circulation. *Newsday* had run shorter but similar stories. The *Times* ran a strong editorial on November 3 condemning union leaders for so far making only "barely dutiful" statements opposing violence. The *Post* had been far less thorough.

Within days of the rally, the *Times* and *Newsday* began to lose interest, mostly confining their coverage of violent or intimidating tactics to brief mention in other stories about the strike. The *Times* ran its last full-length story treating violence as a major and clearly credible problem in the strike on November 7. Next, all three rival papers began to offer a steady drumbeat of stories that either cast doubt on the extent of the violence, suggested the *News* might be faking or provoking it, or otherwise supported police inaction.

The cost of the strike to the city in police overtime became a major theme, particularly in *Newsday*'s coverage. In an October 30 story headlined "Strike Costs City $465,000 in Police OT" *Newsday* reporter Mitch Gelman pointed out that "for many of the cops it is not an assignment they enjoy."[5] Two days later, Peg Tyre, also of *Newsday*, reported that members of the elite Tactical Narcotics Team and other high-level NYPD narcotics investigators had been temporarily reassigned to such strike duties as supervising pickets. She quoted several anonymous officers upset at being reassigned: "We're supposed to be fighting the war on drugs, not taking the side of a newspaper that has declared war on itself," said one.[6]

On November 8 the *Times* ran the headline "Daily News and Police Vary on Degree of Violence." The story, by David Pitt, revealed that NYPD police records showed only 119 strike-related incidents, far fewer than the *News*'s count of 665 serious incidents. The reported discrepancy did instant, lasting, and serious damage to the *News*'s credibility. The caption head for the accompanying photo was worse: "Despite Daily News's Claims, Little Harassment Reported to Police." Pitt made no serious effort to explain the gap between company and police counts, other than briefly noting that not all crimes are reported to the police. He need not have looked far for at least a partial explanation: the *News*'s incident counts included not only New York City but the rest of New York State (including Long Island and Westchester), as well as all of Connecticut and all of New Jersey. That difference alone, final counts suggest, would account for about a third of the discrepancy. There also may have been a lag between police and *News* counts, since the *final* NYPD count of more than 560 incidents was more than half the *final* *News* count of about 1,000 serious incidents (for all jurisdictions), rather than less than a quarter, as in Pitt's November 8 story. Thus the *Times*'s dramatic and damaging headline rested largely on statistical glitches, some of which should have been easy to discover. And though the "discrepancy" between the company's and NYPD's incident counts became a major ongoing issue in the strike, neither Pitt nor any other *Times* or *Newsday* reporter ever offered a serious assessment of either the NYPD's or the *News*'s methods of counting.[7]

Pitt, who did much of the *Times*'s day-to-day coverage of the strike, was later disciplined for basing stories unfavorable to the company on the word of a source whose identity was unknown (even to Pitt) but who had claimed to be a senior *News* executive.

In Pitt's story for the next day, November 9, the *Times* began to refer to Hoge's claim that union violence was driving the *News* off newsstands as a mere "allegation." Just a few days earlier the *Times*'s own stories had treated that "allegation" as established fact.[8]

In the same story Pitt also mentioned a George McDonald claim that any organized violence was the work of management provocateurs. Pitt noted that McDonald said he could not prove this. Nevertheless this alternate theory of the violence soon became a common press theme. Two days later the *Times* noted: "The unions deny the attacks and blame some of them on out-of-town guards hired by the News since the strike began."[9] From then on for the next several months a reader of the *Times*, *Newsday*, or the *Post* who had missed or forgotten the coverage of the early days of the strike would almost certainly have gotten the impression there was some genuine confusion about the degree, source, or effect of the violence.

Backing off from active reporting, all three rival papers soon contented themselves mostly with reporting each side's claims, as if it were impossible for reporters to assess their relative credibility. After the first few weeks, the most a reader would learn was that the *News* was "claiming" that the paper was being kept off the stands by violence and intimidation. But the reader would also learn this was somehow difficult to establish, and besides, the unions had their own perhaps equally credible "claims." Yet even a casual check of arrest records would have made clear the violence was one-sided. Moreover, although union spokesmen continually floated the notion that the company was doing its share of the violence, the unions offered hardly any concrete examples, true or not.

Of course a casual check of arrest records was not what was called for: systematic investigative work by a good reporting team might have been able to resolve the mystery of the violence relatively quickly. Apparently it was never done. Of those I was able to speak with, no reporter at either New York *Newsday* or the *Times* knew of any systematic effort to answer what became the central political questions of the strike: Was the violence and harassment as pervasive and crucial as the company claimed; and was it organized, condoned, coordinated, or in any way sponsored by the union leadership or a faction thereof? John Kifner's solid and often enterprising stores for the *Times* did make clear how powerful an effect the violence was having on the newsdealers and gave intriguing hints as to who was responsible. In one story he quoted a striking driver named Carlos explaining that the way to "get" the *News* was to go to newsstands and "tell them not to take the *News*. Or else I am going to take down the whole stand."[10] But Kifner, who was never the *Times*'s main guy on the story, knew of no systematic effort at the *Times* to trace the violence to its roots. One of the most obvious steps for reporters to take would have been to stake out or talk their way into the roofers' union hall in Brooklyn, the apparent staging area for much of the violence. Kifner, however, like several other reporters I spoke with who were more deeply involved in the story, had never even heard of the roofers' hall, despite *Post* columnist Mike McAlary's column about a strikers raid staged from there (see previous chapter).

Kenneth Crowe, *Newsday*'s labor reporter, whose coverage of the conflict in the months leading up to the strike was superbly informative, did some of *Newsday*'s more important stories on the violence. Although he defends his newspaper's failure to systematically investigate the sources of the violence, he concedes that the violence "was decisive" in the strike. "One store owner," he says, "told me he had $300 in plate glass he would have to replace and there was no way he was going to risk that against the pennies he would make by selling the paper." He also says that it is "a safe assumption the unions were behind the violence, but you cannot prove it."

You cannot prove it, that is, using the ordinary methods of reporting as defined by Crowe: "Reporters report what George says and what Harry says, that is why they are called reporters." If George and Harry disagree, that is not the reporter's problem. "I don't go into the credibility of witnesses," says Crowe.

This approach was behind a story Crowe did on November 10 that proved damaging to the company. The first story *Newsday* had done on the violence in more than a week, it had nothing to do with intimidation of newsstand dealers. The headline read: "News Guards, Strikers Arrested." The lead informed readers that "Six Daily News security guards, all brought in from other states, and two strikers were arrested yesterday in separate incidents involving a near riot at the Port Authority bus terminal and an assault on a strike supporter." But before offering any details on the incidents, Crowe spent several paragraphs explaining that the incidents coincided with union claims that the *News* had hired "a private army of 'goons and thugs from out of town' to attack and harass strikers and otherwise provoke violence," and that Assembly Labor Committee chairman Frank Barbaro, "after hearing a litany of firsthand complaints from strikers," had announced his intention to investigate the *News*'s use of out-of-town guards.[11]

Finally, eight paragraphs into the story, Crowe gave some details of the actual incident. He must have caused readers to wonder what he had meant by a "near riot" in the lead, since the incident as he described it seemed to involve only a brawl between two strikers and four security guards. In fact there were some dozens of strikers at the scene, who, the company claimed, had attacked the guards. That both guards and strikers were arrested suggests the police themselves were unsure who was at fault. This was a politically crucial story because it seemed to support the notion that the violence was something for which both sides were at best equally responsible, or which at worst was being deliberately provoked by the company. Nevertheless Crowe says he did not attempt to delve into how the incident started. He felt that was not his job. "You report the story and move on."

For an incident as confused and confusing as a multiparty assault that attitude surely is defensible. But it puts reporters at the mercy of spot news sources, especially the police, who Crowe says were not being very helpful. "We would call up the police and ask 'Do you have anything on the *Daily News*?' and they would say 'No, nothing.' Then you call the company and they would say . . . such and such a dealer had his windows broken. So then you would call back the cops and ask and they would say 'Oh yeah, that did happen.' " As far as the police were concerned, he says, "in a city where people get machine gunned on street corners, broken windows don't matter. That's not violence here; that is vandalism." But it was not just the police who seemed to feel that a certain amount of union violence was only to be expected—and accepted. Crowe himself points out, "A strike is a war. It is a class warfare, the owners vs. the workers or the unions. Find me a war where there is no violence." Moreover, he says, the company really started it by "declaring war on its own workers . . . people's lives were really on the line here." The implication is clear: the unions were just evening up the odds and it was not up to reporters from the other papers to effectively cripple their attempts at self-defense.

On November 15, Crowe and reporter Mitch Gelman did do the *Newsday* story on what they called the "most serious act of violence" in the strike so far, "a guerrilla assault" in which "twelve men attacked a Daily News delivery truck early yesterday, dragged out two non-union workers, beat them with bats and sticks" and then pipe-bombed the truck. Crowe and Gelman put the violence in the lead, which also got the headline. But then they spent roughly half the story either floating the union theory that the *News* had staged the attack or rationalizing union violence by quoting union leaders saying the *News* had started it and arguing that "most attacks have been directed at delivery trucks and newsstands rather than people."[12]

In early February, more than three months into the strike, and long after the outcome had been effectively decided, the *Washington Post*'s Howard Kurtz did a story sharply questioning whether the New York papers had underplayed what the *News* claimed was a violent conspiracy to shut down the paper. Prompted by Hoge's complaints about local coverage, Kurtz's story noted that the *News*'s rivals had "largely reported strike-related violence in brief articles, or two or three paragraphs in larger stories, that have done little to convey [the] cumulative impact." Though the violence had slowed significantly by the time of Kurtz's story, he had only to turn to the previous week's papers to find an example. On the previous Tuesday a pipe bomb had exploded under the car of a *News* supervisor. Kurtz noted that incident got little coverage, and the *Times* headline read "No Evidence to Link Bombing of Car to Daily News Strike." "No evidence has been found" was a favorite phrase of both the police and the press during the strike. It did not of course mean that no evidence existed or that evidence pointing in any other direction had been found.[13]

Joseph Lelyveld, the *Times*'s managing editor, conceded to Kurtz that Hoge's complaints had some merit. "Nobody has succeeded in pulling together all of these incidents in a way that would confirm [Hoge's] charges of a union conspiracy through hard reporting," he told Kurtz. But he added, "Part of the problem is the attitude of the police department, which has just seen it on an incident-by-incident basis." He told Kurtz, "I am not satisfied with our performance." He added, however, that he was "satisfied that we tried," a point on which some of his own reporters contradict him.[14] James Toedtman, managing editor of *New York Newsday*, also interviewed by Kurtz, was less apologetic: "The reality is that bombs by the dozen go off in the city of New York every day. We don't print a story every time a bomb goes off."[15]

The press's passive approach meant that the quality of reporting on the violence would depend on the quality of the police work: reporters would report what they were fed by the cops and not much more. As both Crowe's and Lelyveld's comments suggest, however, the cops were not being much more vigorous. The company had feared all along that the NYPD rank and file, strongly unionized, would hesitate to crack down on all but the most egregious strike violence. Comments from the police themselves and union sources confirm that this was not an idle fear. As PBA spokesman Joe Mancini told *New York Newsday*'s Mitch Gelman, "The cops are treading a thin line between being union members and doing their jobs. . . . The cops are in a bad situation. They have to protect the scabs."[16] One former senior official of the drivers union says flatly, "As far as the violence went, the unions outsmarted the *News* because they knew that law enforcement officials were going to turn a blind eye." In the New York area, he says, not only cops but firemen could usually be counted on to support labor because "they feel like victims in a poorly run city." He tells stories of firemen giving striking drivers tips on how to firebomb trucks, and of cops concealing evidence of union violence. During one strike some years earlier, he says, one young driver threw a hatchet at some scabs in plain view of some cops. "One of the cops kicked the hatchet into the tall grass and instead picked up a rock," he says. The cop, he claims, "showed the rock to the kid and told him if he threw 'another rock,' he would be taken in." During the *News* strike, this former official says, he saw a group of men, including an officer of the drivers union, drive up to a newsdealership in Newark and smash the windows with a shovel. Four cops were standing right there, he says, but they "were scared out of their wits. They did not want to pull out their guns and kill a guy for breaking a window." The strikers simply drove away.

Within a few weeks of the start of the strike Hoge, Tribune Chief of Security Paul Stellato, *News* security chief Grover Howell, and the rest of the *News* team were convinced that the New York police had in at least one important respect effectively sided with the strikers. The police performed well, they agree, in restraining or arresting violent or rowdy strikers on the picket line or caught in the act of attacking dealers or trucks. But they believed the NYPD's investigative effort was almost nil. The *News* security team, they say, gave NYPD vast quantities of data on dealer harassment, including descriptions of men and license plate numbers of cars involved in repeated incidents, the plate numbers in many cases, the company claims, belonging to officials or men of influence in the drivers union. That data, says Stellato, ought to have made it easy for the cops to identify the ringleaders and stop the activity. But when he and Howell would periodically ask about the progress of the investigation, they got the impression that little was being done. They would turn out to be right.

Police spokesmen, along with other New York public officials, encouraged the notions that either the company was exaggerating the violence or that it was of ambiguous origin. For instance, after one news replacement worker had his arms broken in several places by strikers armed with baseball bats, police spokesman Sergeant Edward Burns reportedly told *Newsday* reporter Rose Marie Arce the incident "would hardly be considered a crime of major significance in New York City."[17] A November 18 *Times* story announcing that the NYPD had spent $3.2 million on strike-related overtime quoted New York City Corporation Counsel Victor Kovner saying, "There has been relatively little actual violence" in the strike so far. In fact, "It's been quite modest, given the acrimony attendant to this dispute."[18] And when in early November Hoge publicly asked Dinkins to "set the right vigorous tone for denouncing this criminal conspiracy," Dinkins merely replied through a spokesman that Hoge's comments "do not seem to reflect the circumstances."[19]

The cops, the press, and the pols helped create an atmosphere fraught with surreal possibilities. One was that the union leaders and their advisors could almost deny the violence by almost admitting it, by making it seem so matter-of-course that it might as well not have happened at all. Kheel, who had orchestrated the cardinal's absolution of the unions, at one point dismissed the violence by telling reporters that "when a great big, strapping Daily News driver comes and politely pleads with you not to sell the paper, that is intimidating in itself."[20] When Mike Alvino by way of pooh-poohing the violence told the *Times,* "I myself have gone to dealers in my neighborhood and said to them in a nice way please do not buy The News,"[21] reporter John Kifner did not bother to help readers decode this message by pointing out that Alvino was a confessed bag man, running a union with a history of using violence and intimidation to get its way and known to be mob-influenced.

The surreal soon became a reality for the *News* as the unions time and again deflected the company's repeated requests for a serious investigation back on itself.

On November 12, McDonald called on Dinkins and Brown to investigate alleged attacks by management provocateurs. The next day at a union breakfast rally, union leaders asked New York State Attorney General Robert Abrams to look into whether the *News* had encouraged its out-of-state security guards to attack strikers and whether the *News* had violated laws governing the licensing of security guards. Abrams, who never took concrete action against union violence, immediately agreed, telling the rally, "We are going to see if there are laws being violated here,"[22] which was enough to produce a *Times* headline.

When striking reporter Eddie Borges was arrested on the picket line for interfering with an arrest, New York Civil Liberties Union executive director Norman Siegel accused the police of taking sides in the strike, harassing strikers and preventing them from exercising their First Amendment rights. The Borges story and the NYCLU angle got heavy and repeated play in the press. On November 20 a *Newsday* headline announced: "Cops to Probe News Unions' Charges." Police Chief Lee Brown had promised union leaders "a thorough investigation into their allegations that city police assigned to the Daily News strike have been openly hostile to workers during picketing and demonstrations."[23]

By then Hoge was regularly meeting with the press and speaking out in public against the violence, trying to build public pressure for a real investigation. But against the drumbeat of stories suggesting the real target for any investigation should be the *News* itself, Hoge's claims sounded exactly like what the company would have said if it had been trying to provoke the violence in order to discredit or legally destroy the unions. So when Frank Barbaro, the Democratic chairman of the New York State Assembly's labor committee and a lifelong labor advocate, invited Hoge to testify at a November 26 hearing Barbaro had called to investigate the violence, Hoge was wary. He was sure Barbaro would do whatever he could to discredit the company.

Gold was dead set against it. He accepts Ballow's dictum that management could never win the hearts and minds and should never try. Besides, preparing for the hearings would take up lawyers' time, precious time. There was a RICO suit to prepare, there was an enormous daily volume of defensive legal work to keep the company from falling into inadvertent unfair labor practices, and they were trying to get negotiations back on track with the drivers. As Gold remembers it, "Everything stopped. All my time, and the time of several other lawyers and people from the security team, went into preparing Hoge's testimony. It had to be not only persuasive but absolutely, impregnably accurate. The last thing we could afford was to go on Barbaro's turf and make a mistake, which would then be the only story to come out of the hearing."

Ultimately Hoge decided to go and Ballow supported his decision. Hoge got one concession from Barbaro. He would testify first. It didn't help. Hoge got slaughtered.

In an opening statement Hoge argued that the evidence suggested to any fair-minded person that the unions had "orchestrated" a "campaign of unlawful violence and intimidation" that amounted to a "criminal conspiracy." In but four weeks there had been, by the company's count, 700 incidents of harassment, assault, and damage to persons and property. There had been over one hundred arrests, a substantial majority of which were of striking workers. Only seven *News* security personnel had been arrested, mostly for what Hoge called acts of self-defense against violent strikers. The results of this violent campaign, Hoge argued, were clear as well: the vast majority of the *News*'s 12,000 regular dealers were afraid to carry the paper.

Neither Barbaro nor other members of the committee showed much interest in Hoge's testimony. Instead they preferred to explore the theory that the company had caused the violence by using replacement workers. At one point Barbaro asked Hoge rhetorically, "The only two countries in the world that have legalized the use of permanent replacement workers are the U.S. and South Africa. How do you find yourself in that company?"[24]

After Hoge left the stand, Barbaro called the NYPD's highest-ranking uniformed officer, Chief Robert J. Johnston, and the chief of detectives, Chief Joseph Borelli. Both men said that they had found no support for the theory that the violence was coordinated by the unions or factions thereof.

Johnston offered far lower figures of the total number of incidents (though his arrest figures matched up pretty closely with Hoge's). He testified, "To date our investigations show that the acts of violence and other types of criminal behavior are the acts of individuals and are not part of a coordinated effort."[25]

Borelli backed Johnston up, saying that out of all the incidents the police investigated, "Each one seems to have involved someone getting upset and doing what they did." He added, "We don't see a conspiracy, at least not just now." Police investigations, the two men claimed, showed no evidence the unions were organizing the violence.[26]

One reason the police may not have had such evidence, however, is that apparently there had been no thorough investigation of a possible union conspiracy or other union "agency" in violence. It seems that the type of investigative work that was done would have made even the possibility of the discovery of a union conspiracy unlikely.

The *News* security team had been told by the NYPD to turn over all evidence to the Major Cases Squad, an elite investigative unit that takes responsibility for high-profile crimes such as bank robbery and jewel theft. The press reported that Major Cases was to coordinate an investigation. And NYPD Deputy Inspector Dennis Cunningham, to whom Major Cases reported, and to whom I was referred when I requested an interview with Borelli, confirmed that any such investigation would have been the responsibility of Major Cases. In this case, however, coordinating an investigation, he says, meant little more than providing "an accurate accounting" of incidents because "they were scattered throughout the city." Major Cases, he says, did not investigate the violence as a whole. They had simply made sure that individual incidents were referred for follow-up to the detective squads in the precinct where the incident occurred. The precinct squads were to follow up on each incident individually. "There was a political situation," says Cunningham. "The unions were pressing on one side and the company on the other. So we needed to be aware of all the incidents and to refer them to the proper units for investigation and to be able to check up and make sure they were being investigated."

Asked whether Major Cases or the precinct squads ever investigated the larger question of whether the violence was coordinated, planned, or in any way directed by the unions or the union cadre, Cunningham's answer is a flat no. He was under the impression the FBI might do that sort of thing (it did not), but he says that no unit of the NYPD would have done so: "We don't investigate union activities. That comes under the category of political matters. It would be like investigating someone for political beliefs. We have to remain neutral."

Cunningham says, "Our only job was to track cases. . . . All Chief Borelli wanted was to make sure reports had been prepared and forwarded to the precincts for investigation."

Borelli's characterization of each violent incident as "someone getting upset and doing what he did" should have set off alarms in the press corps. Someone "getting upset" is not a plausible description of numerous incidents, many involving the same dozen or so cars, perpetrated by men working usually in the early hours of the morning and rather tiresomely returning to the same newsdealers again and again. If these men had simply lost their tempers they had gotten up pretty early in the morning to do it and apparently could never locate their tempers during the hours it took to meet up with their associates, prepare Molotov cocktails, find baseball bats, and follow route lists to ensure thorough coverage of the dealers, not just once, but over and over again.

These were not crimes of passion; by the end of the strike they were very nearly crimes of habit.

Every reporter in the room should have known that. But the next day, the *Times* story was "Police Rebut Daily News on Violence." In the lead David Pitt reported that "senior NYPD officials yesterday rebutted accusations by the Daily News that the newspaper's nine striking unions were engaged in a criminal conspiracy to disrupt circulation through violence and intimidation."[27]

No reporter I spoke with at either the *Times* or *New York Newsday* ever investigated the alleged police investigation; neither paper's reportage even hints it undertook such an investigation. I asked *New York Newsday*'s Kenneth Crowe why not:

"You mean did we interview the police, go down there, and ask them how they performed their investigation? No."

"Why not?"

"It was not practical."

"Why not?"

"What do you mean? It was just not practical. If you are a reporter you know what I mean. I shouldn't have to explain to you why that is not practical."

"I found some of them forthcoming."

"Well you asked the question and I answered it. My answer is that it was not practical. Next question."

Having failed to interest local police, the Tribune Company would have loved to get the FBI on the case. The New York metropolitan area office of the FBI has more than 3,000 agents, some of whom were working on a separate racketeering investigation of the drivers union's Newspaper Delivery Mob that, two years later, would lead to the indictment of dozens of union members and leaders. Paul Stellato, the Tribune Company's security chief, tried to persuade the FBI to enter the case. But the Justice Department shot it down, citing as a legal barrier a Supreme Court case called the *Enmons* decision.

The FBI would have primary responsibility for investigations based on violations of the Hobbs Act, the federal anti-extortion statute under which much labor racketeering is prosecuted, the statutes covering interstate theft or destruction of vehicles, and the RICO Act, all of which were conceivable legal bases for an investigation of the violence. But under the *Enmons* precedent, the FBI can investigate possible racketeering only if *both* the union's means and its *ends* are illegitimate. In other words, if the drivers struck to get illegal no-show jobs for union officers, any illegal union activity during the strike would be a legitimate object of FBI inquiry. But if the strike was a bona fide union activity aimed at maintaining legitimate jobs and wages, the FBI could not investigate even illegal union activities.

The *News* argued that *Enmons* should not apply in this case on several grounds: first, they argued, the drivers had a record of illegally extorting no-show jobs, and some jobs they proposed to secure through the strike undoubtedly would be so used. *Enmons* moreover applied only to the FBI's Hobbs Act jurisdiction, but there was also room to come in on the stolen or destroyed vehicles grounds or RICO. The Justice Department rejected each argument.

Aware that New York District Attorney Robert Morgenthau's office was investigating the drivers union's mob-related illegal activities, the *News* also tried repeatedly to get that office to investigate the strike violence against dealers. But as one senior official within the district attorney's office told me, the imperative to appear neutral in a labor dispute overwhelmed any interest the office might have had in investigating whether the campaign against the dealers might be directed by the same mob-linked cadres that ran the NMDU's corrupt activities. "We don't get involved in anything that will give inadvertent support to strikebreaking," the source told me. But he also said that at the time the office did note "overlaps" between the NMDU members involved in racketeering activities and those involved in violence against replacements and newsstand operators.

Ultimately Andrew J. Maloney, U.S. Attorney for the Eastern District of New York (Brooklyn), did assemble a task force to look into strike violence, using Alcohol, Tobacco and Firearms agents from the Treasury Department. But ATF's resources are minuscule compared to the FBI's, and the investigation focused primarily on individual crimes of the sort particularly interesting to ATF, such as firebombings, rather than on whether the unions were coordinating the violence.

On Long Island, Nassau County District Attorney Douglas Dillon's office did prosecute the three union drivers who set off the small bomb in the 7-Eleven store that refused to stop selling the *News*. All three pled guilty to felony charges. But Long Island was not the ideal place from which to look into broader issues. Pat McCormick, the Nassau D.A.'s chief of rackets, says the Nassau office did mount an investigation but "never had enough evidence to link the union to the activity." He says that the fact that the acts were repeatedly committed by groups of men from the union "is not proof of union involvement," though such in-

volvement "is a reasonable assumption." Proof, he said, would have
required "somebody willing to testify to what he did, or said, or . . . a
conversation overheard for instance in a wiretap."

Finally, the *News*'s own detective unit, some fifty investigators strong,
was not able to investigate union involvement in the violence effectively, for the simple reason that it was illegal for them to do so. Federal
law forbids a company from keeping union members under surveillance,
for the very good reason that such surveillance might be used to harass
or intimidate strong union leaders or to chill union organizing. As a
result, however, the company force was legally forced into the same
stance for which the police opted: they would stop violence under way,
or videotape acts in progress, and take reports on individual incidents,
but they could not pursue leads that might prove union complicity.
Thus, for instance, though the company believed the roofers' union hall
in Brooklyn was being used as a staging area for the violence (where cars
repeatedly implicated in attacks on dealers could be seen by any casual
observer, night after night), the company security force could not place
the area under formal surveillance. Or if they did, they certainly could
not turn the evidence over to the police.

Barbaro's hearing effectively ended the central political battle of the
strike: union violence became a null issue, hardly ever mentioned in the
press, and no bar to any public figure publicly taking the unions' side.
The *News* might present reams of evidence, but no matter: the violence
had become a nonstory, purged as cleanly as a Soviet apparatchik air-
brushed out of a grainy black-and-white photo.

In the odd, half-unconscious way that such things happen, society
had granted the unions the right of revolution. But because there was no
legal or even public mechanism to do this (as there had been, for
example, in the 1930s when the governor of Michigan declined to send
the National Guard into automobile factories to break up sit-down
strikes), it was accomplished by a communal denial of reality, an un-
spoken agreement to act as if the obvious were not happening.

In the days immediately after the Barbaro hearing the number of
violent incidents, which had been tailing off, suddenly increased again.
The *News*'s little remaining pull with the other papers, the police, or the
political establishment deteriorated pathetically.

On December 6, Carlos Chacon, a replacement driver, was waylaid by
more than a dozen men, badly beaten with baseball bats and bottles,

and stabbed in the chest, abdomen, and buttocks. His wounds required emergency surgery. It was the second time Chacon had been attacked. The day before he had testified to a grand jury against his first set of attackers. The company was convinced the second attack was to punish Chacon for his testimony. Hoge, furious, called a press conference the next day to describe the assault and denounce the Dinkins administration's and the press's now openly lackadaisical response to union violence, and to ask the press to look into the Chacon incident thoroughly. Pounding a lectern and shouting at the assembled reporters, Hoge told them, "The gangsters are running free and nobody is willing to say what is really occurring." Yet none of the papers seriously examined Hoge's charge that Chacon had been attacked because he had testified before the grand jury. The *Times* mentioned the attack on Chacon only in the context of Hoge's press conference. Dinkins did not respond personally. His spokesman Leland T. Jones blandly remarked that the mayor would continue to condemn violence "regardless of the side from which it comes. . . . If Mr. Hoge is aware of any incidents which he does not believe have been examined appropriately by the police department we would encourage him to talk to the Police Commissioner."[28]

Union officials, all but required legally to condemn the violence so as not to appear to be condoning it, weren't even bothering anymore. McDonald called the incident "not a union problem." Lipton commented that "the highest police officials of this city have refuted [the conspiracy] charges."[29]

Is it possible now to answer the question: Did the unions organize the violence? Or did they exhibit "agency" by encouraging violence? Tribune executives remain convinced of it to this day. Union leaders are more equivocal, some staunchly maintaining the unions' innocence, others proudly hinting at union complicity. But no union leader or senior advisor I asked was at all abashed at winning through violence; most roughly seconded Lipton's comment to me: "I am comfortable doing whatever we had to do to win."

It is not possible for one writer, at least not this one writer, to do what whole squads of NYPD detectives, FBI agents, or professional investigative reporters should have done. The evidence available to this one writer suggests but does not prove that the campaign of violence against replacement drivers and newsdealers was led by a cadre of drivers with significant influence within the union. The statement of the NMDU officials or former officials cited in the previous chapter certainly tends to support this view, though of course anonymous sources are less creditable than those willing to speak on the record.

That the effort was organized seems clear from its vast extent and from certain patterns of activity—for example, the cars that kept showing up in illegal incidents; the use of the roofers' union hall as a staging area; the tendency for incidents to occur in the early hours of the morning in the immediate wake of *News* delivery trucks, suggesting a familiarity with the *News* route system. Of course, any given driver would have known his own route. But the dealers' testimony makes clear that the harassers were not always working their own routes, which means they had to get route information from an informed source. Moreover as in an organized protection racket, much of the activity was regular and nonviolent—for example, the frequent repeat visits to vendors who had already agreed not to sell the *News* (though the repeat visits were often made by men who threatened or actually committed violence, and who referred to their previous threats or acts). Such behavior is more tedious than spontaneous and suggests not only considerable organizational efforts but indeed a certain amount of management skill and group discipline.

Similarly, the magnitude and complexity of the effort, and the resources available to those undertaking it—for instance, the roofers' hall—support the view that the effort was led, assisted, or at the very minimum condoned by people with significant influence within the union. It is almost impossible to imagine that some portion of the union leadership (which is very large, amounting to dozens of men, including the entire executive and negotiating committees and all the union foremen, who, under union rules, are officers of the union) was not aware of the details of the campaign. Indeed, arrest records compiled by the *News* and spot-checked by me show that the vast majority of strikers arrested for serious incidents of violence or harassment were drivers, and also show that a significant portion of those arrested were in fact members of the leadership or men known to be politically influential in the union.

Even speaking anonymously, there were limits to what anyone within the NMDU could tell me, especially the harder guys suspected of having mob ties, who speak that elaborate elliptical dialect of men whose touching pride in their work strives with their lifelong need for discretion. Of course the drivers union official cited in the previous chapter absolutely, positively, never ever personally harassed any of the "rag heads" himself. It was other guys who "had certain tasks to do what they had to do." But of course, he tells me, he cannot name any of the other guys.

Frustrated, I try to explain to him that a book has to have details in it to be credible. Readers want specifics.

Undaunted, he says he has an answer to my readers' problem. You know us, he explains. "You know the kinds of stuff we would do . . . you could imagine what guys did." So when you write your book, he tells me, "you just have to use your surmise."

On December 10 there was another union rally outside *News* headquarters. For the first time both Governor Cuomo and Cardinal O'Connor attended, a clear sign that neither the unions' behavior nor the criminal pedigree of the union responsible for the violence was considered politically unhygienic. Cuomo told the crowd, "Stay strong, you are fighting for all of us," and "We need to establish a balance in this country between the people who work and the people who invest and manage."[30] The cardinal suggested the company's use of replacement workers was immoral. Kheel argues that with O'Connor's and Cuomo's appearance at the rally the political battle over the violence was over, a decisive victory for the unions.

The company's last hope was gone. All that happened next was merely a denouement, a slow, elaborate dance toward an inevitable end. The rage of men the company thought it could ignore had in the end overwhelmed all the impressive resources the Tribune Company had marshaled: the money, the expertise, the lawyers, and most of all the vision: Freedom Center would not make it to New York.

CHAPTER 18

Cold Comfort

THE company lost the battle for the hearts and minds about as badly as it is possible to lose. The *News* looked like a loser without ever looking like an underdog. It became pathetic without ever being sympathetic, a pariah it cut no one's conscience to kick.

No one ever said publicly, "Yes it is right to let a mob union terrorize innocent immigrants, and prevent citizens of a democracy from buying the newspaper of their choice, so the mob can hang on to its rackets, the unworked overtime, no-show jobs, and blatant featherbedding, thereby threatening the paper with bankruptcy and their own workers with unemployment."

No one had ever said such a thing. But that is what happened, and New York, and the mayor, the cardinal, the governor, the state attorney general, the Manhattan district attorney, the police force, the federal Justice Department, the press, the entire labor community, even the business community, effectively acquiesced.

That the violence was random, or equally attributable to the company and the strikers became conventional opinion in the most literal sense of the word. Like etiquette, it prevailed not because it was believed to be true but because all concerned acted as if it was true, with some of that same unquestioned conviction usually reserved for such august principles as putting the fork on the left. Once its truth ceased to be an issue, the *News*'s campaign to persuade people of the opposite became irrelevant.

The battle was over. All the company could do was try to cut its losses. These were huge. The company itself admitted that the paper had been losing at least $750,000 a day since the strike began. The *News* had already lost at least $80 million on the year and was on a pace to lose almost $120 million by January 1. Overall, the Tribune Company, which in the fourth quarter of 1989 had earned $119 million before taxes, would barely clear a million for the fourth quarter of 1990. The strike had speedily reduced an essentially conservative, hugely profitable company to a perilous, barely break-even status.

On December 11, the Tribune board gave Hoge a last vote of confidence. Thirty-five days and roughly another $30 million later, Hoge could not report $30 million worth of progress. He could not name the month that when it came would not cost another $30 million. He could not foretell a time when the $30 million would be well spent either because it would recapture enough dealers to turn the advertisers around or because it would be the $30 million that finally convinced the unions the company was tougher than they were and they should make a deal. He and Brumback agreed to recommend to the board that the *News* should give notice that if a settlement was not reached in the next two months the paper would be either shut down or sold. The board agreed.

The announcement did bring one last dramatic effort to settle with the unions, under the aegis of "super mediator," former U.S. Secretary of Labor William Usery. The Usery negotiations were different from those that had gone before. Hoge came to the table. Even Brumback, at Usery's insistence, came to a formal "kickoff" session held at the Waldorf-Astoria on February 15. With some forty people in the room, including all the union presidents, Hoge, Brumback, and legal counsel for everyone, the kickoff looked a little like one of those pictures one sees on the front page after a long strike has been settled: the negotiators, exhausted after a long night's rumble, but now happy and victorious on both sides, some shaking hands across the table, others in shirtsleeves telling tales, now finally beginning the great manly reconciling task of reducing the thing to a sport and the stuff of sportsmen's stories.

It was an illusion. The Usery negotiations, though dragged out for some weeks, failed almost as soon as they started. Both sides allowed their most stubborn and unreconciled players to dominate the game.

The unions wanted a group negotiation, all the unions at once facing the company. No one in the company wanted that: it would be too unwieldy, and in a group session the most stubborn unions could easily dominate. The company proposed a compromise: the other side should name a lead union to go first. The company's one hope was that if there was real sentiment in the Allied for compromise, the group would choose any union other than the pressmen, the union with whom there was least chance of compromise because it was their power on the plant floor the company most needed to crack. It didn't work. Almost inevitably the unions chose the pressmen.

Even before the strike, the pressmen's lawyer Mike Connery had been convinced that the only sensible solution was for the Tribune Company to sell the paper. Now his and Kennedy's greatest concern was to position the pressmen for negotiations with a new owner. Says one union advisor, "We had already come to the conclusion that Hoge was not going to move. So we were not going to put our bottom line on the table because a buyer would use that as a jumping-off point."

Meanwhile Ballow was also playing defense, trying to convince Hoge, Brumback, and the rest of the company team to stand fast.

Ballow had very carefully constructed what he regarded as an impregnable legal position for the company. He could show that the company had bargained in good faith and with great patience. He could prove that the drivers had struck, not been locked out as they claimed. He had an array of potential lawsuits still to file against the unions. The civil RICO suits the company had brought might destroy the NMDU forever. Ballow told Jim Longson, among others, that he had never had a more perfectly prepared legal position.

Now, Ballow explained to Hoge, Brumback, and others, this perfectly defensible legal position could be upset. If the company moved too rapidly off its position it would certainly destroy impasse. More perilously, if the company altered what it had repeatedly described as bottom-line positions, that might be used as evidence that the company had not been negotiating in good faith before the strike, perhaps transforming it into an unfair labor practice strike, and exposing the company to huge liabilities.

Some of Ballow's opponents regard his elaborate legal theories as little more than excuses for his inflexibility. In short, they think, he froze. "Ballow only had one play," comments one union legal advisor. "He was not multidimensional. When things went south he could not adapt." Says another, "Ballow seems to live in his own world. . . . He has a game-playing approach to negotiations" to which he brings his own rigid "rules of engagement," rules by which the other players are not necessarily playing. "It is like the patriots vs. the redcoats. The redcoats march up in perfect formation and they expect the patriots to do the same. But the patriots aren't interested, they just want to win."

Right or wrong, Ballow persuaded Hoge and Brumback they had no alternative but to play defense. One person Ballow did not convince was his protégé Gold. With Hoge and Usery in the picture, Gold had ceased to be a major player in the negotiations, and was excluded from crucial meetings. Besides finding this irritating he was frustrated because he felt he was in a position to "tell Bob he was full of shit" and encourage Hoge to challenge him. Unlike Hoge, Gold had followed the legal strategy closely from the beginning. With just Hoge and Usery in the room, he felt, Ballow was putting too much work into defending his position, acting not as a strategist but as a debater and, what was worse, doing too good a job at debating, especially against Hoge, who had no legal experience. Gold wanted the company to make a reasonably substantial last-ditch offer to the pressmen. He believed that he could strengthen Hoge and show Ballow he was being too careful.

He never got the chance. Within a few days it was clear neither side was willing to take the risks necessary to pull off a last-minute settlement. On February 28 Usery ended the talks. A sale was now the only way to save the *News*.

For almost a year after Robert Maxwell's death the first thing a visitor to the *News*'s Brooklyn plant would see as he entered was a round bronze plaque featuring a bas-relief portrait of "The Man Who Saved the Daily News." It was the unions' idea, and if a visitor should make the mistake of uttering an unflattering remark about the late press baron, who had also been one of the greatest frauds and embezzlers in the history of the world, he would be firmly rebuked. Whatever others might say about Maxwell, the visitor would be told, he was a hero here and always would be.

He was a fantasy hero: a thief, a bully, and a publicity hound who created a myth of himself as an entrepreneurial genius, and by the force of a tremendous will and a considerable, if depraved, intelligence made the world believe it.

Born in poverty in Czechoslovakia in 1923 as Jan Ludvik Hoch, he first came to the attention of the world as a perfectly genuine war hero, a member of the Czech Legion of the British army in World War II. In a pattern he would repeat all his life, he used that genuine achievement to capitalize a piece of the fantasy, transforming himself from a poor Czech Jew into the perfect model of an Oxbridge-accented British officer, named Ian Robert Maxwell.

He went into publishing after the war. By the late 1950s he had transformed himself again into the business prodigy who had built a fortune supposedly by "revolutionizing" scientific publishing, the main business of his Pergamon Press. In fact, both Pergamon and Maxwell's fortune owed their rapid rise largely to what Maxwell's biographer Tom Bower calls Maxwell's "long and shadowy relationship with the Communist rulers of Russia and Eastern Europe."[1] In exchange for a lifetime of toadying, and rather pathetic attempts to propagandize for Eastern Bloc leaders in the West (Pergamon often published such hit titles as *Nicolae Ceausescu: Builder of Modern Romania and International Statesman*), and perhaps for other services to the KGB, Maxwell secured, for a pittance, exclusive rights to publish Russian and Eastern European scientific journals in the West.

The deal with the Russians gave him a tremendous advantage in the sort of business he was genuinely good at. Maxwell was no publisher. Later in life when he made himself a press baron his papers lost money as often as not. Unlike "rival" Rupert Murdoch he was tone-deaf editorially. And he was a brutal and disruptive manager who over the years lost or fired far too many talented editors and hung on to too many yes-men. He once fired his own son Kevin for being late picking him up at the airport.

He was, however, a good printer, a ferocious cost cutter, at least when he was paying attention, and a devastating negotiator: charming, brutal, and with no scruples about going back on a deal. One British unionist remarked, "He could charm the birds out of the trees. And then he would shoot them." These are not the skills of a man who would "revolutionize" scientific publishing. But they served well for a printer of monopoly editorial products obtained at a cut-rate price.

In 1964 he used his Pergamon fortune, and the myth of even greater wealth, to land a seat in Parliament. In the late 1960s, however, after hyping Pergamon's stock to record highs at a time when it was losing huge sums, he tried to unload the company. His machinations were exposed and in 1970 a government inquiry declared him "unfit to exercise top stewardship of a publicly quoted company." He lost his seat in Parliament. With his finances apparently in ruins the curtain seemed to have come down on Maxwell's elaborate staging of his own life.

By the mid-1970s, however, he had partly repaired his financial position. In 1980 he got control of the nearly bankrupt British Printing
Corporation, then Europe's largest printer. He turned BPC around by
crushing its unions and then in 1984 used it to finance a $170 million bid
for the Mirror Group Newspapers, a purchase which made him the
second biggest newspaper publisher in Britain, trailing only his longtime "rival," Rupert Murdoch.

The rivalry, with which he was obsessed, existed largely in his own
mind. His furious publicity mongering—his wife kept annual scrap-
books collecting every story written about him and presented them to
him on his birthday—had helped persuade the press to constantly pair
Maxwell and Murdoch as the world's leading media moguls. But Maxwell was not in his rival's league. Murdoch built his empire by making
his newspapers hugely popular and hugely profitable. By contrast, the
Daily Mirror lost half a million in circulation immediately after Maxwell's takeover. More than a dozen newspapers went bust under his
ownership. His two most important new ventures, *The European*, a sort
of *USA Today* for the Continent, and a twenty-four-hour paper for London were hugely expensive failures. Murdoch created three new television networks. Maxwell never went beyond some modest and not
particularly adventurous cable TV holdings, though he remorselessly
touted himself as a diversified media magnet just like Murdoch.

In the late 1980s after a number of failures in Britain, Maxwell announced that 80 percent of his future business interests would be located in America. In practice that meant coming in—late—on the great
leveraged-buyout fad. By the time Maxwell got into the game, fad had
degenerated into mania, Michael Milken was already advising his own
clients to pull back, and prices were, as Crazy Eddie used to say, insane.
In 1989 Maxwell bought Macmillan for $2.6 billion and the *Official
Airlines Guide* for $750 million, far too much money, in the opinion of
most analysts, and much of it borrowed.

Still, the new investments might have worked out if Maxwell had had
the resources to hang on through the coming recession. But Maxwell's
largely mythical publishing empire could not support his new ventures.
He was making some money as a printer, but many of his media properties were consumption items, like the caviar he used to eat by the
soupspoonful during staff meetings, or his 180-foot yacht, the *Lady
Ghislaine.*

Then, suddenly, as the Soviet empire collapsed, the profitable East

Bloc connections were gone. The man who, on the twentieth anniversary of the Berlin Wall, had proclaimed it an "honor" to publish the autobiography of East German President Erich Honecker, and in Warsaw in 1985 had stood next to General Wojciech Jaruzelski and proclaimed "Solidarity is dead," suddenly found himself patronless.

Still, in one sense, it had all worked. He was a press baron in his own mind, in the eyes of his family—to which he was morbidly devoted, though he often treated them viciously—and in the eyes of the world. He dined with presidents. He had the means to indulge his enormous and varied appetites for food and sex. He cut a huge figure in the media. One year the clipping book weighed over sixty pounds. It was not only the tabloid press that hailed him as a financial wonder; the financial press, or most of it, agreed. In the last few years of his career, at the same time that he was frantically shuffling assets to make himself appear solvent, secretly pledging the same holdings as collateral to nine different lenders, and stealing almost $1 billion from the employee pension funds of his companies to boost the prices of the stock he had pledged as collateral, a group of the world's most important commercial banks lent him over $1 billion.

On the day Usery declared further negotiations useless, the fantasy had only eight more months to run. On November 5, 1991, only a few hours before he would have been exposed as one of the greatest frauds and embezzlers in history, Maxwell would be found dead, drowned at sea, an apparent suicide who could not bear to watch the curtain come down.

Embezzlers are not ordinary thieves. They are fantasists, sleight-of-hand artists whose art is to steal the money and make it appear as if it is still there. Maxwell embezzled an entire life. With his purchase of the *Daily News*, now he brought the fantasy to New York.

The company had been scouting for buyers since January and held serious discussions with real estate baron and *U.S. News & World Report* publisher Mortimer Zuckerman, who would come to own the paper almost two years later. The Tribune Company knew it would have to pay someone to take the paper over, but Zuckerman, in the company's view, wanted too much and the talks broke down very quickly.

By March 5 Maxwell had signed a letter of intent to buy the paper. He would take the *News,* accepting all assets, liabilities, and obligations of the paper along with a payment from the Tribune Company of $60 million—assuming he could make satisfactory deals with the unions.

The $60 million was a pittance, the first indication that Captain Bob, as he liked to be called, was more desperate to make one more big splash than ready to put together a realistic deal. On the day of sale the paper still had shutdown liabilities of between $100 and $150 million. It was still losing about $750,000 a day. Its losses in circulation and advertising might take years to repair. Maxwell would have to cover the cost of any buyouts—roughly $30 million as it turned out—out of his own pocket. And the paper still would not be viable without a color printing plant that would cost somewhere between $75 million (done on the cheap, using used no-longer-state-of-the-art equipment) and $300 million for the new computer-assisted plant the *News* really needed.

Still, Brumback had thought the paper worth at least half a billion with the right contracts or with the unions busted and the right plant. Maxwell started meetings with the unions two days later on the 7th. From the beginning his strategy was as unlike the Tribune Company's as he was unlike Hoge.

Obese, garrulous, crude, plebeian despite his wealth, cavalier about details, Maxwell loved confrontation as much as Hoge hated it. In the short term, he had two enormous advantages over Hoge in dealing with the unions. Hoge, the careful strategist, the future editor of *Foreign Affairs*, had been quick to see the company's differences with the unions as an inevitable and intractable contest for power—"people don't surrender power voluntarily," he was fond of saying. And so believing, he had quickly given up on the unions and turned to Ballow and war. Maxwell, on the contrary, had based his life on the belief that a deal was always possible. And because making the deal was always more important to him than running the business afterward, he was not obsessed with possible long-term contradictions in the interests of the parties.

Maxwell was the ultimate optimist. He had to be, since he was not a great manager. He did not fix broken companies. He was not an innovator. He did not make his people or his workplaces more productive, except by cutbacks. His fortune was based on a few good deals: the original one with the Soviets, buying British Printing at a bargain basement price, and a string of concessionary contracts and broken unions. The deal, for better or worse, was everything.

Moreover, in part because Maxwell himself was a man of tremendous and quite unbusinesslike appetites—for food, for sex, for praise, for respect—a man with far more vanity than pride, he knew instinctively what the coolly rational Hoge would never admit: the unions were not businesses and in making a deal with them the human, irrational, and emotional elements were of inestimable importance. Maxwell growled at the unions a great deal and he asked for enormous concessions, larger in some ways than what the Tribune Company had asked. But he also flattered them. His first act was to agree to dismiss every replacement worker if and when he assumed control of the *News*. He agreed to dismiss all the new nonunion floor supervisors, effectively giving control of the shop floor back to the unions.

Rather than insisting on meeting at hotels where the unions would have to share a bill they could not afford, Maxwell provided what the union leaders cheerfully and admiringly called "lavish" or "first-class" accommodations in the Macmillan building, turning over to them most of an entire floor for the duration of negotiations, including a private office for each union. One wag called the sessions the "most well fed negotiation in history" as Maxwell not only marched in endless rounds of pizza, hero sandwiches, and other takeout delights but had the Macmillan chefs on call throughout the night to serve up gourmet meals.

Leaders of small unions do not wallow in expense account luxury. Their own offices are drab at best. When you go to interview Barry Lipton, a friendly and hospitable man whenever he is not at a negotiating table, he will offer you a muffin with your coffee and then politely ask an assistant to go downstairs to the deli to get it, handing him 75 cents. These are not jaded men, and they were impressed by Maxwell's hospitality. And Maxwell clearly lusted for the *News*. He had been parading around town as a tabloid Messiah, feted by the mayor and local dignitaries from the day he arrived. He gloried in the role. The unions had lived for years with an owner they believed wanted to be rid of the *News*; the simple fact that Maxwell wanted the paper seemed like a bargaining concession.

The concessions the unions gave in return were huge, in some ways at least as large, at least on paper, as what the Tribune Company had asked for. As he had when acquiring the Mirror Group, Maxwell started by demanding that a minimum of a third of the *News* work force be cut, for an annual labor savings of between $73 and $84 million a year, somewhat more than the $50 to $70 million Hoge had cited more than a year before. He got it or even a bit more, at least on paper. The butcher's bill came to 870 jobs. Most of the unions lost at least a third of their total job slots, some did much worse. And those were only the contractual losses. In the coming year it would become clear the *News* had lost a third of its circulation as the result of the strike. That meant fewer presses running, less work all around, and big layoffs. The pressmen, for instance, ended up losing not one-third but half their jobs, counting layoffs.

Lipton's union, which had struck reluctantly, having little to strike for, faced devastating cuts, where Hoge had planned to make substantial increases. Out of a prestrike work force of 759, the Guild sacrificed 238 workers. The newsroom, under Maxwell's plan, would shrink from 425 reporters, writers, editors, photographers, and clerks to 340. And the advertising and circulation sales departments would lose 150 people. Almost two years later, with the *News* in Chapter 11, its current owner, Mortimer Zuckerman, would take advantage of his legal right to override contracts during bankruptcy and fire 170 more Guild members regardless of seniority, a devastating setback for a union. When the Guild resisted, Zuckerman effectively destroyed that union at the *News*.

Maxwell agreed to a $40,000 buyout for each departing employee. Departing Guild members could take their severance instead if it came to more. Nearly all the departures were voluntary. The bought-out craft workers remained eligible to work at the other New York papers, and in the case of the drivers, other wholesalers or distributors as well.

Maxwell was able to do a deal in days that the Tribune Company could not do in two years, union leaders say, because he showed them respect, because they believed he really wanted the paper, and because with the *News* at death's door at the end of a brutal strike they were ready to make even a fairly draconian deal with almost anyone, except the Tribune Company. But they also agreed because Maxwell's cuts did not trim their power. The Maxwell contract contained no dramatic enhancements of management rights, it trimmed manning tables rather than eliminating them, it did not downgrade seniority, or eliminate the shape, or remove the pensions from union control.

The Maxwell deal was the bluntest of instruments. In typical Maxwell style, the contracts were not really about running the paper or changing the way it was run. Maxwell had made his fortune as a commodity manufacturer. He more or less took the product and the production process as a given, a long-standardized process of a "mature" industry. A good deal—for materials, for workers, for facilities—could make the process cheaper but that was the most that could be hoped for.

He was a firm believer in that most destructive of myths, everywhere cherished by firms on the long march to bankruptcy, the belief that success can be built by cuts alone.

He was full of plans for more cutting. He would, he said, get big tax and utility concessions from the city. He knew where he could get used German color presses on the cheap, refurbishing the paper for a fraction of what the Tribune Company had planned to spend, or so he bragged to reporters. But not only had he made no contractual commitment to modernize the plants or build new ones, the contracts actually restricted his right to do so without further negotiations.

And yet if the contracts were blunt, they were also, at least by some accounts, fantasies. Maxwell fancied himself a brilliant negotiator in part because he could make deals happen when his lawyers or his lieutenants or his rivals could not. But increasingly in his last years this magical ability to get the deal done meant only that he was willing to pay too much or let himself get rolled in the details. In the ten-sided negotiations with the *News* unions, Maxwell was constantly striding into deadlocked sessions, asking one of his negotiators what the difficulty was, and dictating a compromise the unions quickly accepted, or Maxwell dismissed his own people's objections as nitpicking. Since most such details had to do with procedures or issues of management control that would in the end do as much as the broadbrush reductions in job slots to determine how many people it really took to produce the *News*, hasty compromise could be enormously costly. The unions were far better positioned to create loopholes than Maxwell was to recognize and close them. Gold and Hoge painstakingly explained to Maxwell the progress Deering and his corps of nonunion supervisors had made before the strike in reducing theft, no-shows, phony overtime, and sheer inefficiency among the drivers. They made it very clear what the NMDU was, and emphasized that it would be impossible to keep the drivers in line without abundant nonunion supervision. Maxwell said he understood and promised, Gold says, that he would not eliminate the nonunion supervisors. But when the unions made an issue of the supervisors Maxwell caved almost immediately.

On March 20, 1991, the strike officially ended and Maxwell became the owner of the *News*. Hoge, who stayed on as publisher for some months, claims the loopholes started opening up immediately and within a few months much of the labor savings Maxwell thought he had secured began to slip away. Kennedy and other union leaders, and even some *News* executives such as Barbara Kalish, say Hoge does not know what he is talking about. Whoever is right about the numbers, the unions certainly regained complete control of the shop floor.

Maxwell, the rest of his empire besieged by creditors and investigators, almost immediately abandoned his oft-repeated promise to spend six months or a year in the United States devoting the bulk of his time to rebuilding the *News*. He returned to England almost immediately and ran the *News* either by telephone or on flying trips to New York or did not run it at all. Circulation almost immediately jumped back to between 700,000 and 800,000, far more quickly than expected. But it stalled there and Maxwell gave no evidence of having a plan for rebuilding it to the prestrike level of more than one million. He did, in the first few days after he bought the paper, personally call most of the *News*'s major advertisers and invite them back on board, recording it as a great personal victory that so many said yes so quickly, prompted by huge discounts. But there was no systematic effort to expand the *News*'s advertising base into the neighborhood zones in Queens and Brooklyn where *Newsday* was running rampant.

Some *News* executives believe Maxwell would have put the paper in the black eventually. But the $60 million Maxwell had gotten from the Tribune vanished quickly. The morning Maxwell died, the *News* was effectively bankrupt. With no visible means of support the *News* was in Chapter 11 within days.

Still, Maxwell had propped up the *News* for a time. It is possible that had he not done so the Tribune Company would not have found another buyer and the *News* would have been shut down immediately, though Mort Zuckerman, who eventually bought the paper after it languished in Chapter 11 for more than a year, and may yet save it, had first approached Hoge in the waning days of the strike, and Conrad Black, the Canadian newspaper magnate with a track record of successful turnarounds, had also been interested.

In every other way the Maxwell tenure was a disaster. As the folks in AA might say, he enabled denial on a massive scale, letting the unions go on pretending the *News*'s only problems were old presses and perhaps too many workers, but never suggesting that the union culture itself, the hatred of work, the extremes of solidarity that protected the beatouts and the buddy system, the opposition to any reform that might challenge union control, the relentless fight for turf, and the petty sabotage against any attempt by management to assert itself on the floor, stood in the way of saving the *News*. Maxwell surrendered any hope of real reform, squandered a year, and made it far tougher for his successor to turn the paper around.

And yet Maxwell the fantasist was exactly what the unions had wanted, had been begging for, and resented the Tribune, Hoge, Brumback, and Ballow for not being. Kheel's October 1990 lecture on "two contrasting styles in labor relations," comparing the *News* unfavorably with Kalikow's *Post*, could have been a brief for Maxwell. He had every virtue Kheel cited. He did not blame the unions for the paper's problems. He did not accuse them of "featherbedding and other flagrant labor abuses." And most of all he limited his "demands to labor cost reductions that would not destabilize the structure of labor-management relations established in the newspaper industry through years of bargaining." He bore none of Ballow's dark messages of change abroad in the world. He did not ask the unions to change; he merely asked them to shrink—and that they had been doing for forty years.

He flattered the unions, but at bottom the flattery prescribed by Kheel, and demanded by the union leadership, was a deadly insult. To say that the unions and their members could not be blamed for the state of the *News* was to say they could not fix it either. To say the conditions in the Brooklyn plant were none of their fault was to say the work force was as good as it could be expected to be. At bottom the Maxwell-Kheel view despairs of workers as assets. They are what they are, said Maxwell, said Kheel, say cynics and pessimists and "realists" everywhere, union and management alike. And since they can't be assets our only hope is to have fewer of them. The only thing the cynics have to disagree about is how much the company should pay for the men who leave.

The unions beat the company. But what did they win? Not jobs, since with the circulation losses from the strike there are fewer jobs at the *News* now than there would have been under the Tribune Company's most draconian proposal. By going with Maxwell, they sacrificed their best chance of saving the paper, increasing (eventually) the job base, and, most of all, replacing the horrors of the *News* printing plants with a more humane, decent, fulfilling, and satisfying workplace of the sort in which most Tribune Company papers are produced.

It is possible of course to blame the unions' choice on the company: on Brumback's inflexibility, Hoge's lack of the personal touch, Ballow's extraordinary intransigence and unwillingness to settle for half a loaf from the drivers or the Guild, the whole team's absurd (or deliberate) stubbornness in those last few hours when they could still have avoided a strike. In some sense the company did force the unions to total war.

The deeper truth, however, is that the unions gave all for a principle, a principle from which they could not escape because it defines them: the principle of solidarity. Ultimately, the unions rejected the company's post-industrial paradise not because they hated the messengers but because the company's new paradise would have been hell for the unions. All that is best about the new workplace runs directly contrary to the ethic of unionism as we have known it.

In this era of an almost supine and slowly vanishing labor movement, the *Daily News* war was anomalous in many ways: in the unions' willingness to fight, in the violence, in the fact that the unions won. But the deeper moral conflict in the *News* war, the conflict of values that was far more important than the conflict of personalities, is the same conflict faced by the entire union movement today—the resolution of which will define the future of American labor.

CHAPTER 19

Solidarity Forever?

THE *News* unions won by accident. They won by throwing away their carefully planned no-strike strategy; by abandoning prudence and cunning, and bowing instead to principle and outraged pride; and by going into the streets, where they expected to go down fighting, hoping at best, as McDonald said, to take the company with them.

And so they won. But this accident is also the history of the union movement in this country, a history that has shown again and again that if unions cannot win by striking they cannot win at all. Boycotts and other alternative strategies—such as "corporate campaigns" that seek to embarrass or in other ways to pressure companies into giving in—may win a few battles, but usually while the unions are losing the war. Alternative strategies are almost always a sign of union weakness and have been most popular at times when it seemed the union movement might disappear altogether, as in the 1920s and again today.

These eras of union impotence can end suddenly—as happened in the 1930s when the CIO burst on the scene to lead a national uprising of industrial workers and revive American unionism in three years—but only when unions rediscover the strike. Unions succeed when they remember that a cautious, defensive strategy buys you nothing if you are already trailing by two touchdowns.

Here is the dilemma the union movement faces: unions can only defend working people if they are strong enough to strike. But strikes usually don't work if employers would just as happily be rid of their workers, a conclusion an increasing number of employers in recent years have reached about their union employees. Strike busting, union busting, the use of permanent replacement workers, and "preventative labor relations," that is, keeping the union out in the first place, are at fifty-year highs.

Here is an even worse dilemma. The strike is the ultimate expression of solidarity, workers one for all and all for one against the world. But solidarity, the very heart of unionism, is the reason employers are fighting unions harder than ever, and, increasingly, it is the reason more workers are refusing to join unions. Solidarity was well suited to an industrial age in which workers followed highly regimented procedures to suit the needs of the machines, and economies of scale drove out considerations of quality. Under industrial procedures, individual achievement and an individualist work ethic was of less value than conformity to standards. After some initial resistance industrial employers in this country lived very comfortably with their unions for a long time. But today an increasing number of employers and employees are deciding that the old union ethic is little more than a stumbling block in the post-industrial era.

In the 1950s, the high-water mark of American unionism, more than a third of the American private-sector work force was enrolled in unions. By 1992 this figure had dropped to 11.5 percent. In the private sector union organizing has come to a virtual standstill. In the early 1950s the union movement organized an additional 1 percent of the American work force every year. In union representation elections, workers voted union more than two thirds of the time. By the 1980s, unions were losing most such elections and losing more workers each year through job shrinkage in unionized industries and decertification elections than they were gaining through new organizing. Leading labor economists, such as Richard Freeman of Harvard, talk about the emergence of a "union ghetto" in the economy, in which the unionized worker is not a pacesetter for the nation but an expensive curiosity.

A shrinking union movement, terrified of the increasingly common use of replacement workers to thwart strikes, has all but abandoned the strike. In the 1950s there were on average some 350 major strikes a year, involving 1,000 or more workers. Throughout the 1960s and early 1970s the average was almost 300 a year. But in the late 1970s the number of strikes began to fall sharply, averaging only 83 a year in the 1980s. So far in the 1990s there have been but 40 a year on average, with 35, in 1992, being the lowest figure on record.

Some well-meaning "friends of labor" think they know what causes these trends and how to reverse them. The problem as they see it is relatively simple. Employers are fighting unions harder than ever before simply because it has become easier for employers to win. The law has evolved in ways that make it easier than ever to fight union organizers or break strikes. Reagan-era courts and a Reagan-appointed NLRB tipped the balance even further. The causes of union decline are primarily legal and *political*.

The general argument goes about like this. In the 1950s and 1960s employers opposed union-organizing drives relatively rarely, not only because they had made their peace with unionism but also because the law made it hard to beat union organizers. Even after the passage of the pro-company Taft-Hartley amendments to the original Wagner Act, American labor law was understood to impose a virtual dome of silence on companies during union-organizing campaigns. The obligation not to interfere with union organizing was interpreted as an obligation not to oppose such campaigns even by argument. Gradually, however, the courts expanded companies' "free speech" rights, effectively allowing open campaigns against unions so long as they avoided actual harassment (e.g., firing pro-union workers) or bribery and extortion (e.g., promising to raise wages if the union is kept out or threatening to lower wages if the union is voted in).

These new company rights began to mature just as the lavish wage increases of the late 1960s and the 1970s began to punish American firms newly exposed to foreign competition. Desperate to keep wages down or cut them, once lackadaisical employers began to actively oppose union organizing or even try to weaken and decertify already established unions. A new profession of anti-union consultants grew up and forged company free speech rights into coherent anti-union campaigns, spreading anti-union propaganda among the work force, contesting NLRB designations of which workers would be in the bargaining unit and therefore eligible to vote, fighting to legally delay representation elections, knowing that the longer an election is delayed the more likely it is that the union will lose.

The new tactics worked and as they were perfected over time they worked better and better. Richard Freeman and James Medoff in their landmark 1984 book *What Do Unions Do?* cite some dozen studies showing the success of various tactics: If the company can just delay the election by eight months to a year, union success rates fall by 40 percent. Companies that hold anti-union meetings for workers and distribute written anti-union propaganda can reduce union-organizing success rates by more than half. Though unions win more than 70 percent of representation elections if the company does not bring in an anti-union consultant, when the company does bring in a consultant unions win fewer than one quarter of the time.

The professional union busters went even further, however. They began to break the law, and break it skillfully and effectively, particularly by firing pro-union company employees who fought actively for the union during organizing campaigns. From 1960 through 1980 "the number of charges involving a firing for union activity rose fourfold and the number of workers awarded backpay or ordered reinstated rose fivefold," say Freeman and Medoff.[1]

Freeman and Medoff came up with another startling statistic: by dividing the number of workers who voted pro-union in organizing elections by the number of union members fired for union organizing, they showed that by the late 1970s and early 1980s one in twenty union supporters were being fired during organizational drives.

The Bureau of Labor Statistics does not keep records on the numbers of permanent replacement workers used by employers each year, but all the anecdotal evidence suggests these numbers have skyrocketed. This also was the result of government policy, say labor's friends. Perhaps the most frequently written sentence in the thousands of pages of newspaper, magazine, and scholarly articles and books discussing the decline of American unions has gone something like this: "Before the 1980s employers rarely invoked their legal right to permanently replace striking workers, but in the wake of President Reagan's decision to fire the striking air traffic controllers in 1981, the practice has become widespread, dramatically weakening the nation's unions by turning their most powerful weapon against them."

If the problem is simple, in this view, so is the solution: It is politics and law that is hurting unions, so rebalance the law in the unions' favor. For one thing, increase the penalties for firing pro-union workers. Right now the only penalty is back pay for the discharged worker, awarded years later and reduced pro rata for any days spent working for another employer in the meantime. If a company can stop a union drive by firing a handful of workers, that is a bargain.

Another frequently suggested political fix is to eliminate union elections altogether. Under the current rules, an election must be scheduled by the NLRB whenever one third of the eligible workers in a plant sign a petition (actually, fill out postcards) requesting one. Union organizers, however, know that unless they actually get about two thirds of the workers to fill out cards, the union will lose the election, since once the game is out in the open and the company starts its campaign the union will lose votes every day. So, many friends of labor want to make the petition process equivalent to election: as soon as a majority of workers sign pro-union cards the union would be certified, even if the company was never informed that an organizing campaign was under way.

Probably the most popular political suggestion is to simply outlaw the use of permanent replacement workers. Practically speaking such a rule would make it impossible for companies to operate during strikes except by patching together a temporary staff of managers and professional strike- breakers.

In the short term the proposed solutions might strengthen the nation's current unions numerically and revive the power of the strike. But the standard account and the usual solutions divert attention from deeper sources of union decline that transcend politics and law. Both tempt unions to avoid confronting their own profound failures to adjust to post-industrial reality. The standard account begs the hard questions: Why are companies *now* fighting their unions so hard? Why is anti-union propaganda suddenly so effective that simply talking to workers and sending them information sheets can cut union victories by half? Why do unions lose votes every day leading up to an election? And most of all—why are companies willing to undergo the trauma of replacing their entire work force with untrained recruits?

In the great eras of union growth, union men faced far more formidable obstacles than anti-union consultants and company propaganda. Firing a few pro-union workers is profoundly unjust but it does not compare to the old days of the company calling out the Pinkertons or the company guards who had been deputized as state police, or turning machine guns on striking workers, or burning down mining camps. It is not the same as pro-company judges routinely declaring perfectly peaceful strike activities to be illegal, as was done early in this century. The sort of "heightened employer opposition" unions see these days would be a mere annoyance to a movement without deeper problems.

Many of labor's more responsible friends, conceding that legal changes can account for only a portion of union decline, do admit that structural changes in the economy, such as the declining percentage of American workers engaged in manufacturing, the shift of manufacturing to the South, and the rapid decline of the older, heavily unionized plants of the Northeast and Midwest, account for much of labor's losses.

But even the structural explanation falls short. For beneath and behind all these grand historical trends and objective economic forces are men, both workers and managers, men who think and feel and believe, men who know more about their daily work than can possibly be revealed in economic statistics, men whose personal choices, preferences, and beliefs in the end determine those statistics at least as much as they are determined by them. It is the decisions and beliefs of these men that are reducing the old unionism to a mere ghetto in the American economy.

The old unionism, organized for industries in which men served and imitated machines, becoming rule-bound, rote repeaters of mechanical functions, is a disaster today. Today machines, imbued with intelligence, imitate men, and the men who run them best do so by becoming more manly: independent, responsible, good team members, self-motivated, diligent, willing to make judgments rather than merely responding to rules, eager to learn and improve. Most of all, in a quality factory, work requires not mere compliance with the rules, as established in an adversarial, negotiated contract, but a free act of the will, an active personal commitment to quality and to the good of the enterprise. This is an attitude directly at odds with the management and labor institutions of even twenty years ago.

As good a friend of labor as Ray Marshall, former secretary of labor, agrees. "The mass production system organized work so that most thinking, planning and decision making was done by . . . elites" whose job it was to render work as mindless as possible. But flexible, quality-oriented production systems, he writes, require workers who do not simply follow orders but "impose order on chaotic data and can use information to add value to products, improve productivity, technology and quality, and solve problems." The new worker and the new factory are utterly unsuited to "the adversarial and authoritarian systems" of labor relations bequeathed to us by the industrial age.[2]

One of the most respected and imaginative friends of labor, Harvard's Charles Heckscher, author of *The New Unionism*, also argues that the old unionism was intimately tied to "the structure of mass production industry" and for that reason impedes the post-industrial trend "toward flexibility and innovation." As he points out, today many companies "avoid unionization not because of wage considerations—they are willing to pay the union scale—but because they want the flexibility to change work patterns rapidly and between contracts. It is this nonunion sector that has taken the lead in the recent trend toward increasing worker participation and reducing bureaucratic hierarchy."[3]

There are union leaders who understand this better than most managements. Former United Auto Workers vice president Irving Bluestone, in his excellent *Negotiating the Future* (co-written with his son, economist Barry Bluestone), frankly concedes that the industrial model of unionism is outmoded. But then he goes on to argue that the nation's best unions, such as the UAW, are leading the way to a post-industrial work culture, freeing up the production process in the pursuit of quality, and revitalizing the U.S. auto industry.

Bluestone makes a good case, but the UAW, for generations the most progressive and intelligently run large American union, is the exception—the very frequently cited exception—that proves the rule.

Occasional bright spots provided by the UAW and others cannot hide a grimmer truth: *Companies are resisting unions more fiercely today—not just because fancy anti-union consultants have shown they can win, but also because the companies do not believe the unions can make the post-industrial change. And they are winning because more and more workers do not believe it either.*

Freeman, Medoff, and others cite data that suggest unions actually raise productivity, not only by raising wages and forcing managers to use fewer workers and more capital equipment, as has long been known, but by building a better-trained, more stable work force. Though they admit that a company concerned with its bottom line might reasonably oppose unions in order to avoid paying higher wages, they dismiss as irrational or uninformed employer claims that the union work culture is a stumbling block to productivity and innovation. The Bluestones take a similar tack, arguing that there is nothing inherent in unionism that requires the old restrictive work rules, or the old industrial work culture. Employers who pretend otherwise as an excuse to get rid of the unions are being spiteful, self-willed, and arrogant, they imply, even as the *News* union leaders repeatedly described Tribune Company leaders as ideologues, or religious zealots or fanatics, in pursuit of an unbusinesslike, even irrational, course of action.

Yet Freeman and Medoff effectively admit their broad national statistics may not be an appropriate way to measure the effects of traditional unionism in a changing economy. There is enormous variation in results from company to company. Union firms with a high level of labor-management conflict often score badly for productivity, which may mean that many high-productivity but supposedly "union" firms are only weakly or nominally unionized. Moreover, the data suggest that unions do not help productivity *growth*, and may retard it. And we are just discovering now that traditional measures grossly underestimate the productivity of high-tech and service firms, which tend to be nonunion.

Statistical studies that lump together all union firms and all nonunion firms, industrial and post-industrial alike, and measure them at a moment in time, cannot possibly capture the depth of the conflict between the old work culture and the new, a conflict that has yet to be played out in most American firms. Statistics are perhaps the worst tool ever invented for studying human nature, which is what that conflict is about.

If the new culture of work could be established simply by dropping a few old work rules, the Bluestones might be right that unionism is not a stumbling block. But managers and workers are rejecting unions because they sense that such changes are trivial compared to the change the machines evoke in men themselves and in the morality of work. Their concern is not with statistics but with their own experience, which tells them that it is not work rules but the very ethic of unionism that is incompatible with the post-industrial workplace.

The apostles of quality like to say that their goal is not to get men to work harder but to work smarter. But working smarter *is* harder. Working smarter requires far more personal dedication to the enterprise than simply speeding up the pace because the foreman is heading this way. Heckscher, almost alone among the "friends of labor," seems to realize this: "It has become clear only in the last few years that the real problem is not the decline of the old work ethic but the need for a new one. Companies have, in effect, increased the demands on employee motivation. Frederick Taylor sought mere obedience to rules. Managers today seek active involvement and creative input. . . . The growing importance of 'knowledge work' and the need for frequent and rapid innovation to meet international competition . . . reduce the value of routine effort and put a premium on the ability to mobilize active cooperation at all levels."[4]

The industrial workplace wanted the worker's body, the post-industrial workplace wants his mind. Even more, it wants his will, his moral dedication, without which the mind, unlike a muscle, is not much use.

In short, the post-industrial workplace wants the worker to switch sides.

The industrial worker, in the face of fearsome machines that might work him to death, had to be first and foremost on his own side, and if he was lucky he would have a union on his side too. The craft worker's loyalty was first to the traditions of the craft, which he was presumed to know better than his employer. But the post-industrial company, because it needs not only men's bodies but their intellects and their wills, cannot tolerate such divided loyalties.

The union movement is built on *solidarity;* on loyalty not to the enterprise, but to a faction within it, on mutual support of workingmen for workingmen and *on the blurring of differences between them.* Thus promotion by seniority rather than the company's judgment of merit. Thus standardized wages for all men doing the same job or with the same experience and the movement's traditional dislike for bonuses based on performance.

The post-industrial ethic is diametrically opposed to solidarity. The post-industrial ethic is individualistic, but not only individualistic. As befits what is in effect a revival of the Christian work ethic, it is an ethic of *communal individualism,* of people whose *personal* standards of excellence and *individual* desire to excel are shaped and inspired by *common* values and a deep commitment to the *communal* enterprise.

As Charles Heckscher says of "knowledge workers," though their "consciousness is often seen as individualistic, it has a strong moral component that goes beyond individual ambition. The sense is not simply that 'I' should get ahead, but that the standards for getting ahead should be fair and equally enforced . . . [and] reward merit as defined by their common values."[5]

At the very heart of Christianity lies a law that is breathtaking in its individualism—almost, one might say, in its selfishness: that the supreme concern of every man must be his own salvation. Nothing could be more vain and damnable than to compromise one's own soul to save another's, say by lying to preserve another's faith. Even in such paradigms of Christian community and the Christian work ethic as the Benedictine monastery, or the Puritan village, each worker pursued salvation or the evidence thereof, alone. In a powerful paradox of faith, men and women join religious communities to be alone with God.

In the quality factory a similarly harsh law applies: a man cannot hide his performance in that of the herd. For one thing, too much of his compensation comes out of performance bonuses. More important, he is measured not against some "good enough" standard based on the usual performance of the herd, but against the relentlessly demanding standard of constant improvement, a standard he must at least to some extent carry around in his own conscience.

"Every man's soul's his own." And yet in both the quality factory and the Christian community all these *individuals* work according to the same prescriptive and deeply shared *communal* standards; and they do it not only for themselves but for the good of the community.

As the Puritan literature attests—both the Puritans' own and the literature they inspired—the Puritan village was a high-strung place, fraught with nervous excitement arising from the central paradox of what we blithely call Protestant individualism: the Puritan was alone, but surrounded by his ethic; free of the Old World hierarchies, but engulfed in a conscience formed by the community; an individual, but subject to an absolute, demanding, conformist, and communally enforced moral code.

Not every example of communal individualism is quite so forbidding as our literary memory of a Puritan village. Team sports are exercises in communal individualism—a group effort, under a group ethic, but a group ethic of individual competition and the ruthless pursuit of excellence that gives sports their moral purity. A fine sort of football team it would be that chose the starting quarterback on seniority or fellowship. The very possibility would poison every bead of sweat dropped on the practice field.

Post-industrial companies are not necessarily grim places either, indeed far less grim than their industrial predecessors, and more exciting too, even as it is more exciting to join a team than simply to get a job. Yet even in its pleasantest forms the high-pitched excitement of communal individualism is utterly unlike the comfortable companionship of solidarity.

In a paradox as powerful as those of "communal individualism," the true goal of solidarity is to *defeat* conformity, to protect men *from* rigid moral standards or frantic competition, to allow them to live and let live, free and easy. By averaging out the gains of work—every man paid the same, regardless of his productivity, as long as he meets basic minimal standards—solidarity gives every man the freedom *not* to work his hardest, not to sacrifice himself to the enterprise.

Average standards, such as work rules, may seem conformist. But compared to a moral ethic of constant improvement and dedication to the communal enterprise the mere obligation to meet average standards is libertine.

Solidarity is forgiving. It allows the drunk or the slacker, or simply the older, slower, or less skilled worker, to go along and get along as long as he does not go too far.

Solidarity is the very heart of unionism, and with good reason. Solidarity is the most humane, if sometimes all too human, of ethics. And in the inhuman world created by the industrial machine the one thing workers craved above all, needed above all, was to force their masters to make allowance for their humanity.

Solidarity was well suited to the industrial workplace. If the production process is more or less fixed, and the goal is simply to meet current standards, then it does not really matter by how much you meet the standard. You either cross the goal line or you don't—you don't get extra points for crossing the end line too.

In the post-industrial factory, premised on Continuous Process Improvement, the comfortable live and let live of minimum standards is a disaster. Meeting standards will not move the system forward. W. Edwards Deming, the father of the quality movement, argued that "meeting specifications" is one of the great enemies of quality, implying as it does that "anything inside the specifications may be all right." He had a favorite analogy to make the point:

"Down the road there is a music store, and that music store would be delighted to sell you the score for . . . Beethoven's Fifth Symphony. Listen to the London Symphony Orchestra play it. So wonderful. Now listen to my hometown orchestra play it. . . . Same music; same specifications. Not a mistake. Both perfect. But listen to the difference."[6]

The problem unions face, however, is not only that solidarity makes the post-industrial factory inefficient but that it makes the post-industrial worker unhappy.

The machines make the new work ethic possible. Competition makes it necessary. But workers adopt the new ethic because it is a better way to live.

One of Freeman and Medoff's most interesting findings was that even though unionized workers on average quit their jobs much less often than nonunion workers, stay with the same employers for longer than nonunion workers, and are much more likely to believe it would be hard to find a job as good as their current job elsewhere, they are, on average, much *less* satisfied with their jobs than nonunion workers.

Their complaints are not with wages and benefits, but with supervisors and work conditions. They are more likely than nonunion workers to believe that management allows them to work in dangerous conditions, even when their plants are actually safer. They are much more likely to dislike their supervisors. And they are less likely to believe their supervisors take their ideas seriously or treat them with respect.

Freeman and Medoff's suggested explanation of this apparent contradiction is fascinating: this "voiced" dissatisfaction, they suggest, is not a genuine reaction to working conditions but an artifact of the union's politicization of the workplace—a device the union uses to pressure the company for more.

This too is the ethic of solidarity, an ethic of victimhood, which nurses grievance and which so needs a common enemy that it must turn victory and prosperity into dissatisfaction and defeat. Solidarity must have alienation—but the new work ethic will either destroy alienation or be destroyed by it.

"Knowledge workers" have always been hard to unionize. Knowledge workers dislike nearly everything about solidarity: promotion based on seniority, uniform wage scales, detailed rules about how to do their jobs, the notion that loyalty to their fellow workers obliges them to compromise their own standards of quality or restrain their own abilities, and especially the notion that management is "the other side," when in fact knowledge workers all expect to rise through the ranks.

One reason for the drop in union membership, nearly all observers agree, is the rapidly growing number of knowledge workers, whose ranks, according to various surveys and estimates, have doubled and redoubled in the past few decades. Yet these estimates, however generous, are nearly all underestimates. The post-industrial factory encourages nearly all its workers to adopt the attitudes of knowledge workers.

Solidarity nurtured a deep hatred for work. But then, much industrial work was hateful, not only because of the noise and the dirt and the danger, but because the machines robbed men of their humanity by making their minds, their skills, even their virtues irrelevant. Men rejoice in the exercise of their faculties. They become depressed, bored, angry, and hateful when such exercise is forbidden or irrelevant. They drink, and they scheme, and they look for someone to fight.

The great blessing of the post-industrial workplace at its best is that it engages men, even modestly endowed men, in their minds, in their skills and senses, and even in their hearts and their souls. To replace monotony with challenge; mindless conformity with engagement; isolation with human intercourse; perpetual and mindlessly self-righteous confrontation with teamwork; and "specifications" with the opportunity to improve and excel is an infinitely better way to live. In the high-strung atmosphere of a post-industrial factory like Freedom Center, even a new man or woman doing a relatively rote job, like feeding a sorting machine, is part of a team and looks and acts it. Morale runs amazingly high.

The more work engages the worker, the more he becomes a knowledge worker and the more intolerable solidarity becomes. When repetition and fitting in with the machines was the order of the day, then what men got in exchange for work was infinitely more important than what they got out of work. But if men can use themselves in their work they will insist on doing so. If they can do better they will want to.

Knowledge work is incompatible with solidarity because using your mind means making things different rather than making them all the same, and that means being different yourself. Workers in the habit of using their minds to make a difference are not fond of a system that pretends that how well they do their jobs doesn't matter. The same applies even to purely moral faculties like enthusiasm, or diligence, or competitiveness—get accustomed to using them to make a difference and it becomes very hard to accept institutions whose great goal is to destroy difference so that men can hide in the herd.

It is their antipathy between solidarity and the new work ethic that is destroying the American union movement. There are those who are content to say good riddance and not give a second thought to institutions that seem to have outlived their usefulness. Yet the social benefits of unions have been inestimably high. On average unions raise wages by approximately 10 to 30 percent, the biggest increases going to less educated, less experienced, less skilled, and nonwhite workers. They also increase fringe benefits, with older workers particularly benefiting. Unions also force up wages and benefits in nonunion companies eager to stay nonunion. They improve the quality of work life, again, and perhaps even especially, in nonunion as well as union companies. The nonunion companies that have taken the lead in programs to raise the quality of work life, increase worker participation, and raise the dignity of work have done so not only because the gospel of quality demands it but because those are among the best ways to keep the union out.

All other things being equal, by forcing wages upward unions encourage employers to raise the amount of capital invested per worker, use fewer workers, and take other steps that raise the productivity of the workers who remain. High wages, high levels of investment per worker, a relatively low percentage of the population in the work force: these are always and everywhere the signs of a prosperous, modern, First World nation. Insofar as the decline of unionism has contributed to the recent erosion in head-of-household wages and the stagnation in family income it can only be considered a social catastrophe.

As morally flawed as the ethic of solidarity is, the ethic of communal individualism has its own opposite and equally frightening flaws. The New Puritans of quality can be a fiercely intolerant, arbitrary lot, proud in their righteousness, and apt to stumble badly, as the Tribune Company did in New York, by overestimating the advantages of being right. Precisely because the post-industrial ethic is at root so moralistic it can become tyrannical as quickly as a good CEO can be replaced by a bad. One bad boss with a clean conscience can wound a great many families very quickly—especially a nonunion company most of whose workers are "at will" employees, terminable at any time.

Labor unions are one of the least popular American institutions. In survey after survey, Americans rank unions lower in their affections than such perennially reviled institutions as Congress, the press, television, and banks. The number of Americans who have "hardly any" confidence in labor leaders is three times the number who have "a great deal of confidence" in them. A substantial majority of Americans say unions *still* have too much power.

Nevertheless, an overwhelming and apparently growing majority of Americans, 67 percent in 1987 and 70 percent in 1990, still say labor unions are necessary to protect the working person.

We no longer love solidarity. But we still need it, we think, sometimes. Or at least we still want to have it to hand in an emergency.

What, then, is to be done?

CHAPTER 20

Straight on Through to the Other Side

AMERICA needs strong unions. Not perhaps as strong as they were four decades ago, when Congress was so alarmed by union power it passed the Taft-Hartley amendments over Harry Truman's veto to limit it, but strong enough to win fair wages and defense from arbitrary firings and abuse. We do not need unions to run companies, but we need them to herd companies back onto the straight and narrow when they stray. And perhaps most of all we need a union movement strong enough to keep nonunion employers on their best behavior.

There are two ways to rebuild union power and in particular to restore the power of the strike. The first, the one endorsed by most "friends of labor," is purely *political:* rejigger labor law so that unions, without fundamental change, will win more often. Rewrite the rules on elections so that unions routinely prevail. Take away company free-speech rights so unions will not have to defend themselves in open debate. Or even eliminate elections altogether, replacing them with secret petition drives, so the company is not even aware of an organizing drive until the union has been installed. Best of all, make it illegal *ever* to use permanent replacement workers, so that no matter how stubborn, inefficient, overmanned, unreasonable, and abusive the work force, they need not fear that if they strike the company may decide it would prefer they not come back. Strikes would always be called on the unions' terms, and last as long as the union decides, because operating during a strike would be virtually impossible. The unions could bankrupt the company, as the *News* unions were doing, and still the company would have no ultimate sanction against the union.

The pure political solution is the worst possible option.

Rigging elections and taking away free-speech rights are simply tools of denial. Unions may not need messengers quite as dark and menacing as Bob Ballow to awaken them to post-industrial reality. But neither do they need fantasists lulling them into dreams of resisting change forever. A movement that can win elections only by muzzling opposition is in poor health and unlikely to get any better until it learns to beat its opponents in a fair contest.

As for outlawing the use of permanent replacements, if a company has no ultimate sanction against unions at their worst, it is much more likely they will be at their worst. Replacing an entire work force is normally a very expensive proposition, risking years of reduced productivity. Most companies do not undertake such a drastic step unless they are very unhappy with the work force as it is. The threat of replacement is like shock therapy, ugly, but a last-ditch attempt to call unions back to reality.

Outlawing replacements is not only a tool of denial, it is a counsel of despair. It not only protects unions from the harsh message of change, it in effect admits they cannot change. The strike has become impotent not because the law has changed but because the world has changed, devaluing the skills of the industrial worker and robbing them of their market power. To outlaw replacements is to say these men will never be valuable workers again.

All strikes are based on some combination of market and political power. At one extreme, the classic craft union strike is mostly a market phenomenon: the skills of the union members are so valuable the members can win a strike simply by withholding their services. At the other extreme, the paradigmatic industrial strike, the workers have few skills that cannot be picked up in a few weeks of on-the-job training. Replacing the work force is little more than an inconvenience. The industrial strike relies on politics to make replacing the work force more difficult and costly, whether by moral suasion, that is, convincing the public and potential replacement workers to have nothing to do with the company, or by force, as when the auto workers seized their plants in the 1930s and Governor Murphy of Michigan refused to call out the National Guard to evict them.

Most strikes fall somewhere in between. The less the market power of the strikers, the more political clout they need. But political clout has grave disadvantages. For one thing it is not reliable. Hoge argues that if conservative Democrat Ed Koch had won reelection in 1989, instead of losing to liberal Democrat David Dinkins, the company would have won the *News* strike: the police under Koch would have tracked the violence back to the NMDU and provided enough evidence of wrongdoing to break the union.

The more political clout the unions have, the less incentive they have to make settlements that will make their members more valuable to their employers, for instance by letting new technology into the workplace. In the long run, market power is the only guarantee of union strength. All unions augment their power politically, but if they use politics to push the company too far, and the company has no alternative, it will simply shut down.

This is the real argument against outlawing replacement workers. It would move every union in the country to the extreme political end of the continuum between political and market power. It would give all unions all the kind of political power wielded by the drivers in the *News* strike, the power to absolutely and finally forbid the operation of the business (albeit the violence would not be necessary). It gives them the fatal privilege of standing athwart the tide of history yelling "stop"— and stopping it, at least for a while. But history will have its revenge, probably in Chapter 11.

Still, outlawing replacement workers would make some sense if America's blue-collar workers really had permanently lost their market power and would always be as helpless before their employers as many seem to be now.

But what if that is not true? What if American workers are on the verge of a huge increase in their market power? What if American work forces had a way of becoming so valuable that only very stupid employers would risk losing them?

For that is exactly what is happening. In the post-industrial factory computers devalue the formal, physical, or technical skills of many workers, including the instinctive feel for the moods of heavy machines that made so much blue-collar work something of an art. Yet as a part of a team these very same workers can be enormously valuable. Individually their formal skills may amount to little, but collectively their *moral skills*, their teamwork, diligence, enthusiasm, and personal commitment to quality are enormously valuable. Such a team, sharing the company culture and deeply committed to the common enterprise, is far more difficult to replace, as a group, than a moderately skilled industrial work force.

When Deming's ideas, long supreme in Japan, first became popular in the United States in the early 1980s, hordes of desperate American CEOs immediately declared theirs to be quality companies and ordered their lieutenants to impose the rubrics of TQM. By the late 1980s it was clear most of these companies had given little more than lip service to quality and had reaped none of the expected benefits.

To discover why, one need only talk to managers who have done TQM for real. TQM is hard. Making every worker into a manager means waging a political, social, and economic revolution on the plant floor. Continuously improving the process requires a greater commitment to work than most Americans, right up through midlevel supervisors, ever expected to give. The additional technical training in some of the esoterica of TQM costs time, money, and energy.

To learn to run a modern printing press competently takes only a few weeks. To build a quality-oriented, post-industrial work force, by all accounts, takes several very difficult years, and like any delicately engineered machine requires constant, diligent maintenance after that. The *Chicago Tribune* replaced its union work force in 1985. Productivity rose somewhat almost immediately—but most of the immediate improvement came from eliminating featherbedding. It took years of additional struggle to build a work force that could cut newsprint waste to a fraction of the national average, or improve color reproduction so that instead of being in constant danger of losing the *USA Today* account, Freedom Center's color now wins awards.

Freedom Center's work force is irreplaceable, not individually but collectively, for it is collectively that the moral skills matter, and collectively that they are maintained. This is not true of formal or technical skills: A well-trained mechanic does not become a poorly trained mechanic just because he is assigned to a team of poorly trained mechanics—at least not very soon. But diligence and high personal standards, and even the skill of teamwork itself, are all skills that rise and fall with the group. Freedom Center works largely because it is full of workers who under fairly minimal supervision devote their minds and bodies to their work as intently and enthusiastically as if they were playing for the high school basketball championship instead of working for a living. As any good coach knows, the psychology of a championship team is too

valuable and elusive a thing to risk it being torn apart in fruitless conflicts—like a strike that might have been avoided.

The *News* unions lost their market power when the printers gave way
to electronic typesetting in 1974. Lacking market power, they fought
the 1990 strike politically, war being, as Clausewitz said, a continuation
of politics by other means.

But what if the unions had settled with the company, giving the
company most of the prerogatives it wanted in the plants, except the
explicit anti-union clauses, and in return getting healthy buyouts and a
few other protections, while losing no more jobs than they did to Maxwell? And what if the company had built the new plant and used its new
prerogatives to build a new work culture? And what if five years later the
News is making money and the work force is being written up in *Newsweek* as one more example of the American industrial renaissance.

Does the Tribune Company now want to replace this work force?
Does it want this work force to strike? Of course not. Instead of standing
athwart the tide of history, this work force's post-industrial ship has just
come in. Workers that for a generation had learned to think of themselves as a liability would all of a sudden be an asset. No more of
McDonald's whining about how the company is being mean to them, no
more of Kheel's long, slow compromises and retreats, no more long
nights when the main accomplishment is a good beatout at Freddy's. A
union representing a work force of this quality has real power.

Still, if the spirit of solidarity is so utterly opposed to the post-industrial
work ethic, how will unions survive to represent this new, reinvigorated
post-industrial work force?

Union idealists such as the Bluestones—who understand as well as
anyone how different the new workplace must be from the old—have
one answer, which is to give unions, as institutions, broader responsibilities and more power in the company than ever. They see that post-
industrialism requires the cooperation and enthusiasm of the work force,
that every worker must become part of the company team. But they
believe this can and should be done *through the union* by giving the
unions co-management authority at every level in the firm. If the production process must continually change, then it must be changed with
the union's cooperation—and the union must not unreasonably with-
hold that cooperation. In the Bluestones' vision contracts would be
much shorter. Instead of listing detailed work rules they would outline

shared labor-management goals and define the processes by which labor and management would work together to achieve those goals.

The Bluestones have the post-industrial spirit. Even their name for the new arrangement suggests they see that what is at issue is building a new work ethic or restoring a very old one. Noting that contracts are "essentially adversarial in nature," they recollect that founding document of Puritan America, the Mayflower Compact, and suggest unions and companies should make "enterprise *compacts* . . . cooperative document[s], providing for mutual vision and a joint system for achieving common goals." And they hope that our Puritan forefathers "may provide just the right guidance for a new way of building cars and machine tools, or of providing banking services and hospital care."[1]

One cannot dismiss the Bluestones' vision outright; after all they have seen it work, at least in a few plants, at least for a while. At GM's Saturn plant union workers seem to have replaced solidarity with communal individualism: they draw only 80 percent of the industry standard wage, the rest of their income depends on performance bonuses; at the same time more than 80 percent of Saturn workers have lifetime job guarantees, and workers share in every level of decision making, including strategic planning. The Bluestones say it is one of the best-run automobile plants in America.

Over the long haul, however, the Bluestones' new unions may risk falling between two stools. The new unions would still strike. In fact they would have more to strike over than the old unions, since they could go out not only over *contract* issues, such as wages, but over *compact* issues such as quality. In the Bluestones' vision, if GM cars have too many defects the company might lose not only its customers but its work force.

How can the same institution both manage a company and strike against it; maintain solidarity against the boss, and team spirit at the same time; keep workers shoulder to shoulder against the world and get them to give their all for the company in the same shift? The Holy Grail of quality management is "Six Sigma Quality," which translates into no more than 3.4 defects per million units of output, in effect zero. Considering the enormous level of personal and moral commitment required to reach such a goal, the practical difficulties and psychological strains of serving two masters seem like an insurmountable obstacle.

The well-meaning Bluestones et al. who dream of a positive unionism that will act as a full partner with management, or even take the lead in pushing American companies toward the post-industrial future, are nurturing a fond and contradictory hope. Perhaps unions could be helpful in that task, but they are unlikely to be essential. And all that cooperation with management would surely compromise the one task for which unions are essential—fighting bad bosses.

The Bluestones dream of saving unions by broadening their functions. Perhaps the right answer is to do just the opposite. Perhaps unions will survive, and the nation can help them survive, by remembering what they are really for, and what they alone can do, which is not manage companies that are behaving but punish companies that are not. Maybe what we want are unions that are less active in running companies, but much better at striking than today's unions. Perhaps in the post-industrial era solidarity is not forever, but only for the worst of times.

How would we build a union movement that would frighten employers into their best behavior without compromising the post-industrial renaissance?

This is not entirely clear, which may mean that what we really need is a union free-for-all, a radical liberation from current labor law that would allow unions to experiment with new strategies and tactics.

Current labor law prescribes very narrow forms for American unionism. The NLRB, after receiving a petition to hold a representation election, prescribes the "bargaining unit"—those employees who will be represented by the union if a majority vote the union in. In a hospital, for instance, the bargaining unit for a proposed nurses' local would probably include all the RNs and LPNs. But it might also include nurse's aides or physician's assistants, or it might not. Under the current system the NLRB, the company, and the unions spend a great deal of time fighting over this, with the union and the company both trying to gerrymander the unit so they will win the election. Once the unit is defined the election is held. If the union wins, it represents everyone in the unit and the company is bound to bargain with the union on the unit's behalf. The bargaining itself proceeds along rather arcane rules of engagement, the "ritual dance" as the labor leaders call it. In negotiations gone bad, like those between the *News* and its unions, the rules can be as much of an obstacle to settlement as an aid. In hostile negotiations both sides negotiate with one eye on the nearly inevitable court battle over possible violations of the ritual, which if serious enough might take the victory away from one side and award it to the other.

Today this is the only way Americans can have a union, but it is not the only way we could have unions.

Imagine for instance one of the most radical possible changes in the rules, which would be to make "company unions" legal.

Company unions are unions funded, sponsored, established, controlled, or influenced by employers. They were made illegal by the Wagner Act because they were often established by employers in order to discourage workers from forming real unions. Among the friends of labor few notions are more taboo than the company union, which is remembered now purely as a company trick.

Yet company unions actually have a fairly honorable history. They were part of the "welfare capitalism" movement of the 1920s, under which a large proportion of the country's largest industrial employers tried to nurture a happier, healthier, more prosperous, less transient, more orderly, and more productive work force. In addition to company unions, welfare capitalism often included health and hygiene programs, worker participation, profit sharing, and industrial relations departments (today we would call them human resources departments) to make hiring and firing less arbitrary. The company unions had little real power. They could not truly bargain because they could not strike. But they did help articulate workers' needs and concerns and in some cases helped administer the other "welfare capitalism" programs.

By 1933 some 45 percent of American workers in mining and manufacturing were represented by company unions. And though welfare capitalism deteriorated badly in the Depression, some company unions were successful in pressuring companies to maintain job security and other benefits deep into the 1930s.

The most useful service provided by most company unions, however, came in the manner of their demise. The great CIO uprising of 1935–1937 was built in part on the bones of old company unions whose skeletons provided an organizational structure that significantly eased the task of organizing hundreds of thousands of workers in a matter of months.

Why not change the law to allow company unions designed with exactly this end in mind? As long as relations were good, the company union, really a sort of workingman's society, could be an integral part of a post-industrial work culture. It could help coordinate and encourage training and worker participation as well as health and benefit plans. More important, it would help communicate workers' needs, apprehensions, and ideas to the company, serving as a sort of labor relations early-warning system. The company union could, however, if circumstances warranted, call for an NLRB election to be held within sixty days, and if it won the election "go collective" and become a real union overnight. Since the bargaining unit would already be defined there would be no excuse for delay. In reality, the election might rarely be necessary. Company unions armed with the explicit legal right to become independent would serve as a deterrent to bad company behavior. Ideally the board of directors or the shareholders would interpret the call for an election as a persuasive vote of no-confidence in current management and respond by making changes. If nearly half of American workers were enrolled in company unions (as they once were) and those company unions could become real unions at the drop of a hat, surely that would be a great incentive for companies to stay responsive to workers' needs.

Precisely because the company union could not do real collective bargaining it might be a more effective bargaining agent in some circumstances. Not obliged to follow the ritual dance, nor tempted to posture in formal negotiating sessions, a company union might more credibly convey the workers' real bottom-line concerns, the ones that if not met could lead to the union "going collective" and a real fight. So much of "normal" labor negotiation is devoted to testing the other side's position or posturing for the NLRB and the courts that a more informal approach might well be more effective. By the same token, a company union, its position in the company guaranteed, its finances the company's responsibility, would have no need to constantly prove its usefulness to the workers by generating the artificial hostility and divided loyalties so crucial to labor solidarity.

Company unions are among the most radical possible results of a union free-for-all. Yet they provide a clear possible model for a post-industrial unionism: unions as an emergency measure, a tool we take down off the shelf when things go bad, rather than being, as in the Bluestones' model, or effectively in the old industrial model, one more layer of corporate governance encumbering the everyday activities of the enterprise.

Of course emergency remedies, by definition, have to be instantly available. Other less radical measures could also make it easier to take the old unionism down off the shelf in a hurry. One would be to eliminate the often interminable wrangles over defining the bargaining unit.

Currently, appealing and reappealing the NLRB definition of a bargaining unit is a favorite company tactic for delaying elections. Yet it is not at all clear why the company should have a voice in defining the bargaining unit, except for the right to exclude supervisors. The bargaining unit should be defined by the workers who petition for an NLRB election, and then by the election itself. If a majority of nurses and parking lot attendants at a hospital, for some bizarre reason, decide they want to be in the same bargaining unit, surely that is their business. With bargaining unit wrangles eliminated, there would be no excuse not to set a short and inflexible time limit between the time of a successful petition and the election. Freeman suggests fifteen days, but that seems too short for fair debate. Surely sixty would be enough.

One reform clearly we must make: the penalties for firing pro-union workers should be increased sharply. The law now treats such an offense as if the only harm were to the worker fired—only he gets back pay. But the rights of every employee in the firm are violated when the company undermines the election by firing union supporters. Simple justice requires that the fines be heavy enough to deter the offense. And if we are to have emergency unionism it is even more important to keep companies from retarding organizing drives.

For emergency unionism, the rule of thumb ought to be "easy come, easy go." In this vein, we might try another radical reform, such as requiring that every large nonunion company hold an NLRB-supervised representation election every three years, whether the workers petition for one or not. By the same token we might require every large unionized company to hold a decertification election in the same period. If the purpose of unions is not to run companies—or rackets—but to deter bad behavior by employers, the thing to do is keep both employers and union leaders on their toes. It is hard to imagine a more favorable condition for American workers than a nation full of employers constantly worried the union will be voted in, and a nation full of union officials constantly worried it will be voted out.

One long-overdue reform, advocated by, among others, veteran union lawyer Thomas Geoghegan in his brilliant book *Which Side Are You On?* is to finally guarantee union democracy. Under current law one of the easiest things in this country to steal is a union election of officers, which makes it easy for corrupt factions like those in the NMDU to rule for years. The NLRB will "observe" an election if there is good reason to believe it might be stolen, but observation is not always as effective as it sounds. Geoghegan proposes that the Department of Labor ought to directly administer every union election in the country, at least for locals of a certain size. This would be a good idea at any time, but in an era when workers are facing critical changes in the workplace it seems particularly important they be represented by leaders truly of their choice.

Another possibility is to depart from two hallowed principles: that unions must represent all of a bargaining unit or none of it, and that there may be only one union per bargaining unit. There are good reasons for these rules: the framers of the Wagner Act did not want employers to be able to play divide and conquer against their employees. But a half- or quarter-organized work force is a more potent threat than no union at all, and it makes organizing the entire workplace much easier when management goes bad. Giving these half unions legally enforceable collective bargaining rights might be awkward. But even if they simply served as informal associations, waiting for the emergency in which they were needed to organize the entire plant, they might be very useful. Some unions already accept "associate" members; the trend should be encouraged.

Charles Heckscher envisions a whole new labor movement based on "associational unions" that might include any number of worker organizations, some management-sponsored, some not, some established by legislation, some by private initiative, all in the same workplace. On a day-to-day basis most of these organizations would little resemble traditional unions though they would articulate the interests of workers, interests in most cases shared by the firm. A work force organized into such associations should be able to legally switch to confrontational unionism on very short notice, and therefore might never have to.

The percentage of American workers who are union members has declined nearly every year since the merger of the AFL-CIO quashed competition for members. Allowing rival unions, or quasi-unions, in the same shop might be just what we need to reignite the fires of competition and stimulate recruiting.

A list of reforms and experiments could go on much longer. It has even been suggested that we do away with virtually all labor law except those provisions forbidding employers from firing workers who join or help organize unions. A period of radical experimentation would almost certainly be preferable to making the old industrial union straitjacket even tighter, and shielding unions from reality for a few more years.

*   *   *

There will always be times when working men must go to war. But they
cannot do their work at war. They could little enough do this when their
work was so simple that they could work and hate at the same time. But
if the new revival of the old work ethic means anything it means they
can no longer do that.

In extremis, the strike is still the workers' best weapon. But when
both company and workers alike begin to perceive workers as ancient
burdens rather than growing assets, the strike loses its power.

Saving the strike *politically* will not stop history and it will not raise
the value of workers either in the company's eyes or in their own. The
way to save the strike is to join the post-industrial future with a vengeance, a future that might not only revalue the American worker but
restore the moral value of work itself. To save the strike, the one best
weapon men have against work gone bad, men must first make work
good.

NOTES

A NOTE ABOUT THE NOTES

In a bibliographical note for each chapter, I sketch out the main sources for that chapter and draw particular attention to any writer to whose work I owe a substantial debt. I have supplemented the bibliographical note with footnotes in only three cases: Direct quotations from another writer's work, not directly or fully cited in the text, are footnoted even if that work is already credited in the bibliographical note for that chapter. Quotations of characters in the story picked up from news accounts are footnoted if the quotation is unique to a single news account. If the same quotation is cited by several reporters, I do not footnote, but of course the news accounts are listed in the bibliographical note. Whenever feasible, quotations picked up from news accounts have been checked with the person quoted. Finally, there are a few explanatory notes.

NOTES FOR CHAPTER 2: NO MORE GIVEBACKS

This chapter is based substantially on interviews with James Hoge, Jerry Cronin, George McDonald, Lenny Higgins, Barry Lipton, James Longson, Andrew Hayes (Tribune Company VP for Corporate Affairs), Charles Brumback, Terry Teachout, Robert Ballow, Edward Gold, Michael Packenham (former editorial page editor of the *News*), Jack Kennedy, and Barbara Kalish (of the *News* labor relations department).

The principal source for background on the *News* is *The Daily News*, by Leo McGivena et al., published by the *Daily News* for its fiftieth anniversary and available as far as I know only from the *News*. Joseph Allbright's excellent but alas unpublished thesis, "Joseph Medill Patterson: Right or Wrong American," available from Williams College, Williamstown, Massachusetts, was also useful. Also unavailable to the general public but useful to me for certain basic facts about the Tribune Company and the *News*, particularly from the late 1970s through the strike, was the Tribune Company's archival history of the strike, by Kathleen Hale, entitled "They Could Have Had That in New York." Also valuable was William Keeler's *Newsday: A Candid History of the Respectable Tabloid*, New York: Morrow, 1990.

1. Cited in: Allbright, *Joseph Medill Patterson: Right or Wrong, American.*
2. McGivena et al., *The Daily News*, pp. 144–45.

NOTES FOR CHAPTER 3: DEUS EX MACHINA

My education at Freedom Center was at the hands of Jim O'Dell, who runs it, and a flock of his lieutenants and foot soldiers too numerous to mention here. Key interviews for this chapter include O'Dell, Scott Sherman, Gene Bell, John Sloan, Andrew Hayes, and Charles Brumback.

The Weber quotations are taken from the Scribner/Macmillan, 1958/1976 edition of *The Protestant Ethic and the Spirit of Capitalism*, translated by Talcott Parsons.

1. Weber, *Protestant Ethic*, p. 54.
2. Ibid., p. 62.
3. Ibid., p. 176.

NOTES FOR CHAPTER 4: FALL FROM GRACE

Brooklyn plant manager Michael Maloney, and the pressmen's chapel chairman, George Kennedy, were my chief guides there. Other key interviews included Michael Tachi, Kenneth MacAvoy, Raymond Walsh, Daniel McPhee, Jerry Cronin, Richard Casson, Jack Kennedy, George McDonald, Bill Deering, Richard Malone, John Sloan, senior union officials and advisors speaking on condition of anonymity, and present and former *News* employees from the Brooklyn plant also anonymously.

It should be noted that union leaders in conversation often disputed the details of specific listed abuses or instances of featherbedding; therefore, specific instances almost always come from company sources. On the other hand, many of the union leaders and advisors I spoke with admitted and endorsed the existence of such practices in a general way, pointing out, as McDonald did, that many or most such practices existed by agreement with the company and were "bought and paid for" by other concessions.

As usual, the Tribune Company's official archival record of the strike, "They Could Have Had That in New York," by Kathleen Hale, was useful for certain factual details. The Weber quotations are from the Scribner/Macmillan 1958/1976 edition of *The Protestant Ethic and the Spirit of Capitalism*, translated by Talcott Parsons.

1. Weber, *Protestant Ethic*, p. 117.
2. Ibid., p. 119.

NOTES FOR CHAPTER 5: THEY DRIVE BY NIGHT

The history comes mostly from McGivena, Keeler, and Allbright. Crucial interviews were with a senior official in Morgenthau's office speaking on condition of anonymity, Cronin, Longson, and Deering. The indictments themselves are very illuminating. The case has not been tried at this writing.

1. Keeler, *Newsday*, p. 21.
2. The minimum estimate is based on the volume of thefts investigators think they will be able to prove in court; the larger figure is more realistic.
3. Hale, "They Could Have Had That," p. 83.

NOTES FOR CHAPTER 6: BROKEN COVENANT

Key interviews included George McDonald, Lenny Higgins, Barry Lipton, James Hoge, James Longson, Charles Brumback, Andrew Hayes, Michael Packenham (former editorial page editor of the *News*), Jack Kennedy, and Theodore Kheel.

Kheel maintains magnificently complete files on the *News* during the strike period and back through the late 1970s, which he was kind enough to make available to me. Hoge's open letters to *News* employees and their families, the McDonald correspondence, summaries of the McKinsey report, Hoge's turn-around plan, and much other background material for this chapter were found there. Once again the Kathleen Hale archival history "They Could Have Had That in New York," was useful for factual details.

1. Hale, "They Could Have Had That," p. 14.
2. George McDonald letter to James Hoge, 27 March 1989; from Kheel files.
3. Hoge letter to McDonald, 4 April 1989; from Kheel files.
4. McDonald letters to Hoge, 12 April 1989, 17 April 1989, 4 May 1989; from Kheel files.

NOTES FOR CHAPTER 7: WHAT KHEEL KNEW

Key interviews were with Theodore Kheel, George McDonald, Jack Kennedy, Barry Lipton, Charles Brumback, and senior union advisors.

The Kheel files draw a clear picture of the Kheel-McDonald relationship and of Kheel's intimate involvement with the New York newspaper unions. Numerous Kheel letters, press releases, speeches, statements, and notes reiterate and expand on the Kheel theory as explained to me in several lengthy interviews.

The account of Kheel's involvement with the *Post* crisis in 1990 depends in part on *New York Times* reporter Alex S. Jones's 11 Sept. 1990 *New York Times* story, "Post Survives as Last Union Accepts Pact."

NOTES FOR CHAPTER 8: WAR GAMES

Key interviews include Charles Brumback, James Longson, Jim Hoge, Edward Gold, John Sloan, Paul Stellato, Grover Howell, Jack Kennedy, George McDonald, Terry Teachout, Gil Spencer, Richard Malone, Barbara Kalish, John Scanlon, Mike Maloney, Ken MacAvoy, Ray Walsh, and Mike Tachi.

Kathleen Hale's archival history of the strike, "They Could Have Had That in New York," was useful for the summary of strike contingency plans, particularly the advertising department example.

1. George McDonald letter to Stanton Cook, 2 Oct. 1989; from Kheel files.
2. Edward Gold letter to McDonald, 11 Oct. 1989; from Kheel files.
3. McDonald letter to James Hoge, 12 Sept. 1989; from Kheel files.

NOTES FOR CHAPTER 9: A MODEST PROPOSAL

Scott Sherman in several long interviews detailed the vision herein presented of how a quality-oriented, automated newspaper plant should be run and its work force managed; Jim O'Dell and his staff at Freedom Center put flesh and blood on that vision by showing me how it worked in practice. Interviews with Charles Brumback, Richard Malone, Jack Kennedy, George McDonald, Barry Lipton, Barbara Kalish, and senior union advisors were also helpful, as were negotiation minutes kept by Edward Gold for the company and by the pressmen's legal team at Skadden, Arps.

The most frequently recommended short history of American labor is *American Labor* by Henry Pelling (Chicago: University of Chicago Press, 1960).

Also useful was *A History of American Labor* by Joseph G. Rayback (New York: The Free Press, 1966).

1. Peter Drucker, *The Concept of the Corporation*, rev. ed. (New Brunswick, NJ: Transaction Books, 1993).
2. Ibid., p. 151.
3. Ibid.

NOTES FOR CHAPTER 10: RITES OF SPRING

The principal source for this chapter is Edward Gold's negotiation minutes, as checked against the pressmen's minutes taken by Larry Marcus's team. The two sets of minutes were gratifyingly consistent as to substance, but Gold's were more complete and descriptive, and so I more often rely upon them for direct quotation.

Key interviews were with Gold, Robert Ballow, Larry Marcus, Michael Connery, James Grottola, Barry Lipton, Donald Singleton, Sam McKnight, Theodore Kheel, and senior union advisors.

1. Daniel Patrick Moynihan and Nathan Glazer, *Beyond the Melting Pot* (Cambridge, Mass.: Massachusetts Institute of Technology Press, 1970), p. 226.
2. Ibid.
3. Throughout the early and middle stages of the negotiations Ballow's official position was that the company would not propose buyouts but would discuss union proposals. However, when the unions did propose buyouts he often rejected them dismissively.
4. Robert L. Wiley III, 11 May 1990 industry briefing paper for Furman, Selz; from Kheel files.

NOTES FOR CHAPTER 11: A HEARTBREAK AWAY

Once again the principal source is Edward Gold's notes as checked against the union's. I have used the union wording where it was more complete or the context was more clear. Also helpful were interviews with Gold, Robert Ballow, Jack Kennedy, Larry Marcus, Michael Connery, and senior union advisors.

1. Both sides deny the significance I attribute to this meeting, but in each case they deny it because they do not believe the other side was serious about wanting a settlement. Each side claims its own proposal was serious and I believe both are telling the truth.

NOTES TO CHAPTER 12: LA FORZA DEL DESTINO

Again the principal source is Edward Gold's notes. Also crucial were interviews with Donald Singleton, Barry Lipton, Gold, Robert Ballow, Michael Oesterle, Robert Vann, Dave Hardy, Tom Pennachio, Bill Deering, Stephen Guida, Seymour Goldstein, Jerry Cronin, senior NMDU officials, and present and former employees of the district attorney's office.

The reconstructed argument at the sixth Guild session for the most part reflects a consensus of the participants, except that Gold's notes do not show his comment to Vann, and Pennachio says he did not mean to threaten Gold and does not recall saying, "I'll get you in my own way."
1. LaChance was not available for an interview.

NOTES FOR CHAPTER 13: THE BATTLE OF WOUNDED KNEE

The key interviews for this chapter were with Stephen Guida, Seymour Goldstein, Edward Gold, Robert Ballow, James Hoge, Gene Bell, John Sloan, Bill Deering, senior union advisors, and senior NMDU officials.

Several news accounts were of great help in assembling the story of that night, especially after the replacements were called. See especially:

Paul LaRosa and Stuart Marques, "News Unions Strike," *Daily News*, 16 Oct. 1990.

John Kifner, "Picket Signs and Cheers as Drivers Go on Strike, *New York Times*, 26 Oct. 1990.

David E. Pitt, "Drivers Strike at the Daily News and Most Unions Honor Walkout," *New York Times*, 26 Oct. 1990.

Jim Dwyer, "On the Death Watch at the Daily News," *New York Newsday*, 26 Oct. 1990.

William Bunch et al., "This Time the Buses Did Come," *New York Newsday*, 28 Oct. 1990.

Kathleen Hale's archival history, "They Could Have Had That in New York," usefully summarized the company's version of events.
1. Hale, "They Could Have Had That," p. 292.
2. Dwyer, "On the Death Watch."
3. Bunch et al., "This Time."
4. Kifner, "Picket Signs and Cheers."
5. Of course in the exteme version of the Kheel theory, which holds that the company was positively averse to the settlement at the table, that measure of agreement with the pressmen might be considered a setback, taking the company further away from impasse. But if so, the company had stepped back from impasse voluntarily, for it was only Ballow's response to the pressmen's offer that would tend to prove the talks were making progress. Ballow could have supported a drive to impasse by rejecting the pressmen's offer outright, as he had done with previous buyout offers.

Moreover, even if Ballow's buyout offer had been a misstep, a straight-

forward declaration of impasse would still have been a far safer way of
bringing things to conclusion than phonying up a lockout. Gold thought that
impasse had been a safe legal bet by midsummer at the latest. Ballow was
much more cautious; but certainly a few more months would suffice, not a
long time by Ballow's standards. With federal mediators overseeing negotiations an impasse declaration would be less risky than otherwise.

NOTES FOR CHAPTER 14: NO DO-OVERS

The key interviews were with Theodore Kheel, George McDonald, James
Hoge, Edward Gold, Michael Oesterle, Robert Ballow, Charles Brumback, and
senior NMDU officials.

The account of the first few hours of the strike, and especially Alvino's walk,
owes a particular debt to two vividly written news stories, Jim Dwyer's 26 Oct.
1990 column for *New York Newsday*, "On the Death Watch at the Daily News"
and Paul LaRosa and Stuart Marques's "News Unions Strike," *Daily News*, 26
Oct. 1990.

Also see:

Pete Bowles, et al., "Clash at Brooklyn Plant Sparks Walkout at Paper," *New
York Newsday*, 26 Oct. 1990.

David E. Pitt, "Drivers Strike at the Daily News and Most Unions Honor
Walkout," *New York Times*, 26 Oct. 1990.

John Kifner, "Picket Signs and Cheers as Drivers Go on Strike, *New York
Times*, 26 Oct. 1990.

Alex S. Jones, "Unions Play into Management's Hands," *New York Times*, 27
Oct. 1990.

1. This conversation obviously was not conducted in the set-piece fashion laid
   out here. Because the legal and other issues that dominated what the two
   sides said are both crucial and complex I have blocked out the positions with
   a certain rather artificial neatness and have for that reason avoided direct
   quotation, which would be misleading in this context. However, the formal-
   ism in the company's explanation does convey the tone in which the lawyers
   talked when they were being their most infuriatingly lawyerly.
2. Bowles et al., "Clash at Brooklyn Plant."
3. Jones, "Unions Play into Management's Hands."
4. Kifner, "Picket Signs and Cheers."

NOTES FOR CHAPTER 15: THE HIGH GROUND

Key interviews were Barry Lipton, Sal Arina, Don Singleton, and a veteran
News reporter speaking on condition of anonymity. John Roca helped recon-
struct the events of that first night. Elizabeth Jenson and Joel Benenson helped
with details of the playground meeting.

I am particularly indebted to two outstanding pieces of journalism, both from
the *Village Voice:* Of the many published accounts of the moral dilemmas facing

Guild members Joanna Molloy's strike diary is by far the best and most well-grounded. James Ledbetter gave a moving, vivid, and elegantly written account of not only this meeting but Gonzalez's career and his later role in the strike.

1. Joanna Molloy, "The Prisoner of Second Avenue," *Village Voice*, 27 Nov. 1990.
2. Ibid.
3. Ibid.
4. Ibid.
5. Ibid.
6. Tom Robbins, "I Walk the Line," *Village Voice*, 11 Nov. 1990.
7. Molloy, "The Prisoner of Second Avenue."
8. Gonzalez's speech made a powerful impression on many of the people in that room, but of course accounts of his exact words differ. I rely on Ledbetter, and interviews with Sal Arina, Barry Lipton, and a veteran *News* reporter speaking on condition of anonymity. Gonzalez failed to return numerous phone calls requesting an interview for this book.
9. James Ledbetter, "Rockin' the Trib," *Village Voice*, 27 Nov. 1990.
10. Ibid.
11. Ibid.
12. Alessandra Stanley, "Among Striking Reporters, Fear and Misgivings Grow," *New York Times*, 31 Oct. 1990.

NOTES FOR CHAPTER 16: WITH A VENGEANCE

The most important interviews for this chapter were with current and former NMDU officials speaking on condition of anonymity. Other important interviews were with Sam McKnight, George McDonald, senior union advisors, Richard Malone, Richard Casson, Paul Stellato, Grover Howell, Barbara Kalish, Robert Holzkamp, Edward Gold, and James Hoge.

The descriptions of violent and intimidating incidents as well as my sense of their number, severity, and source (crucial and controversial issues during the strike) depend on a wide variety of sources: Published or broadcast news accounts, company records provided by former *News* employees no longer associated with either the *News* or the Tribune Company, my own and my research assistants' interviews with victims and law enforcement officials, and sworn testimony of victims, and interviews with current and former NMDU officials.

The most controversial decision I made was to rely to some extent on company records. The company had an incentive to make the violence appear as serious, extensive, and well organized as possible, not only to help in the war for public opinion but because any showing of "agency" in the violence by the unions could lead to their virtual legal destruction and sure company victory in the strike.

Of the specific incidents described, however, only a few—the attacks on *News* trucks cited early in the chapter—are drawn primarily from company records.

And even in the case of the truck attacks, published news accounts and arrest records make clear there was a great deal of such activity in those early days. The real influence company records had on my conclusions was more general: They helped convince me that the violence was both more extensive and systematic than most public officials or most of the New York press would admit during the strike. In fact, I came to the conclusion that even the company's estimate of 1,000 serious incidents (i.e., actual violence, vandalism, or threats and harassment) was probably a substantial undercount. More likely there were many thousands.

The most relevant company records are collections of "incident reports" and summaries thereof, the latter often in the form of internal memos between members of the company's security and legal teams. Though my collection is necessarily incomplete, these reports show hundreds of news dealers who reported being harassed, threatened, vandalized, or more seriously attacked. Moreover, press reports, dealer testimony, and my own interviews make it clear that many of these dealers were visited dozens of times, a fact not reflected in the company's incident tallies, which may record only one incident in the case of a dealer visited virtually every day. The threats were not necessarily repeated every day, though in many cases they seem to have been repeated very often. But the fact that a man who threatens to burn down your newsstand if you don't drop the paper does not repeat the threat every single time he stops by to check is cold comfort. Moreover, if hundreds of dealers reported being harassed there were probably many others who were afraid to report.

Still, the question remains, why accept the company's incident reports in the first place, since they include incidents not reported elsewhere or reflected in the police count? Well, of course, one cannot rely on them absolutely, say for an exact incident count, without rechecking every single incident, which was beyond my means. But cross checks against other sources, including my own and my research assistant's interviews of victims and spot checks of incidents represented only in *News* records, do show the company reports to be broadly reliable.

The company's system for reporting and tracking incidents also lends credibility to company records. The *News*'s chief security advisor was Richard Koehler, former chief of the New York State Department of Corrections. The head of the security force was Grover Howell, formerly the head of the Communications Division of NYPD (he ran the city's 911 operation). Previously he had served in NYPD's detective division for twelve years, and had taught detective investigation at the police academy. He had also served as deputy inspector and eventually inspector general for the Department of Corrections. He is currently head of security for the Times Square Business Improvement District, one of the city's largest. The man in charge of investigations was Al Cachie, a prominent former NYPD detective. The investigative staff, roughly fifty strong, was itself composed largely of former NYPD detectives. One of the

News lawyers primarily responsible for the process of recording evidence was Barbara Kalish, who joined the *News* labor relations department months before Hoge's decision to go militant and was well known as a "moderate" who strongly disapproved of Ballow, Gold, and the total-war approach to the unions.

The incident reports from which the company counts were assembled were prepared by investigators who, having been notified of an incident by a team of recorders and dispatchers, went out into the field to interview the victims and begin an investigation, the results of which could be eventually turned over to NYPD and law enforcement agencies. Because the two primary goals of the investigations were to supply NYPD with information that could lead to arrests and case closures and later to serve as evidence in lawsuits against the drivers union, the *News* had every incentive to obtain accurate information.

In short, though the *News* team undoubtedly made errors, especially on matters open to interpretation, such as the line between persuasion and harassment, the investigative operation was too large, too busy, and composed of too many people with substantial reputations and little personal commitment to the Tribune Company to make wholesale fraud, such as the faking of incident reports, at all likely.

Useful press reports not cited below include Andrew Maykuth, "Vendors Face Threats and Thievery as Strikers Battle N.Y. *Daily News*," *Philadelphia Inquirer*, 31 Oct. 1990; David Gonzalez and James C. McKinley Jr., "Violence and the *News* Strike: Anger, Blame and Distrust" *New York Times*, 3 March 1991; and Mitch Gelman and Joseph W. Queen, "Fire Set at Store That Was Warned to Drop the *News*," *New York Newsday*, 3 Nov. 1990.

1. David Gonzalez, "Taunts but 'Good Money' for New Drivers at *News*," *New York Times*, 29 Oct. 1990.
2. Quotations are from a lawsuit filed by Naveed against the NMDU. Naveed's counsel was Henry Korn, who successfully prosecuted LaChance in 1980. The suit was eventually dropped.
3. John Kifner, "Striking Drivers Warn Against Selling the *Daily News*, Dealers Say," *New York Times*, 10 Oct. 1990.
4. Ibid.
5. Ibid.
6. John Kifner, "Dealers Cite Warnings Against Selling the *News*," *New York Times*, 11 Nov. 1990.
7. Kifner, "Striking Drivers."
8. The affidavits were provided to me in masked form, that is, with the names removed, by a former *News* employee able to vouch for their authenticity.
9. Mike McAlary, "Behind the Lines as *News*' Drivers Go to War," *New York Post*, 12 Nov. 1990.
10. Ibid.
11. Kifner, "Dealers Cite."
12. Ibid.

13. Curtis Rist, "Unions Go Door to Door to Stop *Daily News* Sales," *New York Newsday*, 11 Nov. 1990.

14. Alex Jones, "*Daily News* Plans for a Strike: a Fundamental Miscalculation," *New York Times*, 16 Nov. 1990.

NOTES FOR CHAPTER 17: GETTING OVER

Key interviews included James Hoge, Barry Lipton, Theodore Kheel, John Kifner, Kenneth Crowe, Paul Stellato, Grover Howell, Edward Gold, Deputy Inspector Dennis Cunningham, a senior official in the office of the Manhattan District Attorney speaking on condition of anonymity, Nassau County District Attorney Douglas Dillon, Nassau D.A. chief of rackets Patrick McCormick, and an NMDU official speaking on condition of anonymity. Both former Chief Johnston and Chief Borrelli failed to respond to requests for interviews.

1. Robert D. McFadden, "Mayor Struggles with Limited Role in Strike at *Daily News*," *New York Times*, 29 Oct. 1990.

2. William Bunch, "*News* Strike at Stalemate," *New York Newsday*, 29 Oct. 1990.

3. John Cardinal O'Connor to Theodore Kheel, 1 Nov. 1990, Kheel files.

4. Richard Rosen and Sharon Rosenhouse, "Getting Louder," *Daily News*, 2 Nov. 1990. Pete Bowles, "13,000 Protestors Rally at *News*," *New York Newsday*, 3 Nov. 1990.

5. Mitch Gelman, "Strike Costs City $465,000 in Police OT," *New York Newsday*, 30 Oct. 1990.

6. Peg Tyre, "Pickets, Rallies, Parades Put Elite Cops on Streets," *New York Newsday*, 1 Nov. 1990.

7. David E. Pitt, "*Daily News* and Police Vary on Degree of Violence," *New York Times*, 8 Nov. 1990.

8. David E. Pitt, "Unions Said to Be Ready to Take Cuts," *New York Times*, 9 Nov. 1990.

9. James Barron, "*Daily News* Uses Homeless to Sell Paper," *New York Times*, 10 Nov. 1990.

10. John Kifner, "Striking *News* Workers Remember Inky Legacy," *New York Times*, 10 Nov. 1990.

11. Kenneth C. Crowe, "*News* Guard, Strikers Arrested," *New York Newsday*, 10 Nov. 1990.

12. Kenneth C. Crowe and Mitch Gelman, "*Daily News* Drivers Bushwhacked," *New York Newsday*, 15 Nov. 1990.

13. Howard Kurtz, "New York *News* Publisher Faults Rivals in Strike," *Washington Post*, 3 Feb. 1991.

14. Ibid.

15. Ibid.

16. Gelman, "Strike Costs City."

17. Rose Marie Arce, "Both Sides Wage War of Tabloid Words," *New York Newsday*, 12 Nov. 1990.
18. Todd S. Purdum, "Police in Middle, on Overtime, in the *News* Strike," *New York Times*, 18 Nov. 1990.
19. David E. Pitt, "Circulation Hurt, *News* Gives Away Many of Its Copies," *New York Times*, 3 Nov. 1990.
20. Pitt, "*Daily News* and Police Vary."
21. John Kifner, "Striking Drivers Issue Warnings on Selling the *News*, Dealers Say," *New York Times*, 30 Oct. 1990.
22. David Pitt, "*News* Strikers Ask Abrams to Step In," *New York Times*, 14 Nov. 1990.
23. Curtis Taylor and Scott Ladd, "Cops to Probe *News* Unions' Charges," *New York Newsday*, 20 Nov. 1990.
24. David E. Pitt, "Police Rebut *Daily News* on Violence," *New York Times*, 27 Nov. 1990.
25. Ibid.
26. Ibid.
27. Ibid.
28. David E. Pitt, "*News* Publisher Strongly Criticizes Dinkins," *New York Times*, 7 Dec. 1990.
29. Ibid.
30. David E. Pitt, "At Rally, Cuomo Supports Unions in *News* Strike," *New York Times*, 11 Dec. 1990.

NOTES FOR CHAPTER 18: COLD COMFORT

Key interviews include James Hoge, Charles Brumback, senior union advisors, Jack Kennedy, Bob Ballow, Jim Longson, Edward Gold, Barry Lipton, and Barbara Kalish. The world's leading expert on the bizarre career of Robert Maxwell is Tom Bower, whose book *Maxwell: The Outsider* (Viking, 1992) was very useful, as was his *New Republic* article of 8 April 1991, "Maxwell's House." Also useful were Edward Klein's "The Sinking of Captain Bob," *Vanity Fair*, March 1992, and two pieces by *New York* magazine's Edward Diamond, "Big Max Attack," 8 April 1991, and "To the Max," 25 March 1991.
1. Tom Bower, "Maxwell's House," *The New Republic*, 8 April 1991.

NOTES FOR CHAPTER 19: SOLIDARITY FOREVER?

Of the works cited below, the Marshall essay and the Heckscher book struck me as the most acute. Freeman and Medoff are indispensable. Useful works not cited below include Thomas Geoghegan's *Which Side Are You On?* (New York: Farrar, Straus & Giroux, 1991); *Bargaining for Change*, Miriam Golden and Jonas Pontusson, eds. (Ithaca, N.Y.: Cornell University Press, 1992); and Barry and Irving Bluestone's *Negotiating the Future* (New York: Basic Books, 1992).

306 of RICHARD VIGILANTE

1. Richard B. Freeman and James L. Medoff, *What Do Unions Do?* (New York: Basic Books, 1984), p.

2. Ray Marshall, "Work Organization, Unions and Economic Performance," in *Unions and Economic Competitiveness*, Lawrence Mishel and Paula B. Voos, eds. (Armonk, N.Y.: M. E. Sharpe, 1992), pp. 288–89.

3. Charles C. Heckscher, *The New Unionism* (New York: Basic Books, 1988), p. 59.

4. Ibid.

5. Ibid., p. 70.

6. Quoted in: Mary Walton, *The Deming Management Method*, foreword by W. Edwards Deming (New York: Perigee Books, 1986), p. 61.

NOTES FOR CHAPTER 20: STRAIGHT ON THROUGH TO THE OTHER SIDE
For useful readings see notes for previous chapter.

1. Barry Bluestone and Irving Bluestone, *Negotiating the Future: A Labor Perspective on American Business* (Basic Books, 1992), pp. 24–25. My emphasis.

INDEX

ABOUT THE AUTHOR

RICHARD VIGILANTE, columnist for *New York Newsday* and director of the Center for Social Thought, was founding editor of the Manhattan Institute's *City Journal*, credited by *The New Yorker* with creating "a new center" in New York politics. A former White House speechwriter, he contributes to numerous national publications, including *The New Republic* and *The Wall Street Journal*. At work on a new book, *The Proletarian Family*, he lives in Queens, New York, with his wife, Susan, who is also a writer.